Wells Manor of Canon Grange

by

DERRICK SHERWIN BAILEY

*Canon of Wells and Prebendary of Ashill
Formerly Chancellor of Wells, and Precentor of Wells*

ALAN SUTTON
1985

Alan Sutton Publishing Limited
30 Brunswick Road
Gloucester GL1 1JJ

First published 1985

Copyright © 1985 D.S. Bailey

All rights reserved. No part of this publication may be reproduced, stored in a retrieval system, or transmitted, in any form or by any means, electronic, mechanical photocopying, recording or otherwise, without the prior permission of the publishers and copyright holder.

British Library Cataloguing in Publication Data

Bailey, Sherwin
 Wells Manor of Canon Grange
 1. Wells Cathedral—History 2. Church lands—England—History
 I. Title
 333.3′22′0942388   BX5195.W4

ISBN 0-86299-089-0

Typesetting and origination by
Alan Sutton Publishing Limited
Photoset in Plantin 10/12
Printed in Great Britain.

To the Dean and Chapter of Wells

ACKNOWLEDGEMENTS

The publication of this work has been assisted by grants from the British Academy, and the Marc Fitch Fund.

I acknowledge most gratefully, the help of Mr Linzee Colchester who checked and corrected all the proofs of this volume and so made possible its publication after my husband's death on the 9th February 1984.

Morag Bailey

CONTENTS

Preface		xi
Introduction i	The Manor of Canon Grange	xv
ii	The Commutation of the Estates of the Dean and Chapter	xvii
iii	Sources	xix
iv	The Liberty	xx
v	The Topography of Old Wells	xxii
Abbreviations		xxvii

PART I Numbered Properties shown on the map of Canon Grange c.1825 [DD/CC 10878] and listed in the Table of References thereto [DD/CC 111748], excluding Canonical Houses, Properties Nos. 2, 4, 5, 6, 7, 7a, 8, and 9.*

1.	Property No. 1, 10 New Street	3
2.	Property No. 3, The Canons' Barn	5
3.	Property No. 10, The 'Corner House'	14
4.	Property No. 11, 5, St Andrew Street	19
5.	Property No. 12, 6, St Andrew Street	22
6.	Property No. 13, 7/7a, St Andrew Street	24
7.	Property No. 14, 8, St Thomas Street	26
8.	Property Nos. 15, 16, 17, 14, 16, 18, 20a (22), St Thomas Street	28
9.	Property No. 18, 30/32, St Thomas Street	33
10.	Property No. 19, 84, 86, 88, St Thomas Street	35
11.	Property No. 20, 20/21, Tor Street	36
12.	Property No. 21, 18/19, Tor Street	41
13.	Property No. 22, 17, Tor Street	44
14.	Property No. 23, 10, Tor Street	45
15.	Property No. 23 (Part), Buttclose	47

* See *CHW*, Articles 1, 2, 5, 6, 7, 8, 9.

16.	Property No. 23A, 15, Tor Street	49
17.	Property No. 24, 16, Market Place	51
18.	Property No. 25, The Camery	55
19.	Property No. 26, 25, Market Place and 1a Cathedral Green	60
20.	Property No. 28,* 23, Market Place	65
21.	Property No. 30, 21, Market Place	66
22.	Property No. 32, 19, Market Place	69
23.	Property No. 34, 17, Market Place	71
24.	Property No. 36, 15, Market Place	73
25.	Property No. 38, 13, Market Place	75
26.	Property No. 40, 11, Market Place	78
27.	Property No. 42, 9, Market Place	80
28.	Property No. 44, 7, Market Place	82
29.	Property No. 46, 5, Market Place	84
30.	Property No. 48, 3, Market Place	86
31.	Property No. 50, 1, Market Place (East Part)	89
32.	Property No. 51, 1, Market Place (West Part)	91
33.	Property No. 52, A House in Sadler Street	94
34.	Property No. 53, 18, Sadler Street	96
35.	Property No. 54, 20–22, Sadler Street	99
36.	Property No. 55, A House in Sadler Street	102
37.	Property No. 56, The White Hart Hotel, Sadler Street	105
38.	Property No. 57, 3, New Street	108
39.	Property No. 58, 1, New Street	109
40.	Property No. 59, 2, Chamberlain Street	112
41.	Property No. 60, 11/13, New Street	117
42.	Property No. 61, 10, New Street	120
43.	Property No. 62, 12/14, Union Street	123
44.	Properties Nos. 62A and 62B, A House and Garden in Union Street	124
45.	Property No. 63, 23, Chamberlain Street	127
46.	Property No. 64, A Cottage in Beggar Street	130

* Properties Nos. 27, 29, 31, 33, 35, 37, 39, 41, 43, 45, 47, 49 were the gardens in the New Works Gardens annexed to properties 26, 28, 30, 32, 34, 36, 38, 40, 42, 44, 46, 48

47.	Property No. 65, Tenements in Beggar Street	132
48.	Property No. 66, 61, High Street	133
49.	Property No. 67, A House at Jacob's Well	135
50.	Properties Nos. 67A and 67B, 7, 8, and 9, Mill Street	137
51.	Property No. 68, 13, High Street	140
52.	Property No. 69, 11, High Street	142
53.	Property No. 70, 9 High Street	146
54.	Property No. 71, Gildenhurst	148
55.	Property No. 72, Castlemead	149
56.	Properties Nos. 73 and 74, Blackman's Well and Broad Close	152
57.	Property No. 75, Land in the South Part of Wells Park	155
58.	Property No. 76, A Paddock at Portway	156
59.	Property No. 77, Paulsgrove	157
60.	Property No. 78, Land in High Mead, West Horrington	158
61.	Property No. 79, Land on Mendip	159
62.	Property No. 80, Land on Haymoor (I)	160
63.	Property No. 81, Land on Haymoor (II)	161
64.	Property No. 84,* A Meadow on Knowle Moor (I)	162
65.	Property No. 85, Land on Knowle Moor (II)	163
66.	Property No. 86, Land in Burcot Mead	164
67.	Property No. 87, Land in Tucker Street	165

PART II Various Unnumbered Properties, Parts of the Manor of Canon Grange.

68.	5, New Street	169
69.	Cristesham's Inn or The George Inn (Now 7, High Street)	170
70.	A Copyhold Tenement in Chamberlain Street	171
71.	Brown's Gate	172
72.	A Messuage in Elm	175
73.	A House in New Street	176

* Properties 82, 83, 87, 88, 89, 90 and 91 cannot be traced; the numbers may refer to properties described in Part II.

ix

74.	A Tenement on the North Side of Chamberlain Street	179
75.	Penniless Porch	181
76.	The Choristers' or Organist's House	182
77.	A House in Sadler Street	185
78.	A House at the North East of the Undercroft	186
79.	St Andrew's Acre, North Wootton	190
80.	Longstring, Clay Furlong, and a Close near Balletrow	191
81.	Lands at Dulcote	194
82.	Three Corner Close	197
83.	A Piece of Waste Land on the East Side of New Works Gardens	199
84.	A Messuage/House in Tucker Street	201
85.	Lands at Wookey Hole	202
86.	A Paddock on Pillmoor	204
87.	Land on Queen's Sedgemoor	205
88.	Various Parcels of Land	206
APPENDIX I	The New Works of Bishop Bekynton	211
APPENDIX II	'The Cedars'	219
APPENDIX III	Compton's Burgages	223

PREFACE

My researches into the history of the canonical houses of Wells[1] brought to my notice the dean and chapter's manor of Canon Grange, among the properties of which were numbered the capitular canonical houses. I set to work, therefore, to identify those properties, and to trace their tenants, so far as surviving records made that possible. The results of my researches are set out in the articles that follow. These are divided into two sections: in Part I are grouped in order, excluding canonical houses, the properties bearing numbers, according to the numeration of the map of Canon Grange c. 1825[2] and the table of reference thereto.[3] In Part II are collected various unnumbered properties in which the dean and chapter had an interest. The three appendices contain material which could not conveniently be dealt with elsewhere.

This survey is not a complete account of the manor. The records refer to several properties, particularly lands, and houses in Chamberlain street and Union street, which defy identification. I hope, however, that this account of Canon Grange, breaking as it does new ground, will contribute usefully to the study of the dean and chapter of Wells, and the history of the cathedral; and that it may throw light upon the city of Wells in the past; as well as proving of interest to genealogists, and students of social and economic history.

Each property, or in some cases (for convenience) each group of properties, has an article to itself. First, the history of the property is set out; and then the tenants are listed.[4] Leases are given in date order, stating terms, rents, and fines, and noting any points of interest, such as special covenants or conditions. The surnames of tenants are shown as they appear in the documents. 'Tenant' denotes a person or persons holding the property directly under the lord – that is, the dean and chapter. In the case of houses, it cannot be assumed that the tenant was the resident; in some cases he may have been, but in others the tenement was regarded as an investment, not a dwelling, and was accordingly sublet. Occasionally residents are named, and these are noted. When a grant was made after the surrender of a previous lease or copy, this is also noted;[5] surrender generally indicates that the person surrendering a lease in favour of a new grant was a subtenant, a devisee, or an assignee, or the purchaser or inheritor of a tenancy. All surnames are shown as spelt.

I have attempted to identify properties with existing houses; this does not, of course, mean that the existing house is the actual property specified in earlier leases or accounts, but only that the property in question stood on the site of an existing house. In some cases the original house may have been pulled down and another built in its place; in others there may be architectural continuity between the original and the modern house, so that in the latter the lineaments of the former may be traced.

The financial officers of the dean and chapter usually showed in their accounts from whom rent was received. The person named, however, might not be the current tenant, but a subtenant or a resident, or a former tenant or resident, sometimes deceased, with whom the property had become identified. Similarly premises might be described in a lease as 'late of ─────', giving the name of a former tenant or resident. This confusing usage seems to have arisen from the practice of bookkeepers copying the framework of accounts from year to year, and from conveyancing clerks copying descriptions from old leases into new ones, without bringing them up to date. No doubt the result was exact enough for immediate practical purposes, but the practice makes it difficult, in some cases, to identify property or to trace a succession of tenants.

The cathedral's financial year ran from Michaelmas to the following Michaelmas. Some dates, therefore, are expressed as years of account, not as calendar years – thus 1631/2, prefixed with C, E, F, denoting reference to the accounts of the communar, escheator, and master of the fabric respectively.

All tenants, unless otherwise stated, are of Wells; likewise references to 'the cathedral', the 'dean and chapter', the 'chapter', the 'city', and all canons, dignitaries, officers of the chapter, and bishops, relate to Wells.

I am much indebted for various kinds of help to Mr. L.S. Colchester, Dr. R.W. Dunning, Miss E.A. Livingstone, Miss Lilian May, Dr. R.D. Reid, and to the staffs of the Somerset Record Office, and of the Records Department of the Church Commissioners; and above all, to my wife, Dr. Morag Bailey.

SHERWIN BAILEY

Wells
March 1981.

Notes

1. See D.S. Bailey, *The Canonical Houses of Wells* (Gloucester, 1982).
2. DD/CC 10878.
3. DD/CC 111748.
4. In a few cases I have conflated the history and the list of tenants, when this facilitated presentation of the material.
5. By the abbreviation, 'surr.'

INTRODUCTION

i. *The Manor of Canon Grange*

The manor of Canon Grange was simply the name given to the Wells estate of the dean and chapter, which had manors in other parts of Somerset. It derived its name from the canons' barn or grange, a tithe barn in which manorial courts were held, and to which tenants came to do service and pay rents as their leases required; in more recent times the audit or exchequer rooms over the west cloister served for these purposes. The mediaeval tenants of the manor were never unfree villeins,[1] but rather, clerics (canons, vicars choral, or chaplains), and burgesses of the city. They were required, as were the tenants of the other manors of the dean and chapter, to take the following oath: 'You shall swear that you will be a true and faithful tenant to the worshipful the dean and chapter of Wells for the estate to which you are now admitted, and that you will from time to time bear, pay, and do all such rents, burthens, heriots, customs, suits, and services therefor due and of right accustomed as other tenants of the said manor are or ought to bear, pay, or do.'[2] Among the duties required of tenants were, to do suit at the court baron on the days appointed, called the 'law days', in order to do homage for their holdings,[3] and to pay rents to the bailiff of the Grange, an officer appointed by the chapter. At these courts also, surrenders were accepted; leases, reversions, alterations in terms or lives, and fines were negotiated; and transfers of copyhold tenancies were registered.

Various regulations, applying to all capitular manors, including Canon Grange, were made from time to time by the chapter relating to leases or their renewal. Thus, on 1st April 1585, it was enacted that 'pursuant to instructions from the queen's counsellors, no lease shall be made and sealed, etc., except on one of the four general and quarter chapter days.'[4] A decree made on 26th May 1580[5] aimed at regulating the nomination of lives in the case of copyhold tenancies. On 7th January 1625[6] five covenants were set out, to be included in all leases, among them, stipulations that tenants must sustain their houses and also their hedges and ditches, and that all rents must be paid on quarter days. Another decree on 24th July 1677[7] related to the payment of rents, while others were concerned with renewals (29th July 1714[8]) and payment of fees (2nd October 1722[9], 2nd January 1741[10]). In addition to the bailiff of the Grange, other officers of the manor were a constable of the Liberty, appointed by the court, and a steward, elected from among the residentiary canons, who held office for a term of two years. The jurisdiction of the last named extended over all the capitular manors, and not only over Canon Grange.

Originally it fell to the steward to sell each year before Michaelmas for the benefit of the common fund, the grain which had been brought into the stores of the dean and chapter in settlement of rents and tithes. In the 17th and 18th centuries his duties became wider in scope and more diversified; he negotiated leases, held manorial courts, inspected properties, and generally supervised the capitular estates, and the reeves who administered them.

In the 14th and 15th centuries the chapter had to take steps to control the steward in the exercise of this duties. On 1st January 1511[11] he was ordered not to grant any reversion, nor to impose fines, nor to devise farms or benefices, without securing the consent of a majority of the members of the chapter; nor might he grant licence to remarry to a tenant's widow to whom a property had been devised, unless she surrendered the holding. A steward who contravened this order would lose half the liberty[12] of twenty days absence granted to him in virtue of his office. By a decree of 2nd January 1602[13] no steward might take from a tenant in consideration of any grant more than 12*d*. for the entry and 10*s*. for his fee; all other sums made by him were to go to the general benefit of the common fund. Another decree made two days later was aimed at curtailing the steward's perquisites: no steward might take for himself any sum of money for a heriot *ex conventione* on the surrender of a lease; any heriot taken on surrender must be sold in order to realize the highest price for the benefit of the dean and chapter 'as yf the same heriott were really sold in their sight and presence'.[14] Evidently the stewardship offered to a sharp witted canon opportunities to make a little 'on the side' if his activities were not detected by vigilant colleagues, who stood to suffer financially.

Rents received on the 'law days' or collected by the bailiff of the Grange were normally transmitted to the communar to be credited to the common fund, or to the master of the fabric to be credited to the fabric fund. In the case of non-repairing leases, the officer who received the rent usually paid for repairs; in certain cases when repairing leases were granted, the rent was reduced accordingly, and the tenant executed repairs at his own charges. There seems to have been no system of regular inspection of the manorial buildings, such as that which operated in the case of the capitular canonical houses.

Like the older canonical houses, many manorial properties, lands as well as houses, originally came to the dean and chapter with the intention that the rents issuing from them should provide, wholly or in part, for the maintenance of the obit of the donor. Such obituary rents were received by the escheator, an official elected annually by the chapter, often from among the vicars choral. After the discontinuance of the observance of obits at the Reformation, these rents contributed to the general revenue of the dean and chapter. Usually these obituary rents were low, and one of the interesting features of the survey made for the Parliament in 1649 is the recommendation by the surveyor of improvements in rent to bring the amounts yielded by the properties into line with current values. It is interesting, too, that at the Restoration the chapter made no attempt, with the survey as a guide, to revise the rents. Thus, even in the 19th century, tenants were paying for their properties no more than their mediaeval predecessors. With no allowance for changed money values, it might seem that the manor was hardly a profitable investment for the dean and chapter. It remained profitable largely because of the system by which fines, often substantial, were exacted at every convenient opportunity – at the granting of leases, and whenever a change was made in the term of a lease, or in the lives nominated.

ii. *The Commutation of the Estates of the Dean and Chapter*

On 1st February 1856[15] the chapter resolved to communicate with the Ecclesiastical Commissioners 'with a view to ascertain the terms upon which they would take into their hands the estates of the dean and chapter' – including, of course, the manor of Canon Grange. No reasons are given for this decision, but undoubtedly it must have been prompted by financial uncertainty, and a wish to be assured of an adequate regular income. The administration of the estates under modern conditions may have been felt as an increasing burden which a secular corporation like the Commissioners could undertake more suitably and efficiently than the residentiaries of a cathedral chapter. Moreover the chapter was only following the lead of other ancient cathedrals, which had made similar arrangements with the Commissioners.

Financial details furnished to the Commissioners showed that for the six years 1849–1855 the total gross income from the capitular estates amounted to £34,637. 7s. 8½d,[16] while expenses came to £13,884. 5s. 6½d., leaving a net income of £20,753. 2s. 2d. from which to pay the stipends of the residentiaries, and to meet the many charges upon the funds of the dean and chapter, including the maintenance of the fabric of the church and the services of the cathedral, charitable donations, and the stipends and wages of its servants and officers. The chapter clerk, in submitting these figures, explained that to provide details of the estates would be a long, complicated, and difficult task, but that 'more than half the property is held by copies of court roll for 5 lives renewable upon the dropping of either [sic] of them, and that with few exceptions of 40 and 21 years leases, the remainder is held by leases of 3 lives, renewable in the same way'.

After careful actuarial calculation and full consultation the Commissioners offered an annual sum of £4,200 for the transfer to them of all capitular property except the canonical houses and about two acres of land situated near the cathedral. That sum was to be payable until the dean and chapter had acquired real estate sufficient to yield a permanent income of an equivalent amount.

The chapter decided on 22nd April 1857[17] that this offer was inadequate and unacceptable, and one residentiary wanted the dean and chapter to retain all capitular property in Wells. After a further exchange of correspondence, the chapter, meeting at the Palace on 1st October 1864[18] resolved that the 'leading and essential condition' of any commutation must be the inclusion of the following stipulations: that the Commissioners shall take the estates subject to the permanent charges thereon; that besides the cathedral church and its appendages, the dean and chapter shall retain the dean's house and the canonical houses, and certain other specified houses and property within the precinct of the Liberty, and shall not be required to account for the annual value of any house or property appropriated to the use of any officer of the cathedral; that the annual sum paid to the dean and chapter shall be such amount as after allowing a fair average for ordinary donations, and after payment of the expenses of repairs and maintenance of the fabric and its appendages, the maintenance of the services, the payment of librarian and schoolmaster, of the choir, and subordinate officers and servants, and other incidental expenses, shall leave for each [residentiary] canonry a net annual income of £600, and for the deanery £1,200; that the houses on the cathedral green[19] shall be subject in perpetuity to the restrictions now expressed in the leases thereof; that a salary for the chapter clerk shall be received, and that the steward and the clerk of the manorial courts shall be compensated for any losses they might sustain as a result of a commutation; and finally, that certain financial arrangements shall be made affecting existing residentiaries.

After further negotiations a settlement was reached, which was announced in the *London Gazette* of the 27th July 1866: the Ecclesiastical Commissioners undertook in return for the transfer of all the capitular estates, excepting certain specified properties, to pay to the dean and chapter by equal half yearly payments, an annual sum of £5,425, and to accept responsibility for the chapter clerk's salary.

The excepted properties were: the cathedral church and the churchyard, and the yards, lands, and appurtenances belonging to the church, and also, those portions of the churchyard enclosed by the lessees or occupants of the tenements adjoining thereto; the dwelling house known as 'The Deanery', the four canonical houses[20] used then as houses of residence for the residentiaries; a former canonical house[21] then in the occupation of a surgeon John Nicholls; the Canons' Barn;[22] a dwelling house[23] then in the occupation of Raguel Selway; the ruinous building known as the organist's or choristers' house;[24] Brown's or Baron's gate;[25] 'Claver Morris's house';[26] the 'corner house';[27] Penniless porch;[28] and the house adjoining Penniless porch on the north.[29] Also reserved to the dean and chapter were all chief rents, redeemed land tax, and all fees payable for gates into the churchyard by occupants of the New Works houses and of the houses on the east side of Sadler street. To the tenants or occupants of these houses would continue to apply the restrictions imposed by the leases.

iii. *Sources*

For the manor of Canon Grange the main sources preserved in the cathedral library[30] are the mediaeval registers (*Liber Albus I, Liber Albus II*, and *Liber Ruber*), the series of chapter act books, ledger books, minute books, and record books; charters and other documents, draft court rolls, bargain books, some steward's books; and the account rolls and books of the communar, the escheater, and the master of the fabric.

After the commutation of the estates of the dean and chapter in 1866,[31] the Ecclesiastical Commissioners took possession of a large number of documents (leases, terriers, rentals, surveys, etc.) relating to Canon Grange. The greater part of this material was eventually transferred to the Somerset Record Office in Taunton, though a few documents were retained by the Church Commissioners. Of particular value among the Taunton documents are the map of Canon Grange *c.* 1825,[32] and the survey of the manor made in the summer of 1649 pursuant to the act for the abolition of the capitular establishments of the Church of England;[33] the latter gives a clear and detailed picture of the manorial properties at the time, with tenants, locations, and recommendations for rent improvements.

Apart from the map of Canon Grange *c.* 1825, that prepared for the Ecclesiastical Commissioners in 1875[34] affords useful information, as do the individual property plans in the survey.[35] Other valuable plans are those by John Carter (1794) of the cathedral and Palace precincts,[36] and that published by William Simes in 1735, conventionalized though this is. There seem to be no plans of the mediaeval city, nor of the surrounding fields; and it is surprizing to find that no plan of Canon Grange was drawn in the early decades of the 17th century, a time notable for the making of estate maps.

iv. *The Liberty*

One of the 'leading and essential conditions' upon which the chapter insisted in negotiating the commutation of the capitular estates was the reservation to the dean and chapter of certain houses and properties in the Liberty. The Liberty, or more precisely, the Liberty of St Andrew, to which the chapter referred probably meant the cathedral precinct, or the district surrounding the church. In earlier time 'the Liberty' appears to have denoted the latter, although later it came to mean the 'extra-parochial township'[37] which lay outside both the 'in' and 'out' parishes of St Cuthbert. Sometimes the name was used vaguely to denote the immediate environs of the cathedral. In this sense it probably described the area that was at one time enclosed, or intended to be enclosed, by a wall.

In 1286[38] king Edward I granted permission to bishop Robert Burnell to surround the churchyard and the precinct of the canons' houses with a crenellated stone wall with gates and posterns, which were to be open every day from dawn to nightfall. On 29th March 1340[39] a similar licence was granted to bishop Ralph of Shrewsbury, but this specifies only a wall round the churchyard for 'the honour of . . . the cathedral church . . . and the saints whose bodies repose therein, and the security and quiet of the canons and ministers resident there'. It appears that this work was never fully carried out, however, for bishop Bekynton, alarmed by the outbreaks of violence that followed Jack Cade's insurrection in 1450, obtained permission on 22nd March 1451[40] 'to execute all things specified (in the licence of 1340) hitherto not executed'. Bishop Ralph certainly built a wall enclosing the churchyard on the west and south sides, for this was left intact in the erection of Bekynton's New Works.[41] But the course of the wall intended by Ralph is nowhere set out; the area which it was designed to enclose was certainly not coterminous with the ' extra-parochial township', but much smaller. It is likely that the area around which the wall was to be built was, in fact, designated 'the Liberty', but there is no evidence to support this assumption; nor is the significance of the term anywhere defined. J.H. Parker[42] suggests that it referred to the privilege of being allowed to keep residence in a house within the crenellated wall, but this is improbable. More likely it related to exemption from liability for secular dues, and from certain kinds of secular jurisdiction. Such exemption does not, of course, obtain today, and in recent time inhabitants of the Liberty were liable to charges for the maintenance of highways and bridges, and also for a poor rate – one of the houses belonging to the manor, situated in St. Andrew street, being used as a poor house.[43]

Impossible though it is to define the bounds of the area which the royal licences of 1280, 1340, and 1450 were designed to safeguard, it is certain that they were not those of Collinson's 'extra-parochial township'. This is an irregular, roughly diamond-shaped district, in area about forty acres, with the cathedral situated in its south eastern part; it now forms a wedge separating the in-parish of St Cuthbert and the parish of St Thomas. In the past, the dean and chapter exercised a certain jurisdiction within the Liberty (the district around the cathedral): thus, offences under the ecclesiastical law, and infringements of the statute law relating to attendance at worship and reception of the Holy Communion, were triable by the chapter. Today, the 'extra-parochial township' of the Liberty has become virtually the 'parish' of the cathedral; according to well-established tradition, residence in the Liberty is regarded as a qualification for baptism and marriage in the cathedral church.

The dean and chapter, however, did not own the Liberty; the 'extra-parochial township' contained other properties than those of Canon Grange – among them some pertaining to the city and the bishop's manor.

v. *The topography of old Wells*

Containing as they do, descriptions of the locations of property, the leases of houses and land belonging to Canon Grange reveal much about the city of Wells and its environs as they were in the past, and many differences between past and present will be noted.

The differences will doubtless be most apparent in the names of streets and roads. Two features gave their names to streets near the cathedral. One was the area of high ground on the north and north east sides of the church, known as the Mountroy[44]; the other was the chantry college founded there.[45] The eastern arm of the road called The Liberty, known until recently as East Liberty, and shown on Simes's map (1735) as 'The Liberty', and on the map of Canon Grange (*c.* 1825) as 'Back Liberty' was known from mediaeval times until the mid-17th century as 'Mountroy lane'[46] because it led from the cathedral precinct towards the Mountroy; it was also known as 'College lane' because it led to the chantry college. The present College road is the northward extension of the old Mountroy lane, and is shown by Simes as Chewton road. The western arm of The Liberty was also (1683)[47] designated 'the road commonly called College lane'. This portion of the The Liberty was also called 'Canons' street' [*vicus canonicorum*] in certain 14th century documents,[48] showing that it was then, as it remained for the next six centuries, principally a street of canonical houses.[49] On Simes's plan this road is named 'Back Liberty'.

At its southern end Mountroy lane made a junction with 'the street leading to Byestwall', as it was known in the middle ages, or simply 'Byestwalls', now the eastern section of St Andrew street and St Thomas street. The western portion of St Andrew street was commonly called 'The Liberty', and occurs once as 'Back Liberty'.

The western arm of The Liberty makes a junction with New street, already in E1372/3 'la Newestrete',[50] which seems to have begun at this junction, for the houses now 1, 3, and 5, New street were formerly in Chamberlain street. At its northern end New Street branched into two roads, between which lay a small meadow, Three Corner close.[51] This field and the two roads were destroyed by a realignment of the turnpike road from Bristol early in the 19th century.

Many changes in street names have occurred. Grope or Gropecount lane was first genteelized into Grove lane, and then became Union street. Priest row is shown on the map of Canon Grange as Prison row; Beggar street has become a westward extension of Chamberlain street. Tor street, formerly Tor Lane, is shown by Simes as Tower lane; Water lane has now become Broad street.

Much of the land in Wells owned by the dean and chapter lay in the east field, on the south side of Bath road (Frome or London road). There is no map of the East Wells field; housing estates cover the land, and the plots cannot now be identified easily; some occur in the records only briefly, such as the half-acre of land in a *stadium*[52] called Dydman, and a half-acre in another *stadium* 'extending towards Dydman and "iii le bushes"', both granted for 60 years to precentor Thomas Cornish on 20th September 1510.[53] Other fields cannot be identified: Sare orchard,[54] Randal's (Randolph's) croft, and Isaacmead, for example.

In some documents crosses are mentioned as landmarks: St. Helen's cross, near the junction of Chamberlain street and Sadler street;[55] the High cross, at the west end of the market place near the site of the conduit; the Fayre cross,[56] apparently somewhere near the junction of Hawkers lane with Bath road; the Ashen cross, in East Wells, possibly in the vicinity of 16–20, St Thomas street;[57] and a cross near Jacob's well.[58]

Among the properties of the dean and chapter were several inns, only one of which now serves its former purpose – the White Hart hotel, formerly the Hart's Head, in Sadler street.[59] Others no longer surviving as inns, were: the Antelope, later the King's Arms (2–4, Chamberlain street);[60] the Three Horse Loaves, later the Globe (11–13, New Street);[61] the Flower de Luce; the Nag's Head (on the south of the White Hart);[62] and the Saracen's Head (at the north end of New street).[63]

Certain properties of the dean and chapter in Tor street were distinguished by signs; these may have been inns, but this is not certain: the Turk's Head (20, Tor street);[64] the Black Dog (19, Tor street);[65] and the Ram (15, Tor street).[66]

Notes

1. That this was not the case on other manors of the dean and chapter is shown by the deeds of manumission recorded in the registers.
2. DCR III, p. 91.
3. In 1665, 1666 and 1669 tenants were fined 3*d*. each 'for default of their suite and service to this Courte' (Docs. ADD/4024).
4. A.1571–1599, f.30. At this time the chapter met four times a year, on 2nd January, 25th March, 24th June, and 29th September, and the meeting was adjourned from day to day until all the business had been completed. See D.S. Bailey, *SRS* 72, pp. xix ff.

5. L.1571–1624, f. 14.
6. Cal. ii, pp. 382–383.
7. SRS 72, pp. 65–66.
8. Cal. ii, p. 497.
9. A.1705–1725, f. 181d
10. A.1725–1744, p. 214.
11. Cal. ii, p. 225.
12. To qualify for his emoluments a residentiary had to keep residence for specified periods, but on account of his duties, which often took him out of Wells, the steward was allowed a remission of 20 days residence. To diminish this period of remission could result in a reduction of his emoluments. On the emoluments of residentiaries see D.S. Bailey, *SRS* 72, pp. xxiii and xxiv.
13. Cal. ii, p. 344.
14. A.1591–1607, f. 172d.
15. M.1849–1859, p. 191.
16. During the same period, and for many years before, the average annual income from Canon Grange was £111 7s. 11½d.
17. M.1849–1859, p. 228.
18. M.1860–1872, p. 197.
19. It is confusing that the name 'Cathedral Green' is applied both to the western churchyard, and to the road on the north of the churchyard, running between Brown's gate and the Chain gate. Here the houses meant are those on the south and west of the churchyard, backing on to it.
20. Properties 4, 6, 8, and 9; *CHW* Articles 2, 6, 8, and 9.
21. Property no. 2, *CHW*, Article 1.
22. Property no. 3, see below, Article 2.
23. St Andrew's Lodge, *CHW*, Article 22.
24. See below, Article 70.
25. See below, Article 71.
26. See *CHW*, Article 21.
27. See below, Article 3.
28. See below, Article 75.
29. See below, Article 19.
30. On the source material in the cathedral library, see *CHW*, p. xiv.
31. See above, p. xvii.
32. DD/CC 10878.
33. DD/CC 111733–5.
34. Ch.C. map 14614.
35. Ch.C. file 51807.
36. In the possession of the Society of Antiquaries of London.
37. J. Collinson, *History of Somersetshire* (Bath, 1791), iii, p. 405.
38. Cal. i, p. 532.
39. Cal. Pat. Rolls, 1338–1340, p. 446
40. Cal. Pat. Rolls, 1446–1452, p. 473.
41. See R.D. Reid, 'The New Works at Wells', in WNH & A Soc. *Report*, 1930, p. 26; E.A. Freeman, *History of the Cathedral Church of Wells* (London 1870), pp. 143–144.
42. *The Architectural Antiquities of Wells* (Oxford & London, 1866), p. 25.
43. See below, property no. 13, Article 6.

44. This name occurs in a variety of spellings: Mounterie, Montre, Muntorie, Montroy, Mountery, Mountry, Monterye, etc.
45. See Appendix I.
46. Mountroy lane must not be confused with the modern Mountery road, which connects New street with Milton lane.
47. Cal. ii, p. 452; Ch. 849 (Cal. ii, p. 716).
48. Winchester College MS 19402 (1307); Cal. i, pp. 249 (1341), 270 (1376).
49. It is also possible that the name may have been derived from the Canons' Barn which was situated in this street.
50. In the 16th century the northern part of New street was known as Pyll street (*SRS* 51, p. 9 n. 18).
51. See below, Article 86.
52. A *stadium* was probably a strip of land about 200 yards long in the open field.
53. Cal. ii, p. 223.
54. See below, Article 86, and *CHW*, Article 4.
55. See *CHW*, p. 114.
56. See below, p. 207.
57. See below, p. 47 and 49, n.3.
58. See below, p. 135 and 137, n.3.
59. See below, Article 37.
60. See below, Article 40.
61. See below, Article 41.
62. See below, Article 36; this house has been demolished.
63. See below, Article 73.
64. See below, Article 11.
65. See below, Article 12.
66. See below, Article 16. For further information see A.J. Scrase, 'Wells Inns', *Notes and Queries for Somerset and Dorset*, xxxi (Sep. 1984), pp 378–95.

ABBREVIATIONS

A.	Chapter Act Book (WCL)
abbr.	abbreviated[1]
BB	Bargain Book (WCL)
Bennett	J.A. Bennett, *Report on the manuscripts of Wells Cathedral* (Historical Manuscripts Commission, London, 1885)
C	Communar's account
c.	*circa* (about)
Cal. i	W.H. Bird, ed, *Calendar of the Manuscripts of the Dean and Chapter of Wells*, vol. I (H.M.S.O., London, 1907).
Cal. ii	W.P. Baildon, ed, *Calendar of the Manuscripts of the Dean and Chapter of Wells*, vol. II (H.M.S.O., London, 1914).
Cal. Pat. Rolls	Calendar of Patent Rolls.
Ch.; ch.	Charter
Chs.; chs.	Charters
Ch.C.	Church Commissioners
CHW	D.S. Bailey, *The Canonical Houses of Wells* (Gloucester 1982).
DCR	Draft Court Roll (WCL)
D/D/B	Bishop's register, deposited with SRO.
DD/CC	Document deposited with SRO by Ch.C.
Docs.	Documents in WCL
E	Escheator's account
EB	Entry Book.
F	Account of the master of the fabric.
Fasti 1300–1541	J. le Neve, *Fasti Ecclesiae Anglicanae (Bath and Wells diocese), 1300–1541*, ed, B. Jones (London 1944)
L.	Ledger Book (WCL)
M	Chapter Minute Book (WCL)
n.d.	No date
n.p.	No page number.

O/S	Ordnance Survey
R.	Record Book (WCL)
R.I	*Liber Albus I* (WCL)
R.II	*Liber Ruber* (WCL)
R.III	*Liber Albus II* (WCL)
Reg.	Register.
Reynolds	H.E. Reynolds, ed, *Wells Cathedral: its Foundation, Constitutional History and Statutes* (Privately printed, 1881)
SNH&A Soc.	Somerset Natural History and Archaeological Society.
SB	Steward's Book (WCL)
SRO	Somerset Record Office
SRS	Somerset Record Society
S1570	Survey of 5th December 1570 (DD/CC 110002)
S1649	*A Survey of all that Mannor, Farm, and Baylywick of Cannon Grange* . . . made and taken in the months of June and July 1649 by vertue of a Commission granted and grounded upon an Act . . . for the abolyshing of Deans and Chapters, Cannons, Prebends, etc. (DD/CC 111733–5).
S1703	Survey of the manor, 1703 (DD/CC 114086).
S1875	Survey of the manor undertaken by order of the Ecclesiastical Commissioners in 1875 (Ch.C. File 51807, parts I & II).
surr.	Surrender
WCL	Wells Cathedral Library
WML	Wells Museum Library
WNH&A soc	Wells Natural History and Archaeological Society

1. Denotes that from an entry in Cal. i, or Cal. ii, material information for this study has been omitted.

PART I Numbered Properties shown on the map of Canon Grange *c*. 1825 and listed in the Table of References thereto, excluding Canonical Houses, Properties Nos. 2, 4, 5, 6, 7, 7a, 8, and 9.

1

Property No. 1
10 New Street[1]

In 1509[2] this property, situated on the east side of New street, was described as a messuage with curtilage and two cottages annexed. About the year 1745 the premises were converted by a Wells mercer, Thomas Bourne, who then held the tenancy, into two dwelling houses.[3] On 1st April 1842 the chapter authorized the purchase by the tenant at the time, Thomas Conway Robins, from Mary Foster, the occupant of the land and house on the south, of a small piece of ground measuring roughly 12 feet by 2 feet 6 inches, which adjoined the rear of the house.[4] At the commutation of the estates of the dean and chapter in 1866 the property passed into the hands of the Ecclesiastical Commissioners.

In the latter part of the 14th century the tenancy was held by Thomas Barbour, and after him by Christine Barbour (? his wife). She was followed successively by:

William Horsford [E1402/3].
John Hull [E1408/9].
John Wethy or Wythy [E1433/4]; repairing lease for 30 years at a rent of 3s. 4d.
John Taket [E1438/9].
Walter Parker [E1440/1].
Walter Baker [The date of this tenancy is not known].
Isabel Baker, wife of Walter Baker [C1504/5].
Peter Carslegh, prebendary of Shalford, grant on 16th May 1509, a repairing lease for 50 years at a rent of 13s. 4d. [Cal. ii, p. 213]; 18th May 1509. grant for 80 years at the same rent, divided between the escheator (10s.) and the communar (3s. 4d.) [Cal. ii, p. 222]. Dr. Carslegh sublet the premises first to John Brimscombe, and then to Giles Wallis, who in 1580 took the tenancy himself.
Giles Wallis, pewterer, grant made on 1st July 1580 [Cal. ii, p. 302]; fine 16l.
Edmund Bower, lease for 40 years made on 1st July 1585 [L.1571–1624, f. 74d]; further grant for 40 years on 1st July 1586 [DD/CC 112474].

William Clutterbooke, lease on surr. for 40 years on 1st October 1625 [L.1624–1681, p. 33]. This lease was produced (by whom is not stated) as proof of title when the survey ordered by Parliament was made in 1649; an increase in rent from 6*s*. 8*d*. to 2*l*. 13*s*. 4*d*. was suggested by the surveyor [S1649, p. 13].

Richard Stacey [E1660/1, E1668/9, E1670/1].

Ann Clinton, widow, grant on surr. for 40 years made on 7th January 1687 [DD/CC 112115; L.1681–1701, f. 73; A.1683–1704, f. 98; E1670/1, E1672/3].

The Revd. John Paine, grant on surr. for 40 years made on 1st April 1704 [L.1701–1739, f. 14d; A.1683–1704, f. 334; DD/CC112361]; regrant on surr. for 40 years made on 25th May 1721 [DD/CC 112402; SRO, DD/FS box 27 (c/648) – in this document the date of the lease is shown as 20th May 1721, doubtless in error; A.1705–1725, f. 162d; L.1701–1739, f. 200].

John Paine, esq., lease for 40 years on 10th June 1732 [A.1725–1744, f. 174d] regrant on surr. for 40 years, on 10th June 1737 [L.1701–1739, f. 303].

Stephen Stringer of Stawell, Somerset, is found in legal possession of the property in 1748; he was a subtenant of John Paine.

Thomas Bourne, mercer, purchased the lease from Stringer for 90*l*. Lease on 1st July 1748 for 29 years, being the unexpired portion of Stringer's subtenancy under John Paine, which Bourne purchased. [DD/CC 112165]; further grant on surr. for 40 years on 1st July 1780 [DD/CC 112165; cf. Docs. ADD/4219 – grant to Martha Bourne].

Martha Bourne, daughter of Thomas Bourne, lease on surr. for 40 years on 6th December 1804, fine paid, 15*l*. [L.1761–1777, f. 95; A.1777–1792, p. 72; EB 1771–1780 (DD/CC 110009), p. 299; L.1790–1807, f. 510; A.1792–1817. p. 301, cf. Docs ADD/4132, cf. 4219 fine 80*l*.].

Thomas Conway Robins, E1807/8; lease for 40 years on 2nd January 1819 [A.1817–1832, p. 33] regrant for 40 years on 1st April 1835 [A.1832–1840, p. 146].

Edward Thomas Whitacre, of 12 Lincoln's Inn Fields, Middlesex, grant for 40 years on 17th September 1859, on payment of a fine of £76 [R.3, p. 315].

At the time of the survey made in 1875 for the Ecclesiastical Commissioners, the house was occupied by a surgeon, John Gabriel French. [Ch.C. file 51807, pt. 1, ref. leasehold property 17; for a plan of the premises see Ch.C. file 51807, pt 2, p. 58a].

Notes

1. Now occupied as offices by Messrs Cluttons.
2. Cal. ii, p. 213.
3. DD/CC 112165.
4. R.1, p. 387; DD/FS, box 69 (c/648).

2

Property No. 3
The Canons' Barn

The canons' barn, often designated Canon Barn, stood between the grounds of 3, the Liberty[1] and those of 11, The Liberty;[2] it lay on the north of the former charity school.[3] It was a mediaeval structure, and has been described as 'an exceedingly early example of Early English'.[4] To the original building modern additions had been made before it was partly incorporated into the new building of the Cathedral School – known as the 'Bernard Building', having been provided by the munificence of chancellor T.D. Bernard. On the occasion of the opening of this new building in 1884, the barn was described, in the only account we have of it, as 'a large nave 15 feet 18½ (*sic*) in the clear with aisles 6 feet 6 inches wide the nave being separated from the aisles by columns 1 foot 9 inches square, which have chamfered caps and bases. These columns . . . rose some 18 feet above the old ground line, and were about 12 feet 6 inches apart longitudinally. The roof was of one pitch the rafters being continued over the aisles, and the ridge was about 28 feet 6 inches high from the ground'.[5] From time to time the property was also described in leases and surveys; thus from a lease of 1592 we learn that adjoining the barn there were two 'bartons, courts, or yards, one on its north side, and the other on its south side'.[6] Adjoining the barn were a prison, for the erection of which the communar paid 54*s*. in 1448/9, and a pinfold for impounding stray animals.

Nothing is known of the early history of the barn nor of the site on which it stood. It may originally have been episcopal property,[7] and this supposition gains support from a charter of bishop Reginald, granting the barn to the canons and relieving them of all service connected therewith, and particularly of a rent of 12 coins [*nummi,*] probably 12*d.*, which they had paid to him annually;[8] this implies that at first they held the barn on lease from the bishop. A bull of pope Alexander III, dated 16th June 1176 confirmed the dean and chapter in possession of the site on which the barn stood.[9] The same instrument confirmed the assignment to the capitular common fund of the tithes of the produce and wine of the whole parish of Wells, for the reception and storage of which the barn was principally used.

From at least the 13th century it was the practice of the chapter to lease the greater tithes (mainly grain) of the parish of Wells (St Cuthbert's), for which each lessee or farmer paid to the communar an annual rent of 100 marks (66*l.* 13*s.* 4*d.*). This rent was increased to 80*l.* by an ordinance of the chapter made on 27th March 1332 in pursuance of a mandate issued by archbishop Simon Meopham of Canterbury during a visitation of Wells which he made at that time.[10] It appears from an ordinance of bishop Jocelin in 1226 that the treasurer of the cathedral was entitled to a share of the rent issuing from the canons' grange, as a contribution towards the expenses incurred by him in the discharge of his responsibilities.[11]

In an *inspeximus* by bishop Jocelin dated 12th January 1240, Robert Gyfarde, chaplain, is named as entitled to the tithes and obventions of the church of St Cuthbert.[12] At the end of the 13th century dean William Burnel had the farm of the grange, but at the request of the chapter he demised the revenue to the common fund for the relief of the cathedral; in gratitude for his benevolence Burnel was promised the next vacant farm, and in 1295 he received accordingly the manor of Winscombe belonging to the dean and chapter.[13]

On 13th April 1300 the farm of the grange was granted to Peter de Insula, archdeacon of Wells, for as long as he should remain a canon. The rent on this occasion was slightly increased to 101 marks (67*l.* 6*s.* 8*d.*)[14] Peter did not long hold the farm, for on 3rd March 1303 it was granted at the usual rent of 100 marks to dean Henry Husee.[15] On 6th April 1305 the farm was granted to the successor of de Insula, Thomas Charlton,[16] who made an agreement with the chapter to hand over to it all the rents and profits of the farm in return for an annual pension of 20 marks; he would continue to pay the rent of 100 marks, which the chapter undertook to pay into the common fund of the vicars choral. It was also agreed to take no action against him in respect of defects in the building of the church of St Cuthbert, the chancel of which he was bound, as farmer, to maintain.[17]

In an undated document, which appears to belong to the first part of the 14th century, Thomas Haselshaw[18] alleged that he ought to have received a certain farm, but that it had been granted to another canon, in defiance of the custom at Wells. This custom was to assign farms in rotation to canons residentiary as they completed their residences. To this complaint a memorandum is appended apparently citing instances where this custom was not followed, and first among them we read that 'Iterius Bucard, canon of Wells, who never kept residence, had to farm the common grange of Wells by assignment of the dean and chapter'.[19] Bucard was prebendary of Wanstrow in 1213, but the records contain no other reference to him which would enable us to date his tenure of the grange.

On 7th June 1332 the farm of the grange was granted to Thomas Haselshaw,[20] presumably the canon mentioned above. The next farmer of whom we have record is M. Robert Stonor, to whom the grange was assigned on 28th February 1348.[21] In documents of 1352[22] and 1357,[23] John Huish is mentioned as farmer of the grange. On 26th April 1386 the farm was granted to M. Edmund Saynteloo,[24] prebendary of Combe XIII, and from this grant it appears that the previous farmer was William de Odecumbe,[25] prebendary of Combe VII. According to C1372/3. C1392/3, and C1394/5 the rent for the grange in those years was paid by Arnald Brocas, prebendary of St Decuman.

Most of the 15th century references to the grange and its farmers occur in the communar's accounts. The farmers' names, their prebends (when known), and the amounts of rent paid, are set out below; in some cases the account shows only the name of the farmer's bailiff or agent:

1400/1	Gregory Butleye (canon, prebend not known)	66*l*. 13*s*. 4*d*.
1407/8	Richard Drayton (Combe IX, Whitelackington)	66*l*. 13*s*. 4*d*.
1408/9	Richard Drayton	66*l*. 13*s*. 4*d*.
1414/5	Richard Drayton	66*l*. 13*s*. 4*d*.
1416/7	William Calf (North Curry)	66*l*. 13*s*. 4*d*.
1417/8	William Calf	66*l*. 13*s*. 4*d*.
1418/9	William Calf	66*l*. 13*s*. 4*d*.
1421/2	John Or[26]	66*l*. 13*s*. 4*d*.
1428/9	John Lygh, *custos firme hoc anno*	37*l*.
	due from the farmer's bailiff	44*l*. 14*s*. 1*d*.
1430/1	John Lichfield[27]	66*l*. 13*s*. 4*d*.
1437/8	John Lichfield[27]	60*l*.
1445/6	John Grene[28]	48*l*. 13*s*. 4*d*.
1446/7	John Grene – due from farmer	18*l*.
1448/9	William Lasewell (bailiff)	61*l*.
1449/50	William Lasewell	61*l*.

1455/6	John Parker (farmer)	52*l*. 6*s*. 8*d*.
	due from John Parker	7*l*. 13*s*. 4*d*.
1470/1	Richard Hayne (vicar choral)	54*l*.
1473/4	Richard Hayne	50*l*. 8*s*. 5*d*.
1478/9	William Dyke (bailiff)	51*l*. 3*s*. 4*d*.
1490/1	William Dyke	12*l*. 2*s*. 9*d*.
1497/8	John Stevyns (North Curry)	33*l*. 19*s*. 0*d*.
	William Chamberlayne (bailiff)	3*s*. 4*d*.

It will be observed that despite the mandate of archbishop Meopham, and the consequent chapter act of 1332, no increase in rent to 80*l*. was imposed during the first part of the 15th century, and that the tendency was for the rent to diminish in the course of the century. This may indicate a decline in the value of the farm, reflecting perhaps a change in the agricultural economy, such that neither the customary nor the recommended rent could be obtained. According to the *Valor Ecclesiasticus* of 1535 the grange was valued at 43*l*. 17*s*. 2*d*.; before this valuation, two further leases of the grange had been made. On 28th February 1504 it was granted to John Merler, master of the hospital of St John Baptist in Wells for a term of 6 years at a rent of 37*l*. 6*s*. 8*d*.,[29] and on 5th January 1509[30] for a term of 7 years, a grant was made to William Capron, vicar choral, and communar for that year, at an annual rent of 36*l*.[31]

Capron was not the first vicar choral to hold the farm of the grange, for it will be remembered that more than thirty years before it had been assigned to another vicar, Richard Hayne. It seems that the rule requiring the farm to be granted to residentiaries on completion of their residences was not strictly applied. Indeed, the next grants to be noted were made to laymen; possibly no canon or vicar wanted the farm when it fell in hand, so that it was offered to any one who would take it. Thus, on 26th July 1537[32] a grant of the grange was made to two husbandmen, William Evans of Bristol and William Lovell of Chilcote, for 60 years at a rent of 40*l*. A new lease was made on 20th November 1570 for a like term[33] at the same rent to Geofrey Upton of Worminster,[34] who was a person of some consequence in Wells, being keeper of the bishop's prison and bailiff of the store at the Palace. He died in 1683, and on 1st July 1585 the farm of the grange was granted to his son George,[35] who surrendered this lease in favour of a regrant dated 1st April 1586.[36] In 1586 further grants were made to George Upton – on 1st July, for three lives;[37] on 13th August;[38] and on 27th September, for three lives.[39] In each case the rent was set at 40*l*. On 1st July 1588 a change in tenancy occurred, a grant being made for three lives to George Upton and

William Bowerman.[40] By another grant on 16th October 1592[41] the tenancy reverted to George Upton for three lives.

The last lease is interesting because of its stipulations. These require that the lessee 'Shall repair and maintain the chancel of St Cuthbert's church as the dean and chapter may think necessary; . . . shall sett the pound doare at Canon Barne in the place where it was wont to be; . . . shall not stande within the compass of Canon Barne or the backside thereto belonging any cattle agaynst any wall abuttinge upon any of the Canons' howses or groundes adioyning thereto, or (against) the wall abuttinge upon the Ludborne,[42] nor keep any swyne within the precincte of the same barne and grounds . . . ', on pain of a fine of 10s. for every such offence. On 2nd January 1593[43] the barn and the rectory of St Cuthbert's were granted for three lives to George Upton and William Morgan *alias* Williams, a woollen draper of Wells; the stipulations were similar to those in the lease of 1592.

Towards the end of 1600 Upton entered into negotiations with the chapter for a further lease, under which he would pay, not an annual rent, but only a fine at the inception of the contract. The dean (Herbert) was then at Court, so the proposition was referred to him by letter, and on 27th November he replied: '. . . whereas Mr. Upton hath been and is a sutor to have a further state in the parsonadge of Wells and the Canon Barnes, I am content the same be propounded (in chapter), to th'end his offer may be knowen, and uppon notice thereof and your liking of the same, I will as then further impart my resolucion therein.'[44] Subdean Philip Bisse conveyed the dean's views to the chapter on 2nd January 1601, and a lease to Upton was approved for a fine of 400*l*.[45] A year later the question of this lease again arose; this time Upton sought a grant of the farm for his former co-lessee, William Morgan, and it appears that the chapter promised Upton that this would be made, for, hearing of the matter, dean Herbert wrote from Court to his colleagues: 'towching the graunt yow have made[46] of Canon Barne, though in some respect I could have wished yow had made longer staye, yet seeing yow thought it convenient soe to doe, I will not impugne the same, but yeld my consent to that yow have done.'[47] On 2nd April 1602 Upton accordingly surrendered his lease with a view to the granting of a new one to William Morgan,[48] to whom a grant was made three days later for three lives at a rent of 40*l*.[49] No fine was exacted, the grant being made in consideration of the fine of 400*l*. paid by Upton,[50] but we do not know what arrangement had been made between him and Morgan.

Upton died in 1608, and despite his surrender in 1602 had assigned the lease of the rectory of St Cuthbert's to his brother in law, Edward Bisse of Spargrove.[51] We hear nothing of William Morgan's interest. On 2nd April 1610 Bisse surrendered his estate in the grange, and a grant of the rectory and barn for three lives was made to him at the (by now) customary rent of 40l.[52] Seventeen years later Bisse surrendered this lease in favour of a grant for three lives at a rent of 40l. made on 2nd April 1627 to Edward Bisse the younger,[53] a fine of 240l. being charged, payable by eight annual instalments.[54] Edward Bisse the younger eventually surrendered his interest in favour of a grant, made on 4th January 1660 to George Bisse of Spargrove for three lives at a rent of 40l.[55]

Meanwhile the surveyors for the Parliament in the summer of 1649 had taken note of 'the parsonage and rectory of the parish and parish church of St Cuthberts,' together with all that Barne called Cannon Barne and two curtillages to the said Barne belonging . . . and all the tithes of corne, graine, hay, and other tithes . . .'; and had recommended an improvement of the rent to 180l. annually.[56] George Bisse having surrendered his interest, a new lease for three lives at a rent of 40l. was made on 7th April 1681 to his son Edward Bisse,[57] who was then living in Lechlade's house (17, The Liberty)[58] as a tenant of the dean and chapter. Ten years later, on 7th October 1681, Edward Bisse was permitted to change the lives nominated in his lease.[59]

On 15th April 1680 the chapter ordered its prison in the canons' barn to be repaired.[60] There is no record of any committal of offenders to this prison, though the barn itself was used once as a place of detention. A vicar choral named William Gale was charged on 18th February 1587 with negligence in the performance of his duties, and with frequenting a certain house of ill fame in Tor lane belonging to one Wallis. He admitted the charge, and was ordered from thenceforth to 'better behave himself in his demeanor in amendemente of his lose and lycentious life'.[61] On the following 1st March, Gale was again charged that notwithstanding the order made only a few weeks before, he did 'openlie in disguised order in the companie of others goe in a maske, with a visarde uppon his face, into the parish of Pileton and thence to Croscombe to the evil example of others servinge in the . . . churche.'[62] He confessed to the truth of the charge, whereupon he was ordered to 'goe presentlie in the Canon Barne, and there continewe in fastinge and prayer untill he weare by the deane and chapter againe remitted', after which detention he had to perform a prescribed penance in the chapter house and in quire.

The tenants of the grange farm after Edward Bisse were:

Matthew Hale of Alderly, Gloucestershire, jointly with Clayton Milborne of Bristol, grant on surr. for three lives at a rent of 40*l.* on 17th March 1704 [L.1701–1739, f. 27d; DD/CC 112605].
Gabriel Hale of Cottles, Wilts, one of the lives named in the previous lease, grant for three lives at a rent of 40*l.* on 2nd July 1715 [DD/CC 112606; A.1705–1725, f. 103; L.1701–1739, f. 87d].
John Wayte, of the parish of St Margaret, Westminster, grant for three lives at a rent of 40*l.* [DD/CC 112607; L.1701–1739, f. 287].
James 2nd duke of Chandos, grant for three lives at a rent of 40*l.* on 2nd July 1734, after surr., John Wayte having died. [DD/CC 112608, 112609; L.1701–1739, f. 617]. It appears that the farm of the grange was sublet by the duke to Peter Taylor, of the parish of St Clement Dane, Middlesex, brother of William Taylor of Wells [EB 1745–1755 (DD/CC 110006), p. 271].
John Wilcox, innholder, grant by the above in June 1731 for one year at a rent of 190*l* from 25th March 1731 [Docs. ADD/4081]
Peter Taylor, grant on surr. for three lives after payment of a fine of 240*l.*, on 1st October 1754 [DD/CC 112610; A.1743–1760, p. 198]. This grant was renewed for three lives at a rent of 40*l.* on 1st July 1774; at this time Taylor was living at Purbrook park, Hants. [EB 1771–1780 (DD/CC 110009), p. 94; L.1740–1760, p. 452]. Late in 1777, Taylor having died, the farm was vested in three trustees named in his will, who surr. the lease of 1774 in return for another for three lives, which was sealed on 1st October 1778 after payment of a fine of 240*l.* [A.1761–1777, p. 322; L.1761–1777, p. 425; EB 1771–1780 (DD/CC 110009), p. 253; Docs.ADD/4111, 4126].
Alexander Popham, a master in Chancery and the surviving trustee of the three named in Taylor's will, grant for three lives after surr. at a rent of 40*l.* on 1st October 1800 [A.1777–1792, p. 21]; regrant after surr. in May 1800 for three lives (fine 450*l.*) [Docs.ADD/4194d].
Francis Popham, Alexander Popham's heir, received the lease of the grange when the latter died in October 1808.
Henry Rycroft of Curzon street, Mayfair and Thomas Lewis of Nassau street, Soho, took the lease from Francis Popham, and obtained a regrant on surr. for three lives at a rent of 40*l.* on 15th May 1813 [L.1790–1807, p. 356; A.1792–1817, p. 179; DD/CC 112615; DD/CC 112617, cf. 112614, 112616; A.1792–1817, p. 502].

On 28th April 1858 the chapter resolved to allocate to the Revd

George Blisset, vicar of St Thomas's church in East Wells, an annual sum of £30 from the rent received from the rectory of St Cuthbert.[63]

In 1856 the chapter began negotiations with the Ecclesiastical Commissioners with a view to the transfer to them of all the capitular estates in return for an annual allowance. The lease of St. Cuthbert's rectory came under discussion, and after considerable correspondence it appeared that neither Sir Charles Taylor, the son of Peter Taylor and one of the lives named in the lease made to Messrs Rycroft and Lewis, nor Sir Charles's trustee, had power to renew the lease, according to a minute of a chapter meeting held on 1st April 1858.[64] No further reference to the rectory or the barn occurs in the correspondence between the chapter and the Commissioners, and when arrangements were finally concluded in 1866 for the commutation of the capitular estates, the barn (but not the rectory) was included in the schedule of exempted properties.

On 13th September 1876 it was resolved to let the barn on a yearly tenancy from 25th December 1875 at a rent of £12 to a Mr. Garrod.[65] Six years later the question of accommodation for the Cathedral School arose. It was decided on 18th October 1882 to erect new school buildings on the site of the old tithe barn, 'retaining as far as may be the structure of the barn', and to make application to Mr. Garrod with a view to the termination of his tenancy, if possible, at Ladyday 1883.[66] He was reluctant, however, to surrender this lease before Christmas 1883,[67] but it was considered that if possession of the barn could be obtained before the summer of 1883, work could be put in hand. Towards the cost of the dean (Plumptre) offered £100 and chancellor Bernard £500 – the balance required was to be raised by an appeal.[68] On 2nd July 1883 the chancellor increased his offer to £1,000, and the dean promised £100 if it should be required.[69] The dean and chapter donated the site, and the school building was opened in 1884.

Eventually, in the course of improvements to the facilities of the building, the canons' barn was incorporated into the Ritchie hall.

Notes

1. See *CHW*, Article 1.
2. See ibid, Article 2.
3. 7, The Liberty (St Andrew's Lodge), see *CHW*, Article 22.
4. WNH&A Soc. *Report* 1873, pt. 1, p. 42. It was built before 1191, L.S. Colchester and J.H. Harvey, 'Wells Cathedral', in *Archaeological Journal* 131, p. 203 and n.21.
5. *Wells Journal*, 8th May 1884.

6. Cal. ii, p. 325; cf. DD/CC 112596; a survey of the rectory of St Cuthbert's refers to 'two curtilages to the same barn belonging', DD/CC 112618a.
7. C.M. Church, *Chapters in the Early History of the Church of Wells*, London 1894, p. 78.
8. Ch. 8 (Cal. ii, p. 547); cf. Cal.i p. 27 (ch. lxxx) and Cal. i, p. 67 (ch. ccxxxviii).
9. Cal. i, p. 534.
10. Cal. i, p. 230.
11. Cal. i, p. 36. The treasurer had to supply all that was required for the due performance of the services in the cathedral. The effect of this ordinance was to create a fund on which he could draw for this purpose.
12. Cal. i, p. 135.
13. Cal. i, p. 153.
14. Cal. i, p. 170.
15. Ibid.
16. Cal. i, p. 169.
17. Cal. i, p. 214.
18. There were two canons so named. One held the prebend of Combe X in *c.* 1305, the other the prebend of Worminster in 1343 (*Fasti 1300–1541*, pp. 31, 78). The former is probably the one referred to here.
19. Cal. i, p. 192.
20. Cal. i, p. 222.
21. Cal. i, p. 242.
22. Cal. i, p. 456; Ch. 324 (Cal. ii, p. 618).
23. Cal. i, p. 383.
24. In *Fasti 1300–1541*, p. 36, the name is shown as Edward Seylo.
25. Cal. i, pp. 297–298.
26. Possibly John Orum, prebendary of Holcombe.
27. One John Lichefield was collated to the prebend of Dinder on 1st July 1476.
28. One John Green held the prebends of Holcombe and Milverton II, but not in these years.
29. Cal. ii, p. 175.
30. Cal. ii, p. 211.
31. W.P. Baildon, ibid, n.*, doubts that this sum was a rent, and suggests that it was a fine; but it is clear from C1513/4 that it was the rent.
32. L.1535–1545, f. 65.
33. Cal. ii, p. 291 has 50 years.
34. L.1571–1624, f. 1.
35. Cal. ii, p. 308.
36. A.1591–1599, f. 30.
37. L.1571–1624, f. 83; Cal. ii, p. 309.
38. See A.1571–1599, f. 35d
39. L.1571–1624, f. 88.
40. Ibid, f. 103.
41. A.1571–1599, f. 86d.
42. The Ludbourne was one of the subterranean watercourses or drains in Wells, see H.E. Balch, 'The Old Watercourses of Wells' in WNH&A Soc. *Report*, 1925, pp. 29–30. It appears from this stipulation that it flowed in the open near the barn.
43. Cal. ii, p. 325.
44. Cal. ii, p. 342.

45. A.1591–1607, ff. 158d–159.
46. This is evidently a slip for 'promised'.
47. Cal. ii, p. 345.
48. L.1571–1624, f. 182.
49. DD/CC 112596.
50. cf. L.1571–1624, f. 182d.
51. DD/CC 112597.
52. Ibid.
53. DD/CC 112598. The lessee was probably the elder son of Edward Bisse of Spargrove, who had two sons, Edward and Upton, see F.T. Colby, *Visitation of Somerset* (Harl. Soc. XI). London, 1876, p. 8.
54. Cf L.1624–1681, p. 45, where no mention is made of a fine; Cal. ii, p. 386.
55. DD/CC 112600. In 1688 George Bisse failed to pay the rent, Cal. ii, p. 715.
56. DD/CC 112618a.
57. SRS 72, p. 30; L.1624–1681, p. 628.
58. See *CHW*, Article 6.
59. *SRS* 72, p. 89; DD/CC 112604.
60. Cf Docs. ADD/4019. This document also notes that the common pound needed repair, another notice was to be served on the bishop's bailiff 'to remove the Soyle that lyeth agt the wall over agt Cannons Barne'.
61. Cal. ii, p. 310.
62. Ibid.
63. R.3, p. 175.
64. M.1849–1859, p. 269. No reason is given for this conclusion.
65. M.1873/1886, p. 85. Presumably C.W. Garrod, the chapter clerk.
66. Ibid, p. 199.
67. Ibid, p. 203.
68. Ibid, p. 214.
69. Ibid, p. 218.

3

Property No. 10
The 'Corner House'

The 'corner house' [*domus angularis*] stood at the south western corner of a plot of ground known in the 14th century as 'La Purihey'[1] (pear close or pear orchard). It was situated at the junction of Mountroy lane (The Liberty) and the road leading to Byestwalls (St Andrew street). In the late 13th century 'La Purihey' was in the tenure[2] of Walerand de Welleslegh, from whom it passed to John de Welleslegh, knight and from him to subdean Walter de Hulle. On Hulle's death 'La Purihey' came into the hands of his kinsman and heir, William Iwayn (or Ewayn) of Mudford, from whom it was purchased by John Wareyn, prebendary of Combe X, and canon residentiary. From Wareyn, another residentiary, Ralph Canon, prebendary of East Harptree, acquired 'La Purihey'. From the communar's accounts for 1414/5 and 1416/7 it appears that there was a house *situata cornerio ex parte orientali sicut itur versus la Mountrey et ex parte boriali sicut itur versus Byestwall* . . .[3] This corner house, with Lymington's or Surrey's house on the north of 'la Purihey', seems to have constituted a single tenement at that time. It was in the joint possession of Ralph Canon and William Bye, who paid for it a rent of 4*d*. From 1418 to 1431 the two components of this tenement were separated, and according to the communar's accounts William Bye paid a rent of 4*d*. for a *hospicium iuxta hospicium Radulphi Canon*.

From a charter of 30th November 1422[4] we learn that Bye's house was inhabited by a tailor named John Ekharte, while in C1437/8 a cleric Mr. Richard Thomas is shown as holding the house for life at a rent of 4*d*. His tenancy, however, was not long, for on 30th September 1440[5] a grant at an increased rent of 10*s*. was made to another tailor, John Coton, for the lives of himself and his wife Juliana. For the next fifteen years Coton occurs as the tenant in the accounts. In C1470/1 and for the following seventeen years rent was received from William Grene, and in C1497/8 and C1504/5 from his wife. Mrs Grene's tenancy appears to overlap a little with that of John Plummer, who paid, instead of 10*s*., 13*s*. 4*d*. in C1497/8 and C1513/4; he may have been at first a subtenant.

The next tenant disclosed by the communar's accounts is Peter Grantham *alias* Cole. He was followed by a widow, Margery Colwey, who occurs first in C1534/5. In this account appears an entry: 'paid for repairs to the house formerly Peter Grantham's in which Margery Colwey now dwells – *nichil*'. It would seem that the cost of the repairs was not known when the account was drawn up, for in C1537/8 we find: 'repairs, entered but not previously charged – 2*s*. 0½*d*.'

At court baron held on 13th August 1535[6] a bargain was made with William Haymen, Roland Dogeon, tailor, and precentor George Dogeon, to take a lease of 'the corner house now in the tenure of Marjorie Colwey'. The consideration was 6*s*. 8*d*. but the lease does not appear to have been taken up immediately, for according to C1547/8, C1549/50, C1550/1, and C1553/4, the house was in the tenure of John Kynge, tailor. In C1557/8 and C1559/60, however, we find Roland Dogeon in possession of the premises. In C1560/1 he paid a rent of 13*s* 4*d*. *pro duabus domibus* from which it would appear that the house had been divided into two dwellings. For C1561/2 the rent of 13*s*. 4*d*. was received from John Norman.

15

C1568/9 shows that the property was then in the tenure of one John[7] Chedsey *alias* Emery, who paid a reduced rent of 12s. This sum was received in C1587/8 and C1602/3 from Marian Chedsey *alias* Emery. She was probably the widow of John Chedsey, and appears to have been a recusant, for she was cited to appear before the chapter, having omitted to receive the Holy Eucharist. She failed to answer this citation, and on 20th May 1598 was excommunicated,[8] and cited again.[9] In C1625/6 the receipt is noted of 12s. rent from John Niblett for the house held by John Rytherche.

In 1630 a lease of the property was surrendered by Ann Atkins *alias* Emery, evidently a married daughter of Marian Chedsey; Ambrose Morton, a clothier, then secured a reversion of the premises for three lives, paying a fine of 4*l.*[10] In the Steward's Book, where this transaction is recorded the house is identified as being 'opposite the precentor's stable'. Morton paid rent for C1626/7, C1627/8, C1634/5, and C1636/7. On 27th October 1636, he was confirmed in possession of the 'corner house' by copy of court roll,[11] but he had already taken a lease of Lechlade's house (17, The Liberty[12]).

At a court baron held on 28th April 1642,[13] ratification was sought for a grant of the house by Morton to William Lewis by means of the transfer of a copy of the grant of 1636; it is not stated whether the chapter consented to the proposed change of tenancy. On the same day (28th April) Morton was permitted on payment of a fine of 40s. to change a life under his lease, which suggests that no transfer of tenancy was sanctioned.

In the summer of 1649, Morton was unable to produce to the parliamentary surveyors any proof of his title to the house, simply claiming to hold it from the dean and chapter at an annual quit rent of 12s., which the surveyors recommended should be raised to 3*l.* 10s. The description in the survey refers to the house as 'Commonly called the Decoy house', and not as 'the corner house'.[14]

During the Interregnum the house came into the possession of the Corporation of Wells. For the year 1658/9[15] the receiver of the Corporation collected a rent of 10s. from a carpenter, William Britten, and from the same tenant, 5s. for six months of 1659/60.[16] After the Restoration Britten continued to hold the property, and in 1703 was granted by the chapter a further lease. In this the house is designated 'Decoy-Pool', and 'Fountain'.[17] In his account for 1703/4 the communar also notes that it is 'now called the 'Fountain', formerly the 'Decoy-pool' in the Liberty'.[18] These names are nowhere explained, but they may have been derived from the pool into which St Andrew's well flows, and which is situated on the east of the cathedral church, at no great distance from this house. There is no evidence that the pool was used as a decoy.

William Britten may have been a puritan, for on 4th January 1667 he was brought before the chapter and charged with one John Brethers 'for causing a paper to be read at the high altar in the cathedral'. Both men admitted the offence, but no action appears to have been taken against them; and the contents of the paper are not disclosed.[19] Britten died in 1705 or 1706, and apparently was buried in the cathedral churchyard, for in his account for 1705/6[20] the communar recorded the receipt of 5s. 4d. in respect of the burial of William Britten.

After Britten it appears that the tenancy passed to Anne Thomas and her husband. On his death and her remarriage, her second husband Abraham Parsons, a glazier, acquired the tenancy in her right. On 15th June 1719 Parsons sought a reversion for three lives, the fine being agreed at 13l. In the following November Parsons granted the house 'called the Decoy Poole house, being at ye Sign of ye Fountain' to George Moore for seven years from the ensuing 25th March at an annual rent of 11l.[21]

The next tenant of whom we have record is Thomas Thacker, who in 1774 claimed to hold 'the corner house', then the Fountain inn, for two lives by virtue of a copy of court roll dated 17th October 1743.[22] On Thacker's death an involved series of transactions ensued. The premises passed to his brother Robert, and eventually to the nephew of Robert's wife Ann, John Trutch of Greinton, who claimed possession for two lives by a copy dated 6th December 1774.[23] On 1st October 1798,[24] Ann Thacker purchased the reversion for three lives, one of whom was her grandson, John Hill Thacker, who inherited the house under Mrs. Thacker's will. She had previously assigned the house as security for a mortgage for 200l. grante by Charles Bacon,[25] which J.H. Thacker took over. At the time of his death (c.1808), the amount due to Bacoon was 280l., and Thacker's trustee agreed to settle the equity of redemption to Simon Davidge Witherell for a payment of 80l.[26] Witherell then took a lease of the house for three lives from the dean and chapter at a rent of 13s.[27] He then repaid the mortgage to Bacon, and for a fine of 50l. assigned the property to a grocer, Henry Giffard, who at a court held on 2nd October 1826[28] took a reversion of the lease. Giffard seems to have assigned the lease of the house to John Giffard Everett, to whom a grant for five lives at a rent of 13s. was made on 6th September 1862,[29] for a fine of £125. This lease was renewed on 19th July 1910.[30]

On 1st January 1918[32] the chapter declined an offer of purchase for £750 from a Miss Swainson, but offered her a seven-year lease at a yearly rent of £45, provided she contributed £50 towards dilapidations. On 6th April 1918[33] Miss Swainson offered a quarterly tenancy at a rent of £45; finally on 1st July 1918[34] she was granted a yearly tenancy at a rent of £50. It was reported to the chapter on 6th June 1919[35] that Miss Swainson had offered to purchase 4, St Andrew street, as the house was now known;[36] she was told that no offer under £1000 could be considered. Eventually a lower price was agreed upon, and the conveyance to her was approved in chapter on 1st January 1920;[37] the sale was completed on 26th June 1920[38] for a sum of £850.

Thus the corner house passed from the hands of the dean and chapter. Some years later it was pulled down in order to improve an awkward and dangerous corner, and on part of the site was built the house called 'The Grange'.

Notes

1. See *CHW*, Article 9.
2. See ibid for details of the tenancies of 'La Purihey'.
3. 'on the E. side of the road to la Mowntrey and on the N. side of the road to Byestwall.'
4. Ch. 566 (Cal. ii, p. 665, abbr.)
5. Ch. 604 (Cal. ii, p. 671)
6. SB. 1535, f. 32d.
7. See L.1571–1624, f. 228.
8. A.1571–1599, f. 115.
9. Cal. ii, p. 335.
10. SB. 1625–1637, p. 45.
11. See S1649, p. 24. A reversion for three lives to be named had already been granted by the steward for a fine of 40s. on 1st October 1636.
12. See *CHW*, article 6, p. 67.
13. DCR II, p. 149.
14. S1649, p. 24.
15. WML, *Wells Corporation Receiver's Book* 1652–1681, f. 22.
16. Ibid, f. 29d.
17. S1703, p. 175.
18. Cal. ii, p. 484.
19. *SRS* 72, p. 3.
20. Cal. ii, p. 474. In the cathedral register his burial is recorded on p. 31: '7 March 1705/06. William Britten of East Wells in the parish of St Cuthberts.'
21. Docs. ADD/4075, 4076.

22. EB 1771–1780 (DD/CC 110009), p. 120.
23. EB 1798–1815 (DD/CC 110011), p. 35.
24. Ibid.; DCR. XXIV, pp. 51, 52; Docs. ADD/4188.
25. See DD/CC 111801. Bacon sought a reversion by copy of court roll for one life on 1st October 1806, a fine of 20*l.* being agreed (Docs. ADD/4207)
26. Ibid.
27. DCR XXIX, pp. 12, 13, 14. cf. Docs. ADD/4233.
28. Ibid, p. 48.
29. General Terrier (DD/CC 114080/2), p. 143.
30. R.5, p. 175; A.1900–1923, p. 95; M.1904–1918, p. 207.
32. Ibid, p. 379.
33. Ibid, p. 382.
34. Ibid, p. 390.
35. M.1919–1938, p. 11.
36. At one time La Purihey was thought to be on the opposite corner of Mountroy Lane; so W.E. Daniel, in a note in his transcription of the Communar's rolls, associated this house with 'The Towers', i.e. Tower House.
37. M.1919–1938, p. 23.
38. Ibid, p. 30.

4

Property No. 11
5 St Andrew Street ('Trinity Cottage')

This house appears to stand on land which in the 14th century, was in the possession of Alice de Welleslegh.[1] Property No. 11 originally consisted of two tenements,[2] one (here distinguished as tenement A) fronted on to the street and comprised a dwelling house and garden, and the other (here distinguished as tenement B) seems to have been situated at the rear of tenement A, to which it was adjacent, and comprised a dwelling house with a small barton pertaining thereto. About the year 1735 both tenements were united and converted into a single house with garden and backside. At the time of the commutation of the estates of the dean and chapter (1866) property no. 11 passed into the hands of the Ecclesiastical Commissioners from whom it was later purchased for the sum of £215 by John Giffard Everett.

The earliest tenant of this property known to us is

John Godwyn, grant for 80 years on 2nd October 1549 [S1570, f. 8]. Godwyn assigned the lease to Richard Roberts, and Roberts to a notary, John Smith. At this time it is stated that William Personns lately dwelt in tenement A, and that Thomas Sherman once dwelt in tenement B. These were doubtless subtenants.

After John Godwyn and his assignee John Smith, we find the following tenants:

Elizabeth Smith, John Smith, and W[illiam?] Smith, children of John Smith, grant on 1st April 1584 for their lives at a rent of 12s. 4d. (8s. 4d. for tenement A, 4s. for tenement B) [L.1571–1624, f. 68]. From this grant it appears that a widow Margery Burton, deceased, had dwelt in tenement A; the grant also included a house in Tor lane, where John Smith's father George Smith, then dwelt.

William Morgan, grant for three lives on 1st October 1619 at a rent of 12s. 4d. (8s. for tenement A, 4s. 4d. for tenement B [L.1571–1624, f. 228]. In the communar's accounts it is recorded that Morgan paid rent [C1625/6, C1626/7, C1627/8] *pro domo nuper Augustini Badgeworth*, and that for C1634/5 and C1636/7 rent was received from Edward Pit[t]man; Badgeworth and Pittman were probably Morgan's assignees or undertenants.

Robert Chute is named as the tenant in the survey of 1649, but no evidence of his title is recorded. The surveyor considered the whole property worth an improved rent of 70s. 4d. [S1649, p. 15]. Before Chute the premises, according to the survey, were in the occupation of Robert Morgan.

John Sheppard, pewterer, grant for three lives on 16th January 1690 [L.1681–1701, f. 117]. In the survey of 1703 there is a note with reference to this property: 'late Robert Charles', of whom nothing is known; he may have been a subtenant [S1703, p. 190].

Welthin[3] Sheppard, widow, is mentioned as tenant in leases of adjoining properties dated 31st May 1714 [DD/CC 111969], and 6th April 1736 [L.1701–1739, f. 680].

Owen Parfitt, joiner, grant after surr. for three lives on 25th June 1741 [L.1740–1760, f. 44; A.1725–1744, f. 216d; DD/CC 111974]. From a marginal note in the ledger book 'Mr. Owen Parfitt's new house', it would appear that Parfitt was responsible for the conversion of tenements A and B into one house during his subtenancy.

Owen Parfitt and his son Owen Parfitt, cabinet maker of Bristol, lease for three lives on 1st January 1756 [L. 1740–1760, f. 492; DD/CC 111980].

Francis Squire, chancellor, purchased the tenancy for three lives at a cost of 40*l*. [Docs. ADD/4085].

Edward Trent, grocer, grant for three lives on 5th May 1760 [Docs. ADD/4130]; regrant for three lives [L.1761–1777, f. 137; A.1761–1777, p. 149]; regrant on surr. for a fine of 13*l*. on 14th December 1779 [L.1777–1792, f. 83; L.1777–1792, p. 55; EB 1771–1780 (DD/CC 110009) p. 274; Docs ADD/4130];

Henry Brookes, grant on surr. for three lives on 1st April 1805 [L.1790–1807, f. 529; A.1792–1817, p. 313; Docs. ADD/4220]; regrant for 40 years on 13th February 1832 [A.1817–1832, p. 592]. From this regrant we learn that a subtenant, William Collins, was in occupation of the premises. The rent is stated to be the 'ancient rent' of 9*s*. 4*d*. (this would appear to be an error), plus an additional 8*d*., making 10*s*.

The lease of 1805 included the adjoining house on the east (property no. 12), and carried the stipulation that 'neither premises shall be made use of as a public inn or alehouse, or in carrying on the trade of a blacksmith or any other trade or business that shall or may obstruct the people passing by the street doors of the houses'. The adjoining premises on both sides of property no. 11 had been held by tailors, and those on the east by a staymaker and a blacksmith; those on the east had been used as an inn, while property no. 11 itself had been in the tenure of a pewterer and a joiner; but there is no evidence that these tenancies had given rise to any public nuisance, or that trade had been carried on in, or from these premises; though it is not improbable that tenants had in the past permitted some use for the purposes of trade. The stipulation may have been nothing more than a routine precaution.

The same stipulation was included in a lease for 40 years granted to a surgeon Richard Hawkes on 28th April 1847[4] in consideration of a fine of £66. Like the last mentioned lease, this grant covered properties nos. 11 and 12. Both premises were granted for 40 years to John Giffard Everett on 2nd. April 1864[5] in consideration of a fine of £68; property no. 11 at this time was, or had lately been in the occupation of Perrins Russ, presumably a subtenant.

Notes

1. See *CHW*, Article 9, p. 83.
2. L.1571–1624, f. 68.
3. This name also occurs as Welthian and Welthiana.
4. R.2, p. 163.
5. R.4, p. 78.

5

Property No. 12
6 St Andrew Street

The earliest known tenant of this property was Thomas Everett of Bristol, from whom the communar received 9s. rent for the year 1557/8. On 1st October 1588,[1] a grant of the house for three lives was made to Edith Everett, Thomas Everett's widow. When she died the lease passed to her son Gamaliel Everett, yeoman, to whom a grant after surrender was made on 20th October 1602[2]. On 30th January 1603[3] Roger Borne took a lease of the property for 40 years at a rent of 9s. The next tenant was a vicar choral, Anthony Mowry,[4] to whom a grant for 40 years was made on 2nd April 1623.[5] For the year C1625/6 the rent was received from William Taylor for the house *modo Anthonii Mowrie*, while for the next two years payment of the rent was attributed in the account to Anthony Mowrye 'late William Taylor'; Taylor was probably a subtenant of Mowry. According to the survey made in 1649, the property was then in the possession of Mowry's widow, Mary, who proved her title by production of the lease of 1623. The surveyor considered that the rent should be improved from 9s. to 2l 10s.[6] On 14th January 1662[7] Mrs Mowry surrendered her interest in favour of a new grant for three lives.

Mowry's widow, who on remarriage became Mrs. Meliar, sublet the premises to a tailor, Roger Lambert, who obtained a lease from the dean and chapter for 40 years on 4th July 1690;[8] he was named as tenant in the survey made in 1703.[9] Lambert secured a regrant on surrender for a term of 40 years on 31st March 1714.[10]

Lambert was followed in the tenancy by a blacksmith, John Broad, who was already in possession, probably as a subtenant, when he was given a lease for 40 years on 6th April 1736.[11] After Broad, the next tenant was a staymaker, James Moon, who took a lease for 40 years on 7th April 1752[12] in consideration of a fine of 3*l*. 3*s*. On Moon's death the property passed to his widow Sarah Moon, who was granted a new lease for 40 years on 2nd January 1773.[13] In this lease was inserted a stipulation that the tenant should not use the premises as a public inn or alehouse, or carry on in any part thereof the trade of a blacksmith or any other trade or business that would or might obstruct or prejudice persons passing to and fro before the street door of the house. A similar stipulation was imposed with reference to the adjoining property no. 11 in 1805,[14] and may have been simply a routine precaution, for there is no evidence that objection had been made to the chapter on account of the trading activities of tenants.

On 2nd July 1787[15] Edward Trent, a grocer who was already in possession of the property, secured a lease for 40 years;[16] this was renewed on the same terms, for a fine of 10*l*., on 1st April 1803.[17] The tenancy then passed to Henry Brookes by a lease for 40 years on 13th February 1832,[18] at which time the house was occupied by George Masterman.[19] This lease contained the same stipulation concerning the conduct of business on the premises, as that granted to Mrs. Moon. On 28th April 1847[20] a grant was made for 40 years to the Revd John East of 9, Belmont, Bath and William Hooper of East Harptree, who were presumably trustees.

On 2nd April 1864[21] a grant of the house was made to a wine merchant, John Giffard Everett. This was for a term of 40 years, and Mr. Everett paid a fine of £68 in respect of this grant and of another of the adjacent property on the west.[22] Property no. 12 was then in the occupation of Stephen Richards; with other capitular properties it passed into the hands of the Ecclesiastical Commissioners in 1866, from whom Mr Everett purchased it on 13th January 1881[23] for a sum of £215.

Notes

1. L1571–1624, f. 107d.
2. Ibid, f. 187.
3. Ibid, f. 187d.
4. In a later document (DD/CC 111959) Mowry is designated: the Rev Anthony Mowry; a variety of spellings of the name occur, such as Murray.
5. DD/CC 111960.
6. S1649, p. 8.

7. DD/CC 111959.
8. Docs. V/27; L.1681–1701, p. 106.
9. DD/CC 114086, p. 186.
10. L.1701–1739, f. 77d.
11. EB 1745–1755 (DD/CC 110006), p. 204; DD/CC 111973; L.1761–1777, p. 680; A.1725–1744, f. 155.
12. EB 1745–1755 (DD/CC 110006), p. 204; EB 1771–1780 (DD/CC 110009), p. 53; L1740–1760, p. 377; A.1743–1760, p. 288.
13. L.1761–1777, p. 369; A.1761–1777, p. 288; Docs. ADD/4103.
14. See above, Article 4, p. 21.
15. L. 1777–1789, p. 411; A.1777–1792, p. 262.
16. Docs. ADD/5154.
17. L.1790–1807, p. 484; A.1792–1817, p. 262.
18. A.1817–1832, p. 592; Brookes also held the adjacent premises on the west, see Article 4, p. 00; Docs. ADD/4242.
19. General Terrier of Canon Grange, 1826–1846 (DD/CC 114080[1]).
20. R.2, p. 163.
21. R.4, p. 78.
22. See above Article 4, p. 19.
23. R.4, p. 78.

6

Property No. 13
7/7a, St Andrew Street

This property now consists of two small dwelling houses, one (7, St Andrew street) fronting on to the road, and the other (7a St Andrew street), situated at the rear of no. 7. In the 16th century, however, the premises are described as a house with backside and garden, on which an annual rent of 8s. was charged. The first tenant of whom we have record was Thomas Ploweman or Lawrence, on whose death the lease passed to his widow, Alice, to whom a grant for three lives was made on 1st April 1584,[1] at which time Robert Brooke, doubtless a subtenant, was dwelling in the house. On 1st October 1588[2] the property was granted for three lives to Thomas Morris,[3] who was already in occupation; the premises are described in this grant as a 'house with a shop, backside, and garden appertaining or hitherto appertaining thereto'. Morris was still paying rent in C1602/3; he appears to have sublet the property to Thomas Lowe, to whom a lease for three lives was made on 1st July 1614.[4] The next tenant was a blacksmith, John

Evans, to whom a grant on surrender was made for three lives on 2nd January 1626.[5]

Evans was followed in the tenancy by a yeoman, John Clarke, who obtained a grant for three lives on surrender, on 1st July 1630.[6] When the survey of the manor was made in 1649 by order of Parliament, John Clarke had presumably devised the tenancy to his son, Samuel Clarke, who was in possession at that time, and proved his title by production of the lease made to his father in 1630. The surveyor proposed an improved rent of 2*l*. 10*s*.[7] Samuel Clarke still held the tenancy in January 1662,[8] and on 7th July 1670[9] surrendered and took a new lease for three lives; in this he is described as a miner. On Clarke's death the property fell in hand, and was granted for three lives on 4th January 1713[10] to an innholder, Richard Roode. On 13th December 1743[11] a new grant for three lives on surrender was made to Roode.

On 3rd February 1746[12] Roode assigned the lease for 99 years to John Moss as security for a mortgage of 20*l*. After Roode's death the premises passed to his widow, Susannah, and by her will (proved on 14th June 1748), they were inherited by her children – William, a silversmith of Wells, Francis, a joiner of Bristol, and Mary, the wife of a yeoman William King. Miss Mary Pomeroy purchased the tenancy from these legatees for 70*l*., undertaking to pay off the mortgage and the interest due, to the widow of the mortgagor, Joan Moss, who, on 18th September 1750, assigned the property to James Yorke of Wells, Miss Pomeroy's trustee,[13] to whom a lease for three lives was granted on 10th December 1776,[14] after surrender and payment of a fine of 7*l* 10*s*.

On the death of Miss Pomeroy the property passed to a yeoman, Charles Bendall who, upon surrender, was granted a new lease for three lives on 5th December 1799,[16] paying a fine of 42*l*.

In the general terrier of the manor (c. 1827) the occupants of the property are shown as 'the poor',[17] and in a lease granted in 1837[18] the recital of previous tenants includes the overseers of the poor of the Liberty – hence the name now given to no. 7a, St Andrew street: 'The Old Poor House'. There is no trace of any lease to the overseers, doubtless because the dean and chapter was the responsible authority. The premises were not long used as a poor house, for on 1st April 1837[19] they were granted for three lives to a carpenter, Richard George, being described as a 'house with a shop, backside and garden'. Another lease was made for three lives on payment of a fine of £21 on 29th September 1859[20] to Isaac Brown. In this lease the property is described as two tenements, then in the respective occupation of William Warman and John Hayes; and behind these two tenements, two other tenements with a yard, outbuildings and garden adjoining.[21] At the time (1866) of the commutation of the capitular estates, the Ecclesiastical Commissioners took this property into their hands, and in the survey made for them in 1875 it is described as 'butcher's shop, living room, pantry, and washhouse, and three bedrooms; salting house and loft, yard and garden'. It still yielded a rent of 8s.

Notes

1. L.1571–1624, f. 65d; Cal. ii, p. 306.
2. Ibid, f. 110d; DD/CC 111942.
3. Various spellings are found – Morice, Morrys, etc.
4. DD/CC 111943.
5. L.1624–1681, p. 35; DD/CC 111946.
6. A.1621–1635, f. 99; Docs V/8.
7. S.1649, p. 14.
8. DD/CC 111959.
9. DD/CC 111961; L.1624–1681, p. 623; SRS 72, p. 24.
10. L.1701–1739, f. 78.
11. L.1740–1760, f. 139; A.1725–1744, f. 254d; DD/CC 111975.
12. Docs. V/54.
13. Docs. V/55.
14. A.1761–1777, p. 325; L.1761–1777, f. 530; EB 1798–1815 (DD/CC 110011), p. 71. cf. Docs. ADD/4117.
15. EB 1771–1780 (DD/CC 110009), p. 193.
16. EB 1798–1815 (DD/CC 110011), p. 71; A.1792–1817, p. 164; L.1790–1807, f. 346.
17. Cf. DD/CC 111730.
18. R.1, p. 32.
19. Ibid.
20. General Terrier (DD/CC 114080), p. 106.
21. S1875, Leasehold tenement no. 7.

7

Property No. 14
8, St. Thomas Street

This property may have been part of the estate which Peter Orum gave to the cathedral at the end of the 15th century.[1] From a lease[2] of the adjoining property no. 13,[3] we find that in April 1583 Julian Mudwell was dwelling in the house. According to C1553/4 the rent of 8s. was received from a tailor, Richard Mudwyn;[4] at that time a widow, Alice Bye was the occupant. For C1557/8, C1561/2, and C1602/3 payment of the rent is also credited to Richard Mudwyn, and from leases of the adjacent property no. 13 it appears that property no. 14 was held by the following:

Barnaby Gorman, in October 1588.[5]
William Hawker, in July 1614.[6]
Anne Hawker, widow, in January 1626;[7] she is credited with payment of the rent for C1626/7, C1627/8, and C1636/7.[8]

For 1587/8 the communar received the rent from another widow, Frances Smith.

According to the parliamentary survey of 1649,[9] the premises were then in the possession of William Smallridge. Unusually, the surveyor did not suggest any increase in the rent of 8s. On 8th April 1671 a grant for 40 years was made to James Williams,[10] who was still the tenant when the manor was surveyed in 1703.[11] At a court held on 1st April 1775, James and Joseph Bacon claimed to hold the premises by a copy dated 7th October 1709; on the same day James Bacon took a reversion for two lives, paying a fine of 10*l*.[12] The premises then passed to William Lovell, to whom a regrant was made on 1st April 1775 for two lives. Lovell proposed, on 1st July 1785 to take a reversion for three lives for a fine of 10 guineas.[13]

The general terrier of the manor shows that a lease of this property was made on 3rd April 1835 to a carpenter, Richard George; and another, for three lives, on 29th September 1859, to Isaac Brown, a freestone mason.[14] The property passed to the Ecclesiastical Commissioners at the time of the commutation of the capitular estates in 1866, and in the survey and valuation prepared in 1875 for the Commissioners the premises are described as being divided into four tenements – an east front portion, consisting of a living room, a back kitchen, and two bedrooms; an adjoining front portion, with a kitchen, and back kitchen, and three bedrooms; a tenement in the yard, having a living room and two bedrooms; and an upper tenement, with a living room, a back house, and two bedrooms.[15] Two of these tenements were occupied by William Warman and John Hayes.[16]

Notes

1. Chs. 705, 706 (Cal. ii, p. 691).
2. L.1571–1624, f. 65d.

3. See above Article 6.
4. Doubtless a variant form of Mudwell.
5. L.1571–1624, f. 110d; DD/CC 111942.
6. DD/CC 111943.
7. DD/CC 111946 (in L.1624–1681 – '— Hawker').
8. The entry for C1636/7 may signify nothing more than that for this year rent was received in respect of the house formerly held by Mrs Hawker.
9. S1649, p. 23.
10. *SRS* 72, p. 30.
11. S1703, p. 197.
12. EB 1771–1780 (DD/CC 110009), p. 70; DCR XV, p. 14.
13. Docs. ADD/4151.
14. DD/CC 114080[1].
15. S1875, copyhold tenement no. 1.
16. Williams and Hayes occur as occupants of two of the tenements into which the adjoining property no.13 was divided (see above Article 6, p. 25). There may have been confusion or error on the part of the surveyor, who dealt with properties nos. 13 and 14 at the same time.

8

Property Nos. 15, 16, and 17
14, 16, 18, 20, 20a (22), St. Thomas Street

These properties lay on the south side of what is now St. Thomas street, between a house on the west side belonging to the mayor and corporation of Wells, and certain properties on the east side, part of the estate of the college of vicars choral. Owing to changes which have occurred in modern times, it is difficult to identify satisfactorily these properties with existing houses and shops.

Property no. 15 corresponded to 14, St Thomas street, and is usually described as a cottage; originally it formed part of the estate which Peter Orum gave to the cathedral in 1479.[1]

Property no. 16, described as a mansion house with a shop and orchard attached, corresponded to 16, St Thomas street. The orchard (or garden) was the plot of ground 1½ acres in area, designated in a lease of 1798,[2] and in subsequent leases, 'the wall garden', because it was bounded on all sides by a wall. Properties nos. 15 and 16 generally comprised one holding, both being let together after the middle of the 16th century.

Property no. 17 corresponded to the three premises numbered 18 (demolished in order to make an entrance to the builder's yard of Messrs Hill and Son), 20, and 22 (or 20a).

Property no. 15 yielded an annual rent of 7s., which the communar received for 1545/6 from a smith, Hugh Barton. This, and property no. 16 together were granted for 60 years on 25th February 1552[3] at a combined rent of 27s. to a vicar choral, Walter Nowell. His tenure continued until 2nd January 1586,[4] when the combined holding was granted for 40 years to William Powell, canon residentiary and later, archdeacon of Bath. During the latter part of Nowell's tenancy, the occupant of property no. 16 was John Kirell (or Kyrle). Before Nowell surrendered his tenancy the house had been divided into two dwellings which, in 1586 were inhabited respectively by Thomas Mandley[5] and John Light.[6] The lease of 1586 included a parcel of ground known as 'Buttclose',[7] which thenceforth was always united with properties nos. 15 and 16 to make one holding. Dr. Powell took a further grant on 1st October 1587,[8] at which time the two portions of property no. 16 were still occupied by Mandley and Leigh.

The lease of 1587 was surrendered by Dr. Powell's son Samuel in favour of another for 40 years in January[9] 1592, when Mandley and Leigh were still in occupation of their tenements. On 24th June 1598[10] Samuel Powell again surrendered in favour of another lease for 40 years. Property no. 16 had by now been divided into three parts, two of which were occupied by William Wigmore and his wife, and William Stevens. The tenancy was subsequently acquired by Cornelius Watts, to whom a grant on surrender for 40 years was made on 1st July 1633;[11] the occupants of the tenements comprising property no. 16 at that time were Joseph Jackson and John Dier, while James Sellicombe was in the cottage (property no. 15). In the survey made in 1649 the premises were described as a mansion house with shop and orchard belonging thereto (property no. 16), a cottage (property no. 15), and Buttclose; they were then in the possession of Richard Gorman. The surveyor considered the rent of 29s. 8d.[12] insufficient, and recommended an improvement to 5l. 2s.[13]

The next tenant of properties nos. 15 and 16 was a yeoman named William Smallridge; he was followed by another, James Williams who, on 8th April 1671,[14] obtained on surrender a grant for 40 years. His tenancy was renewed for a like term on 6th December 1679,[15] and in this grant property no. 17 was included, being described as the house

29

where Robert Frye lately dwelt. Also included was a house in Tor lane (Tor street).[16] In the grants of 1671 and 1679, the occupant of property no. 16 was named as Mary Hills, widow, and of the cottage, property no. 15, as Henry White. In consideration of the surrender of his existing interests, a further lease for 40 years of properties nos. 15, 16, 17, and Buttclose was made to James Williams on 2nd August 1688,[17] William Lambert being in occupation of property no. 16, and Henry White of property no. 15. Yet another grant on surrender for 40 years of these various properties was made to Williams on 1st January 1698,[18] at which time William Lambert and Henry White were still in occupation of properties nos. 16 and 15 respectively.[19] They were still living in these houses when the next change in tenancy occurred on 6th July 1716,[20] when a grant on surrender for 40 years of the entire holding was made to James Bacon, yeoman. This grant was renewed on surrender, for 40 years on 13th March 1732.[21]

Joseph Bacon, clothier, came into possession of James Bacon's holding, and surrendered his estate for a new lease for 40 years on 1st April 1751;[22] he renewed the lease for 40 years on 3rd January 1763.[23] A baker, John Hicks, next acquired an interest in the properties and obtained a new lease for 40 years on surrender, on 1st July 1780, paying a fine of 8*l.*[24] On 1st October 1796,[25] he surrendered and took a new lease for 40 years, the fine being set at 21*l*.

The leases of 1751, 1763, 1780, and 1796 do not name the occupants of properties nos. 15 and 16. However, from an indenture of sale drawn on 7th November 1785,[26] by means of which John Hicks, for a sum of 80*l*., conveyed the tenancy of property no. 17 to Robert Bendall, carpenter and joiner, of St Botolph's parish, Aldgate, London, we learn that Elizabeth Gee was then in occupation of property no. 15, the cottage in which Henry White had long dwelt. From a deed of assignment made on 20th October 1798[27] by Ann Hicks, widow, and George Lovell, residuary legatees and sole executors of John Hicks, it appears that an interest in properties nos. 15 and 16 had been acquired by a gardener, Robert Newton. In this document property no. 16 is described as 'the corner house on the east of the gateway or entrance into the passage thereto adjoining called the yard, consisting of a lower room or kitchen and chambers over the same, and one long room behind the kitchen called the pantry, together with a room or chamber over the gateway.'[28]

The cottage (property no. 15) became severed from the total holding about this time, when it passed into the hands of a butcher, William Candy, from whom the lease was purchased for £150 by a widow, Mary

Pearce, on 29th September 1815.[29] This property was granted for 40 years on 4th December 1828[30] to another butcher, James White, to whom the lease gave right of access to a well in the court or yard pertaining to property no. 16.[31] This yard was then in the possession of Elizabeth Newton, who also had the 'wall garden'. The premises (property no. 15) granted in 1828 to James White were described as 'part and parcel of an ancient tenement . . . for which . . . when entire the yearly rent of £2. 2s. 8d.[32] was paid'. On 4th December 1834,[33] a lease for 40 years of property no. 16 at a rent of £1 annually was made to Elizabeth Newton. It appears that running southward from the house there were now four other dwellings inhabited by undertenants of Mrs Newton: Jacob Gould, James Southway, Esau Francis, and Robert Thompson. It will be remembered that at an earlier date, this property had been divided into two dwellings, and then into three; it seems that further dwellings had been built or converted from outbuildings or from the existing houses.

By his will James White left his interest in property no. 15 to John Sheppard, yeoman, in trust for the separate use of his wife Ann White for her life. Thereafter it was to be sold.[34] Mrs White died on 14th May 1857, and on the following 17th July[35] the tenancy was put up for auction at the Lamb inn (now, 25, St Thomas street). The premises were described in the auctioneer's particulars as 'a convenient messuage or dwelling house with slaughter house, stable, piggery, and yard adjoining, where the business of a butcher had been successfully carried out during the last 50 years.' The tenancy was purchased by a yeoman of Coxley, James White, to whom a grant for 40 years was made on 21st October 1857 for a fine of £56.[36] On 30th January 1861[37] property no. 16 was granted for 40 years to a butcher, James Boulton. He is the last tenant of this property of whom record survives, and presumably gave his name to the court in which the well was situated – 'Building's court'[38] being probably a corruption of 'Boulton's court'.

Property no. 17 was granted for 40 years to two butchers, Thomas Raines and Thomas Millard, on 1st October 1830,[39] being described as a tenement used as two dwellings then or lately, in the several occupations of Robert Westcott aand Betty Starr, with a blacksmith's shop adjoining. On 21st April 1849[40] this property was granted for 40 years to Joseph Kiddle of Southway in the parish of St Cuthbert, Wells, in consideration of a fine of £21. The two dwellings were then in the occupation of Thomas Millard and Robert Grandon. This grant was renewed for 40 years to Joseph Kiddle (described as 'of Street') on 2nd January 1864,[41] in consideration of a fine of £77. The two dwellings

31

were then in the occupation severally of Stephen Slade and William Ridewood. A renewal of the last mentioned lease was sought, and a fine of £21 was proposed;[42] Eventually a new grant for 40 years was made to Joseph Kiddle on 2nd January 1864.[43]

Properties nos. 15, 16, and 17 eventually passed into the hands of the Ecclesiastical Commissioners following the commutation in 1866 of the estates of the dean and chapter.[44]

Notes

1. Chs. 705, 706 (Cal. ii, p. 691).
2. DD/CC 111912/3.
3. L.1546–1565, f. 47d
4. L.1571–1624, f. 93d.
5. In a lease of 1698 this name occurs as Mandline.
6. In subsequent leases (and thereafter) this name occurs as Leigh.
7. See Article below 15, p. 47.
8. L.1571–1624, f. 109.
9. Ibid, f. 138; the day is omitted from the record.
10. Ibid, f. 168.
11. DD/CC 111949; L.1624–1681, p. 627; S1649, p. 7.
12. Properties nos. 15 and 16: 27s., Buttclose: 2s. 8d.
13. S1649, p. 7.
14. DD/CC 111957, 111958.
15. L.1624–1681, p. 627.
16. See Article 16 below.
17. L.1781–1791, f. 83.
18. L.1681–1701, f. 220; cf. S1703, p. 196.
19. See the notes in EB 1698–1699 (DD/CC 110005), p. 5.
20. DD/CC 111970; L.1701–1739, p. 102; A.1705–1725, f. 114.
21. A.1725–1744, f. 109; L.1701–1739, f. 574.
22. A.1744–1760, p. 144; L.1740–1760, f. 345.
23. L.1761–1777, f. 33.
24. A.1777–1792, p. 72; L.1777–1789, f. 92; EB 1771–1780 (DD/CC 110009), p. 298.
25. L.1790–1807, f. 262; A.1792–1817, p. 81, cf. Docs. ADD/4184.
26. DD/CC 111908.
27. DD/CC 111912/3.
28. See the plan of leasehold tenement no. 6 in Ch.C. file 51807, pt. II.
29. DD/CC 111856.
30. DD/CC 111856a.
31. For this yard, see above, deed of assignment of 20th October 1798.
32. £1 for property no 16, 7s. for property no. 15, 7s. for property no 17, 2s. 8d. for Buttclose, and 6s. for property no. 23a in Tor lane.
33. A.1832–1840, p. 118.
34. DD/CC 111856b.
35. DD/CC 111857a.

36. R.3, p. 142; Docs. ADD/4202.
37. Ibid, p. 373.
38. See O/S map 1886 (1:500).
39. A.1817–1832, p. 536.
40. R.2, p. 240.
41. R.4, p. 54; for a plan of the premises, see Docs. Add/4273(12).
42. General terrier 1846–1866 (DD/CC 114080/2), p. 21.
43. Ch.C. File 51807 pt. I.
44. See Ch.C. file 51807, pts. I and II, leasehold tenements 6, 13, and 40.

9

Property No. 18
30/32, St. Thomas Street

The earlist reference to this property shows that it consisted originally of a single tenement – a house with curtilage and a close of meadow, about 3 roods in area. It was situated on the south side of the road, now St Thomas street, having on its west side a property of the college of vicars choral. About 1800 the house was divided to make two dwellings.

It is not known when this property came into the hands of the dean and chapter, and the record of tenants begins with:

Oswall [Oswald ?] Daniell, tailor, grant for 40 years on 2nd October 1599. [C1587/8; L.1571–1624, f. 167d].
Richard Oswell[1] [C1602/3].
Oswell Danyell [C1625/6, C1626/7, C1627/8]
Oswall Daniell, tailor, grant for three lives on 1st July 1629 [L.1624–1681, p. 69]
Adriana (Adria) Daniel, widow [of Oswall Daniell] [C1634/5]
Adrya Daniell, widow, grant (on surr.) for three lives on 1st July 1635 [L.1624–1681, p. 249; DD/CC 111951].
Adryan Danyell[1] in possession in 1649, and produced as evidence of title the lease made on 1st July 1635. The property was considered worth an improved rent of 40s. [S1649, p. 16]
Joane Maggs, spinster of East Wells and kinswoman of the above, assignment dated 17th July 1660 [Docs. ADD/4014].
William Smallridge, grant (on surr.) for three lives on 5th October 1660

[DD/CC 111957/8]; the previous tenant is named as Adrian David [DD/CC 111736 25/33].

James Williams, occurs as tenant in a 'new survey' (c. 1700–1710) compiled by the deputy chapter clerk, Dr. Richard Healy [DD/CC 111736]

Lucy Bendall, grant for 40 years apparently made on 1st July 1780; she assigned the lease to a wells goldsmith, George Penny, as security for a mortgage of 14*l*. [DD/CC 111916]

George Webb, tailor, assignment of lease by Lucy Bendall on 27th July 1793 for the residue of the term under the grant of 1780. She held herself responsible for the repayment of the mortgage plus interest [DD/CC 111916].

James Rudge, carpenter of the city of London, and Leah Rudge obtained the tenancy under the will of Lucy Bendall dated 25th March 1800; they were required to dispose of the tenancy at a convenient time in order to discharge the mortgage [DD/CC 111916].

William Grist, baker, purchased the tenancy from the Rudges on 28th March 1807, for which he paid £140 [DD/CC 111916]; grant for 40 years at a rent of 7*s*. made on 1st July 1819 [DD/CC 111917].

George Thorn, grant for 40 years at a rent of 7*s*. 4½*d* land tax, made on 17th November 1840 [R.1, p. 300; DD/CC 111717[1]]. The two dwellings into which the property had been divided were then in the occupation of Joseph Burr and George Urch; regrant for 40 years on 11th September 1855[2] for a fine of £21 [R.3, p. 35; DD/CC 111918, 114080/2, p. 67]. Joseph Burr continued in occupation of one of the two dwellings as Thorn's undertenant.

The property came into the possession of the Ecclesiastical Commissioners in 1866.

Notes

1. Apparently an error for Daniell.
2. For a plan of the premises, see Docs. ADD/4273(37).

10

Property No. 19
84, 86, 88, St Thomas Street

This property, situated on the south side of St Thomas street, consisted of a house, from which a large garden extended southward to the Chilcote stream. In 1866, under the commutation of the estates of the dean and chapter, the property passed to the Ecclesiastical Commissioners, who in 1875 had a survey made of the manor in which the premises are described as a house, formerly in two tenements, of which only a kitchen, pantry and wash-house, with two bedrooms are occupied; the other part – a living room and two bedrooms being in a ruinous state.[1] The house has since been restored, and converted into three dwellings.

In 1587/8 the communar received a rent of 6s. 9d.[2] for this property from a tenant who is not named in the account. The other tenants were:

Joan Loxton [C1602/3, C1625/6].
Francis Loxton [C1626/7, C1627/8; 1629–1637, p. 40].
William Somerton in right of his wife, formerly Mary Loxton, is shown as tenant in the survey of 1649, proving his title by production of a court roll copy dated 24th September 1619. The surveyor recommended an increase in rent to 3l. [S1649, p. 19].
William Lovell is shown as tenant in the survey of 1703 [S1703, p. 186; cf. SB 1636, p. 130]. It is not clear whether Lovell was the tenant or only a subtenant.
William Lovell and John Lovell, masons, grant (on surr.) for three lives on 1st April 1731 [A.1725–1744, f. 85; L.1701–1739, f. 509; DD/CC 111971]. At the time of the grant, William Lovell was in possession. Grant renewed on surr. for three lives on 7th November 1733 [L.1701–1739, f. 592; DD/CC 111972; A.1725–1744, f. 119d; EB 1745–1755 (DD/CC 110006), p. 222] – fine 2l. 2s.
John Lovell, grant on surr. for three lives on 12th December 1752 [L.1740–1760, f. 402; A.1743–1760, p. 165; DD/CC 111976].
James Lovell, mason, son of John Lovell, grant (on surr.) for three lives on 1st July 1780 [EB 1771–1780 (DD/CC 110009), p. 301; L.1777–1789, f. 74; Docs. ADD/4131]; A fine of 4l. was charged.

James Lovell, inherited the tenancy on the death of his father, James Lovell, and relinquished it in favour of

The trustees of John Paine Tudway, grant for three lives sealed on 2nd April 1821 [A.1817–1832, p. 78]. Subtenants under Tudway's trustees: James Lovell and others (1832–1844), H. Gifford's representatives (1845), George Thorn (1846–1851), and James Hutton (1852–1865) [DD/CC 114080/1, 2].

Notes

1. Ch. C. file 51807 pt. I, leasehold tenement 35.
2. This is doubtless a mistake for 6s. 10d.

11

Property No. 20
20/21, Tor Street

The history of this property can be traced back to the early years of the 14th century, when it is described as situated at, or next to, the Tor gate –the gate at the south eastern approach to the city of Wells on the road (now A 371) from Shepton Mallet. The southern boundary of the property then, as always, was the Chilcote stream, which separated it from the field called Tor Furlong, part of the bishop's manor. The stream now passes under the road by means of a culvert, but Simes's map of 1735 depicts a ford at this place, while it appears that, still earlier, the stream was bridged at the Tor gate, for C1559/60 mentions a Tor bridge.

On the site of the Tor Guest House (20, Tor street) there stood originally a dwelling house, the *mansio* or *hospitium apud Torreyate*. From internal evidence it has been inferred that this house had become ruinous by the end of the 16th century, and that between 1600 and 1620 it was restored, thus making the front or western portion of the Guest House; from similar evidence it has also been inferred that about 1700 the rear or eastern portion of the house was added to the restored front part.[1] Leases reveal that from 1751 to 1766 this house was called the 'Turk's Head'.[2]

In the 15th century there appears to have been a cottage and shop on this property; it is not known where they were located, nor their relation to the *hospitium*, but they may in later years have become the outbuildings on the bank of the Chilcote stream which served as a vinegar shop and a brewery in the 19th century, before they were converted into the dwelling called Brook Cottage (21, Tor street)

The eastern part of this property consisted of a garden or orchard, on a portion of which stand the modern houses, 1 and 2, Tor Woodlands. There were also other gardens in the vicinity, but it is not known whether they were connected with this property.

The dean and chapter also had an interest in a chapel built upon the Tor gate, for which the escheator paid to the bishop an annual due of 4*d*. being the monetary value of the original due – one pound of cumin. This payment continued intermittently until E1445/6, at which time the value of one pound of cumin had fallen to 3*d*. For the year of account 1445/6 no payment was made because the gate was totally broken down and ruinous, the Chapel was eventually demolished, and freestone from the building was sold to the precentor, M. William Stefyns, for 6*s*. 8*d*.

The earliest reference to a house at the Tor gate occurs in an assessment of dilapidations made on 25th October 1316 in respect of houses belonging to the dean and chapter.[3] Some of those listed are canonical houses, but it would not appear that this assessment was made in conjunction with the routine annual inspection by the overseers of houses; rather, it seems to have been made in the course of a general survey of capitular properties in Wells. Robert de Derby, a chaplain ministering in the cathedral, was then in possession of a house 'at the gate by the Thorre', which was pronounced to be in good repair.

On 8th April 1337,[4] this house was granted to John de Sobbury (Sodbury), prebendary of Combe IX, and it appears from this grant that Richard de Rodeneye, prebendary successively of Cudworth, Litton, and Worminster, had previously dwelt there. The terms of Sobbury's grant – that he might hold the house so long as he was a canon, do not imply that this was a canonical house; in fact, a grant made in 1372[5] expressly declared that this had never been a canon's house. The terms stated were equivalent to a declaration that the grant was made for life. On 10th April 1342,[6] Sobbury having surrendered his tenancy, the house was granted to a vicar choral, John Treeute de Alta Werthe (John Trote of Highworth), to hold for life, on the understanding that he should not be bound to take a companion to dwell there.[7]

After Trote, the house was held for an unspecified period by Walter Rosesone;[8] it was next granted for life on 6th July 1372[9] to Thomas de Schepton, prebendary of Taunton and rector of Mells, to hold at the same rent (16s.) as it had been held by Rosesone, and on the same terms, these were: that the dwelling must be surrendered as soon as the grantee had been provided with a (canonical) house, because this had never been a canon's house.

Schepton sublet his house at the Tor gate to Peter de Barton, prebendary of Haselbury. In so doing, he may have acted irregularly, for on 13th December 1379,[10] Barton wrote from London asking the chapter to confirm him in the tenancy, and also to defer until after Easter an inquisition of waste, or assessment of dilapidations. Eventually the chapter brought against Schepton an action for waste, in order to recover the cost of the dilapidations for which he was liable. The case was heard at Wells[11] before Henry Percehay, a justice of the common pleas, and a jury. Judgement was given in favour of the chapter, which recovered possession of the property.[12] A grant was made to Barton on 10th September 1380 at an annual rent of 16s. on the same conditions as those in Schepton's lease.[13]

Barton's tenancy seems to have ended in 1400 or 1401; we then find the master of the grammar school in occupation of the house. In his account for 1402/3 the escheator noted a default of 16s., being the rent *domorum quos M. Scolarum modo inhabitat versus Torram*. The rent from the house had been allocated to chancellor Thomas Terry as a subvention to assist him in building a house, on which work he was currently engaged.[14]

According to a surrender made on 10th August 1410, the house at Tor gate was assigned, on the termination of Barton's tenure, to Terry's successor in the chancellorship, Nicholas Danyel, for the use of the schoolmaster.[15] This explains why, during the year E1402/3, the master was in occupation of the house. It had been assigned to the chancellor, who had the supervision of the school, because the building used by the school stood on a site at the Mountroy which had been designated for the erection of a *hospitium* for chantry priests, then in course of foundation pursuant to the will of bishop Ralph Erghum, who died on 10th April 1400.[16] Consequently another place had to be found for the school, and the chapter settled upon the house at the Tor gate, which was conveniently in hand. Possession passed to chancellor Richard Bruton when he assumed office in 1406; he surrendered the tenancy on 10th August 1410, other premises having become available for the school.[17]

The next lease was made to Richard Plasterer and his wife for their lives at a rent of 10s.; they paid rent for C1428/9 and C1430/1, and in the latter account it is noted that the rent used to be 20s.[18] Subsequent tenants were:

John Plasterer and John Bristow [C1437/8 – rent paid, 8s. (noted: used to be 20s.)]

John Cauntelough (Cantlow), grant for three lives at a rent of 13s. 4d., on 11th March 1445 [Ch. 624 (Cal. ii, p. 674, abbr.)]; he paid 8d. for the drawing of the indenture. In this grant the eastern boundary of the property is defined as the wall of the curtilage held under the dean and chapter by Sir John Haydolbie. In C1445/6 Cauntelough paid 6s. 8d.[19] *pro mansione apud Torreyate.*

John Clerke, tanner, grant for life c. ?1447 on surrender by Cauntelough. Distress levied on Clerke for non–payment of the two year rent [C1449/50].

George Smithe, in possession 1576 [L.1571–1624, f. 31d].

John Smithe, notary public, son of George Smithe, grant for 40 years at a rent of 7s. in consideration of a fine of 53s. 9d., on 6th October 1576 [L.1571–1624, f. 31d].

Elizabeth Smithe, John Smithe, and William Smithe, children of John Smithe, grant for their lives on 1st April 1584 [L.1571–1624, f. 31d].

Frances Attwood paid rent [C1602/3].

Edmund Chisman, 'grocyer',[20] grant for three lives at a rent of 7s. on 1st October 1619 (L.1571–1624, f. 226d; DD/CC 112050). Description of property: a messuage with backside, garden and orchard, next to the brook or watercourse on the south side, and next to the house called the 'Blacke Dogge' on the north side.)

John Cheeseman paid rent [C1625/6]

Joan Cheeseman, widow,[21] paid rent [C1634/5, C1636/7].

Thomas Chisman, named as tenant [S1649, p. 16]. Lease of 1619 produced to the surveyor, who recommended that the rent should be improved to 30s.

Mary Lecount, widow, grant for 40 years at a rent of 7s. of the tenement where Thomas Cheeseman, deceased, inhabited, on 4th October 1660 [L.1624–1681, p. 369; DD/CC 112523].

Katherine Rodeney, 'gent' [sic], grant for 40 years on 7th January 1686 [DD/CC 112523; A.1683–1704, f. 98].

Francis Rood, appears as tenant in 'A New Survey' of the manor made in 1703 by Dr Richard Healy [S1703, p. 190]. Rood may have been a subtenant.

- Avy Broderip, innholder, grant on surr. for 40 years made on 3rd November 1710 [DD/CC 112525; A.1705–1725, f. 60; L.1701–1739, f. 61d]. Lease renewed for a further 40 years on 5th December 1727 after surr. [L.1701–1739, f. 390; A.1725–1744, f. 37; DD/CC 112527].
- Daniel Gell, gent., grant for 40 years in consideration of a fine of 5*l*. made on 1st October 1751 [L.1740–1760, f. 370; EB 1762–1771 (DD/CC 110008), p. 199; DD/CC 112589 – endorsed 'Turk's Head in Torr lane'.]
- Elizabeth Evans, widow, grant on surr. for 40 years made on 3rd. December 1766 at a rent of 7*s*. [A.1761–1777, f. 174 (lately called the Turk's Head); L.1761–1777, f. 149; DD/CC 112514.]
- George Crane, paid 7*s*. rent [C1769/70]; he may have been a subtenant.
- Charles Rendall, yeoman, grant of 40 years in consideration of a fine of 10*l*. made on 1st July 1780 after surr. [EB 1771–1780 (DD/CC 110009), p. 304; DD/CC 112515; A.1777–1792, p. 73; L.1777–1789, f. 103; Docs. ADD/4135].
- Amelia, wife of Philip Cock, yeoman, of North Wootton, became legally possessed of the premises on the death of Charles Rendall. [cf. EB 1780–1798 (DD/CC 110010), p. 179].
- Philip Cock, of North Wootton, yeoman, grant on surr, for 40 years in consideration of a fine of 15*l*., on 1st April 1795 [EB 1780–1798 (DD/CC 110010), p. 179; DD/CC 112516; L.1790–1807, f. 188; A.1792–1817, p. 48; Docs. ADD/4179].
- The trustees of Philip Cock, being legally possessed of the tenancy, surr. to the dean and chapter, 30th June 1809 [cf. DD/CC 112512].
- John Hoare, jun., vinegar merchant, grant for 40 years on 1st July 1809 [DD/CC 112517; L.1803–1813, p. 41 (where Hoare is described as 'yeoman'); A.1792–1817, p. 408; Docs. ADD/4228].
- Regrant on surr. for 40 years made on 1st April 1824 (A.1817–1832, p. 139; DD/CC 112518; cf. Docs. ADD/4243]. Grant renewed for 40 years on 23rd April 1838 [R.1, p. 95; DD/CC 112518a].
- John William Hoare stated to be in possession of the premises [DD/CC 112519]
- Martha Cross, of Bristol, widow, grant for 40 years of the premises late in possession of John William Hoare at a rent of 7*s*. + 5*s*. 5*d*. redeemed land tax, on 21st October 1857 in consideration of a fine of £81 [R.3, p. 138; DD/CC 111737]. The occupants of the house in the 19th century were: Dr. Z.N. Paszcowicz (1858–1862), The Revd Mr Lace (1863–1865), Mr Holloway (1863–1865).

The brewery and outbuildings were probably converted into Brook Cottage before 1883; Kelly's *Directory* for that year shows the occupant of the cottage as Mrs Beard. In 1889 the occupant was Charles Sellick, and in 1894, Robert A. Grant.

Notes

1. From information supplied by Mr. E.H. Towers, the present tenant.
2. cf. DD/CC 112589; A.1761–1777, p. 174.
3. Cal. i, p. 157.
4. Cal. i, p. 239.
5. Cal. i, p. 272.
6. Cal. i, p. 247
7. The sharing of houses was sometimes permitted or even required, probably when accommodation was short; cf. Cal. i, p. 225 (R.I, f. 184).
8. It is implied that Rosesone was a canon, but his prebend has not been traced.
9. Cal. i, p. 272.
10. Cal. i, p. 286, where the letter is conjecturally but erroneously attributed to the dean; cf. Bennett, p. 122.
11. Not at Westminster, as in Bennett, ibid.
12. Cal. i, p. 287.
13. Cal. i, p. 281.
14. See *CHW*, Article 18, p. 149.
15. Cal. i, p. 441.
16. See below, Appendix I.
17. Cal. i, p. 441; see *CHW*, Article 3, p. 44.
18. The same note appears in C1437/8 and C1445/6, but there is no evidence to support this repeated assertion; it may relate to a revision of rent proposed at some time past, but never implemented.
19. He had only been in possession for six months when the cathedral's financial year ended.
20. In S.1649, p. 16, he is described as 'husbandman'.
21. Not the relict of Edmund Chisman, whose name was Mary.

12

Property No. 21
18/19, Tor Street

In the earlier part of the 17th century the house on this property was called the 'Black Dog',[1] but the name had fallen out of use by the beginning of the 18th century. In a rent roll compiled after 1660 the property is described as 'house and garden',[2] and in Dr. Richard

Healy's 'New Survey' of the manor it appears as 'a house, stable, and garden'.[3] Early in the 19th century, the house was divided into two parts which, however, were never let separately by the dean and chapter. The general terrier of the manor gives two descriptions of property no. 21 – an ancient: 'a tenement and garden . . . with stable and garden'; and a modern: 'a messuage or tenement now or lately used as two dwellings'.[4] With the commutation of the estates of the dean and chapter the property passed into the possession of the Ecclesiastical Commissioners who, in 1875 had a survey and valuation made of the manor. In this the property is described as a 'tenement lately used as two dwelling houses with stable and garden'.[5] In this survey the two dwellings are also described separately: no. 1082 on the tithe map of 1838[6] (18, Tor street) had two living rooms and two bedrooms; no. 1083 (19, Tor street) had a living room, a large bedroom, a shed, and a work shop. Since the 17th century the annual rent remained unchanged at 10s.

The records relating to this property show that the tenancy was held by the following persons:

William Smithe, capper (capmaker) – the earliest known tenant [E1558/9, E1559/60, E1560/1, E1564/5, C1587/8].
William Smythe, draper, grant (including two tenements in the Market Place) for 40 years on 16th April 1572 [L.1571–1624, f. 9]
Edward Smythe [C1602/3]
Alice Plentie, widow[7] [C1625/6, C1626/7, C1627/8].
William Plenty[7] [paid rent *pro le black dogg* C1634/5].
William Cooke [C1636/7].
William Cooke, mercer, to whom a lease of the house 'commonly called the Blacke Dogg' had been assigned. On 10th October 1636 this lease had 14 years to run and Cooke desired an extension of the term to 40 years; this was approved subject to a fine of 40 nobles [SB 1629–1637, p. 125].
William Cooke, of Frome Selwood, yeoman, grant for 40 years on 1st July 1637 [S1649, p. 12].
Stephen Dosset, named as tenant in the survey of 1649, paying a rent of 10s. which the surveyor recommended should be improved to 2l. [S1649, p. 12].
Stephen Dossett, innholder, grant for 40 years at a rent of 10s., on 6th October 1661 [SRO, DD/X/EX(c/1347)].
Jane Dorset, spinster, named as tenant[7] [DD/CC 112524].
Allen Lawe, gent.[8], grant on surr., for 40 years made on 16th August 1698 [DD/CC 112524; L.1681–1701, f. 218; S1703, p. 186].

Thomas Harvey[9] [DD/CC 112528].

Francis Rood, innholder, after surr. of a lease[10] made to Allen Lawe, grant for 40 years on 3rd December 1723 [A.1705–1725, f. 200; L.1701–1739, f. 257; DD/CC 112526].

Francis Squire, chancellor, grant for 40 years on 13th December 1743, after surr. of a lease[10] made to Francis Rood, deceased [DD/CC 112528; L.1740–1760, f. 145].

Hannah Rood, widow, grant for 40 years on surr. of former lease[10] to Francis Squire, since deceased, made in consideration of the payment of a fine of 3*l*. 3*s*., on 1st April 1766 [DD/CC 112509; A.1761–1777, p. 147; L.1761–1777, f. 134; EB 1762–1771 (DD/CC 112008), p. 180].

George Rawlins, yeoman, on surr. of a lease[10] to Hannah Rood, since deceased, grant for 40 years, on 2nd January 1790 [DD/CC 112510; DD/CC 112511; A.1777–1792, p. 283; Docs. ADD/4162]

John Rawlins, yeoman, on surr. of a lease[11] to Hannah Rood, grant for 40 years on 2nd January 1790 [L.1790–1807, f5].[11]

William Perkins, organist of the cathedral, grant for 40 years of the property (now or lately used as two dwelling houses) 'heretofore granted to one John Rawlins', made on 1st April 1830 [A.1817–1832, p. 513; DD/CC 112512ª]

John Hoare, spirit merchant, purchased the lease from William Perkins for the residue of the term at a price of £140, on 21st December 1838 [DD/CC 112512ᵇ]

James Dudderidge[12] [DD/CC 112513]

Martha Cross, of Bristol, widow, in consideration of a fine of £36, grant for 40 years at a rent of 10*s*. on 21st October 1857 [DD/CC 112513; R.3, p. 140].

Notes

1. L.1571–1624, ff. 9, 226d; S1649, pp. 12,16.
2. DD/CC 111736 25/33
3. DD/CC 111736
4. DD/CC 114080, p. 53.
5. Ch.C. file 51807, pt. I.
6. SRO, DD/LX, box 1, Bdl. 8.
7. Probably an assignee.
8. Lawe was appointed *cursor ecclesiae* on 30th September 1682 (*SRS* 72, p. 99): the *cursor* was the messenger of the chapter and, on occasion, its agent.
9. Probably a subtenant or assignee.
10. No date is given.

11. There appears to be some confusion between this and the previous entry; subsequent documents refer to John, and none to George Rawlins. It seems probable that the tenant after Hannah Rood was in fact John Rawlins.
12. Probably a subtenant or assignee.

13

Property No. 22
17, Tor Street

This copyhold property consisted of a small house and garden. No records of grants have been traced, but the names of some tenants or occupants are to be found in leases of the adjoining property on the south:

1562, 16th April, then in the tenure of Thomas Stopford.[1]
1649, June/July, 'Mr. Elliott's house'.[2]
1661, 6th October, Francis Grimslade.[3]
1698, 16th August, 'where Francis Grimslade now dwells'.[4]
1723, 3rd December, 'now belonging to Mrs. Clements'.[5]
1743, 13th December, 'lately belonging to Mrs. Clements'.[6]

In the survey made in 1875 for the Ecclesiastical Commissioners of the property which they had acquired as a result of the commutation in 1866 of the estates of the dean and chapter, property no. 22 was stated to have been 'heretofore in the successive possession of Charles Bendall, Henry Cook, John Lovell, and Edmund Broderip'.[7] To the last named a grant for three lives was made on 1st July 1829. The annual rent for the premises was 14s.

Notes

1. L.1571–1624, f. 9.
2. S1649, p. 12.
3. SRO, DD/X/EX (c/1347).
4. DD/CC 112524; L.1681–1701, f. 218.
5. DD/CC 112526; L.1701–1739, f. 267.
6. L.1740–1760, f. 145; DD/CC 112528.
7. Ch.C. file 51807 pt. I.

14

Property No. 23
16, Tor Street

For this property, described as a house and garden, few leases or lease copies have survived, but from the accounts of the escheator, and from descriptions in leases of adjoining properties it is possible to compile a list of tenants or occupants:

Thomas Stafford, paid 6s. 8d. rent [E1584/5; E1586/7 – E1592/3].
Richard Stafford, paid 6s. 8d. rent [E1593/4, E1594/5]
John Clark, paid 6s. 8d. rent [E1600/1]
John Elliott, grant for three lives, in consideration of a fine of 10s. in 1620 [DCR I, p. 42].
Widow Elliott, paid 6s. 8d. pro domo . . . in qua ipsa inhabitat [E1633/4]
? John Elliot (one of the lives named in the grant of 1620), grant on 25th April 1637 [S1649, p. 18]
Edward Green [S1649, p. 3; Ch.853 (Cal. ii, p. 716)].
Joyce Elliott, widow (possibly the relict of John Elliott [1637, above]), held the tenancy by virtue of a copy dated 25th April 1637 [S1649, p. 18][1]
Widow Elliott (? Joyce Elliott) [E1660/1].
Francis Greenslet [E1668/9]
Francis Grimslett [E1670/1]
Francis Greenslad [E1671/2]
Francis Greenslade [E1672/3]
Thomas Fuller[2] now dwells, 6th December 1679 [L.1624–1681, p. 701].
Francis Greenslade[3] [E1680/1]
Robert Fry dwelt, 2nd August 1688 [L.1681–1701, f. 83].
Francis Greenslade[3] [E1688/9, E1689/90, E1690/1, E1694/5].
Robert Fry dwells, 2nd November 1698 [EB 1698–1699 (DD/CC 110005), p. 8].
Francis Greenslade[3] [E1699/1700].
Robert Fry late dwelt, 1st January 1698 [L.1681–1701, f. 220; L.1701–1739, p. 102].

45

Joan Taplin, widow (of Thomas Taplin), claimed in 1765 to hold the tenancy for life by copy dated 25th February 1741 [EB 1762–1771 (DD/CC 110008), p. 142, Docs. ADD/2739]. Descriptions in several leases incorrectly refer to this property as 'where Thomas Taplin dwells' [L.1740–1760, f. 345; L.1761–1777, f. 33; L.1790–1807, f. 262]

William Owen, for a fine of 7*l*. 7*s*. was admitted tenant in reversion for two lives on 1st October 1765, the reversion to take effect immediately on the death of Joan Taplin [DCR X, p. 58; Docs. ADD/4095].

William Evans, papermaker [cf. Docs. ADD/4086].[4]

William Rood, goldsmith, assign of William Owen, claimed the tenancy of the property 'sometime Isaac Taplin's[5] but since William Evans's' [EB 1771–1780 (DD/CC 110009), p. 81]; grant on surr. for three lives on 21st May 1773, for a fine of 1*l*. 11*s*. 6*d*. [DCR XV, p. 13].

Thomas Abraham Salmon, prebendary of Combe II, and his wife Frances, administrators of the estate of William Rood, sought a reversion for their lives for a fine of 4*l* 4*s*. to Mark Spicer, baker. They surr. on 10th December 1795 [DCR XXII p. 57; Docs. ADD/4173].

Mark Spicer, baker, claimed to hold the tenancy by copies dated 21st May 1773 and 1st October 1792, each for two lives.

Henry Cook, maltster, likewise claimed to hold the tenancy by copies dated 21st May 1773 and 1st October 1792; grant made for three lives at a rent of 13*s*. 4*d*. (including other properties) on 5th December 1815 [DCR XXIX, p. 9, cf. p. 10]; surr. proposed in December 1815 or 1816, with a view to a new grant [Docs. ADD/4236].

John Lovell (General Terrier [DD/CC 114080), p. 40].

Edmund Broderip, grant on 1st July 1820 [S1275, copyhold no. 2], paying a nominal fine of 10*s*. [DD/CC 114080, p. 40]

It would appear that latterly it was the practice to make grants of property no. 23 jointly with property no. 22. This would explain why both properties are presented together on the plan made for the survey of 1875, each being distinguished by its respective number on the tithe map: 1079 and 1081.[6]

The property was taken in hand by the Ecclesiastical Commissioners in 1866.

Notes

1. In view of the surveyor of 1649, the rent ought to be increased to 1*l*. 4*s*.
2. Probably a subtenant or assignee.
3. It is not to be assumed that Francis Greenslade actually paid the rent; it was a common and confusing practice to refer to property by the name of a past tenant.
4. After Evans it appears that the tenancy passed to John Bendal, gardener, in satisfaction of a loan of 25*l*. [Docs. ADD/4086].
5. No tenant or resident named Isaac Taplin can be traced.
6. Ch.C. file 51807, pt. II, p. 122a.

15

Part of Property no. 23
Buttclose

Buttclose was one of several pieces of ground situated in the area bounded on the north by Byestewalle (St Thomas street), on the west by Tor lane (Tor street), and on the south by the Chilcote stream. Its exact location is difficult to determine, for in recent time this area has been reorganized and built over. We are told that Buttclose lay near the tenement where Hugh Barton lived,[1] that is, property no. 15 (14, St Thomas street). In the 16th century the communar described it as *unus vacuus placius decasiatus ex opposito crucis in Est Welles*.[2] The cross mentioned here may have been the 'ashen cross' to which reference is made in several charters.[3] Unfortunately we do not know where this cross stood, so we have no clue to the precise location of Buttclose. According to various estimates Buttclose contained one acre, three quarters of an acre, and a quarter of an acre. It was part of the estate which Peter Orum gave to the dean and chapter towards the end of the 15th century.[4] In the rent roll of the Orum estate for 1490/1,[5] Buttclose is not named, but a receipt of 7*s*. 8*d*. is entered in respect of rent for land the description of which corresponds to that given in C1561/2, but no tenant's name is shown. Thereafter we find the following tenants, until 1866 when Buttclose, with other capitular property was taken in hand by the Ecclesiastical Commissioners:

William Capron, paid 2*s*. rent 1522/3 [Docs. VI/11].
Laudovicus Shepperde, prior to 1553 [C1553/4, 1556/7, 1557/8, 1561/2].

Roger Edgworth, chancellor [C1553/4, cf. C1568/9].
An assignee of Roger Edgworth [C1561/2].
Hugh Barton, smith [C1557/8].
John Cottrell, archdeacon of Wells [C1568/9].
John Smith, lease (with other properties) for 40 years, on 4th July 1566 [S1570, f. 7d; cf. A.1571–1599, f. 62].
William Powell, archdeacon of Bath, grant for 40 years on 2nd January 1586 [L1571–1624, f. 93d]; lease renewed on surr. for 40 years on 1st October 1588 [L.1571–1624, f. 149]; lease renewed for 40 years on 16th October 1592 [A.1571–1599, f. 86d].
Samuel Powell, son of William Powell, grant on surr. for 40 years, made in January 1593 [day not entered – L.1571–1634, f. 138]; lease renewed for 40 years on 24th June 1599 [L.1571–1634, f. 168].
Cornelius Watts, yeoman, held in 1629 with 19 years to run, desired renewal of tenancy for 40 years [SB 1629–1637, p. 10]; grant on surr. for 40 years on 1st July 1633 [L.1624–1681, p. 196].
James Williams, yeoman, grant (with various properties in St Thomas street – see Article 8) on surr. for 40 years on 8th April 1671 [L.1624–1681, p. 627]; lease renewed for 40 years on 6th December 1679 [L.1624–1681, p. 701]; lease renewed for 40 years on 1st January 1698 [L.1681–1701, f. 220; cf. EB 1698–1699 (DD/CC 110005), p. 8; S1703, p. 196].
James Bacon, yeoman, grant on surr. for 40 years made on 6th July 1716 [L.1701–1739, f. 102]; lease renewed for 40 years on 13th March 1732 [L.1701–1739, f. 574]; lease renewed for a fine of 5*l*. in 1750 (no day or month stated) [L.1740–1760, f. 345 (lessee described as 'clothier'); EB 1745–1755 (DD/CC 110006), pp. 163–4 (grantee described as 'innholder')]; lease renewed on surr. for 40 years on 3rd January 1763 for a fine of 5*l*. [L.1761–1777, f. 33; EB 1762–1771 (DD/CC 110008), p. 24 (lessee described as 'stocking maker')]
John Hicks, baker, grant on surr. for 40 years on 1st July 1780 [L.1777–1789, f. 92; ?Docs. ADD/4133]regrant for a fine of 8*l*. on surr. for 40 years on 1st October 1796 [L.1790–1807, f. 262; cf. EB 1771–1780 (DD/CC 110009), p. 298].
Henry Cook, grant (with other properties) for 40 years on 6th February 1823 [A.1817–1832, p. 115; DD/CC 112530].
Richard Collins, sheriff's officer, grant (with other property) on decease of Henry Cook, for 40 years on 6th April 1847 [R.2, p. 161]; lease renewed for 40 years for a fine of £75 on 30th June 1863 [R.4, p. 10 – lessee described as 'maltster'].

Notes

1. S1570, f. 7d.
2. C1553/4, C1556/7, C1557/8, C1561/2.
3. Chs. 198, 223, 459, and 474 (Cal. ii, pp. 591, 596, 645, 647): these refer to a rood of land situate at 'la Aisshencroyce' in the street called Byestewall.
4. Chs. 705 and 706 (Cal. ii, p. 691), Docs. VI/11, VI/12.
5. Docs. VI/12.

16

Property No. 23A
15, Tor Street

This property, yielding to the escheator a rent of 6s., has been variously described – in 1649, as a messuage or tenement with a little yard and garden adjoining,[1] then 'commonly called the Ram';[2] at the beginning of the 19th century, as a dwelling house and malt house with a garden or little yard adjoining;[3] in 1875, in the survey[4] made for the Ecclesiastical Commissioners, who took the property in possession at the time of the commutation of the capitular estates in 1866, it was stated to consist of a house, buildings and yard, with an old malt house adjoining; the house contained a parlour, kitchen, office, and pantry, and five bedrooms with an attic over.

During the 17th, 18th, and part of the 19th centuries this property was generally held with Buttclose,[5] and with certain tenements in East Wells.[6] The following tenants can be identified:

Fortunatus Archer [E1584/5, E1586/7–E1588/9].
Peter Archer [E1589/90–E1594/5, E1600/1]
William Marshall, paid rent *pro domo . . . in qua ipse inhabitat* [E1633/4].
Thomasine Marshall, widow, grant for 40 years sealed on 2nd July 1633 [A.1635–1645, f. 19.; ?E1660/1; cf. Ch. 853 (Cal. ii, p. 716)].
Robert Pommery (possibly an assignee of Mrs Marshall) in possession, 1649 [S1649, p. 3] increase of rent to 1*l*. 13*s*. 4*d*. recommended by surveyor.
Joseph Norton (Nurton), (possibly a subtenant or assignee) [E1668/9, E1670/1–E1671–2].

James Williams, yeoman, grant (with other properties) for 40 years, on 6th December 1679 [L.1624–1681, p. 701]; grant on surr. for 40 years, made on 2nd August 1688 [L.1681–1701, f. 83]; regrant on surr. for 40 years, on 1st January 1698 [L.1681–1701, f. 220; EB 1698–1699 (DD/CC 110005), p. 8; S1703, p. 196].

James Bacon, yeoman, grant (with other properties) on surr. for 40 years, on 6th July 1716 [L.1701–1737, p. 102]; regrant on surr, for 40 years, on 13th March 1732 [L1701–1737, p. 574 (grantee described as 'innholder'); EB 1745–1755 (DD/CC 110006), pp. 163–164].

Joseph Bacon, clothier, grant on surr. for 40 years in 1750 (no day or month recorded) [L.1740–1760, f. 345]; grant on surr. for 40 years in consideration of a fine of 5*l*., made on 3rd January 1763 [L.1761–1777, f. 33; EB 1762–1771 (DD/CC 110008), p. 24].

John Hicks, baker, grant (with other properties) on surr. for 40 years, on 1st July 1780 [L.1777–1789, f. 92]; regrant on surr, for 40 years on 1st October 1796 [L.1790–1807, f. 262].

Henry Cook, maltster, grant (with other properties) for 40 years on 8th February 1823 [A.1817–1832, p. 115; DD/CC 112530; E1822/3]; proposal for grant (with other properties) for 40 years from 1st July 1868 for a fine of £35. [Docs. ADD/4234].

Richard Collins, sheriff's officer, grant (with other properties) on the decease of Henry Cook, for a fine of £145,[7] for 40 years on 6th April 1847 [R.2, p. 161; DD/CC 114080[2], p. 7]; lease renewed for 40 years in consideration of a fine of £75[1], on 30th June 1863 [R.4, p. 10 (lessee described as 'maltster')].

Notes

1. S1649, p. 3.
2. Ibid, p. 26.
3. DD/CC 114080/2, p. 7.
4. Ch. C. File 51807, pt. I, leasehold tenement no. 12.
5. See above Article 15.
6. See below Article 8.
7. There is no indication what proportion of these fines related to property no. 16.

17

Property No.24
16, Market Place

No records of this property are to be found before the 17th century; it was then described as situate in the New Works,[1] with the Guildhall on the south, Penniless porch on the north, and the choristers' house[2] on the east. The property was augmented from time to time by annexations of land from the choristers' house. In 1683[3] one tenant, Guydo Clynton, received a grant of a 'little plot of ground which belongs to the chorister-house' on which he had built 'an house of office' (probably a privy).[4] It is doubtless to this ground that a lease of 1685[5] refers as 'that little plot of ground adjacent to the . . . dwelling house on the east and north, lately taken out of the backside or garden of the choristers' house.' In 1822,[6] along with the dwelling house a grant was made of 'the plot of ground and coalhouse adjoining the house on the east and north heretofore taken out of the garden of the choristers' house, also one other little plot of ground adjoining the back part of the dwelling house . . . ' The coalhouse may have been an outhouse adapted at some time from Clynton's 'house of office'. These several plots of ground, which are not delineated on any plan, were never actually incorporated into this property, but being regularly granted with it, virtually became part of it. Surrounded by a wall, they now go to make up the garden of 16, Market place, in which a prominent feature is the north gable of the hall of the ruined choristers' house.

Beneath this garden flows an underground watercourse which conveys water from St Andrew's well to the houses on the north side of the Market place. In the winter of 1831 the chapter had to give some consideration to this watercourse, as appears from a minute of a meeting on 6th December:[7] 'The chapter's houses in the Market place having been inundated by water flowing from Miss Parfitt's garden, and the tenants having applied for an additional course[8] to be made in the garden held by the Misses Parfitt under the chapter,[9] and those ladies having by letter and also in the presence of their brother Mr Peter Parfitt refused permission for this purpose, the circumstances were fully explained to the chapter and the tenants having requested that an iron grate should be placed at the head of the drain an order was given for that purpose'.

This property was one of those reserved to the dean and chapter in the commutation settlements of 1866, but on 9th December 1932 it was purchased by the Church Commissioners for £750.[10] The garden, being retained by the dean and chapter, was leased to the Commissioners at an annual rent of £1 from 25th December 1941.[11] The Wells Girls High School, which was held in rooms over the west cloister, was given permission in May 1949 to erect a temporary building in the garden.[12]

The customary rent for property no. 24 was 40s., to which was added an extra 13s. 4d. for the ground taken from the choristers' house. These rents remained unchanged until 1850, though the parliamentary surveyor in 1649 had advised that the property was worth an improved rent of 8l. The rents were allocated by the chapter for the use of the choristers.

In 1629 the steward noted that this property was held by the chapter clerk, Thomas Maicock, and that it was then in the possession of Francis Owen,[13] presumably Maicock's undertenant. About this time, Owen must have died, devising the tenancy to his wife Honoria, who sought to surrender an 'old indenture' (her husband's lease) in favour of the new grant for 40 years. This was approved by the steward, who fixed a fine of 16l. There is no trace of a grant to Mrs Owen, but it seems that one was made, for she assigned the tenancy to Nicholas Willoughby, after whom we find the following tenants:

Francis Willoughby, grant for 40 years made on 2nd April 1630 [L.1624–1681, p. 78; DD/CC 112330; Docs. V/7; A.1621–1635, f. 101d].

Alexander Jett, notary, chapter clerk and bishop's registrar, in possession at the time of the survey made in 1649, when he produced the lease of 2nd April 1630 as evidence of title (suggesting that he was a subtenant or assignee of Francis Willoughby) [S1649, p. 10]; grant for 40 years made on 3rd October 1660 [L.1624–1681, p. 341].

Guydo Clynton, 'register to my lord bishop', to whom on 15th December 1683 was made a grant of 'a little plot of ground which belongs to the chorister-house . . . upon which (he) hath built an house of office' [A.1683–1704, f. 24].[14]

Sarah Cannington, widow of Thomas Cannington, grant on surr. for 40 years, made on 1st April 1685 [L.1681–1701, f. 53; DD/CC 112056; Cal. ii, p. 457].

Thomas Cannington, notary public (possibly the son of Sarah and Thomas Cannington), grant on surr. for 40 years, made on 11th July 1701 [L.1681–1701, f. 236; A.1683–1704, f. 305; Docs. V/35].

Avis Cannington, widow, grant on surr. for 40 years, on 25th May 1721 [DD/CC 112400; L.1701–1739, f. 181; A.1704–1725, f. 162d].

Robert Gresley, bachelor of physic, lease on surr. for 40 years, made on 1st March 1735 [DD/CC 112064; A.1725–1744, f. 153; L.1701–1739, f. 669]; grant on surr. for 40 years, made on 1st October 1750 (grantee described as 'of Bristol', and also as M.D.) [A.1744–1760, p. 136; L.1740–1760, f. 325; Docs. V/56; EB 1743–1755 (DD/CC 110006), p. 148].

Anne, Elizabeth, and Mary Gresley, spinsters of Bristol, grant on surr. for 40 years in consideration of a fine of 10*l*., on 7th November 1764 [EB 1762–1771 (DD/CC 110008), p. 107; A.1761–1777, p. 117; Docs. V/60; L.1761–1777, f. 102]. The Revd Samuel Webb of Winsford (in right of his wife Anne Gresley), Elizabeth Gresley, and Mary Gresley, being legally entitled to the premises surr. on 26th March 1779 in consideration of the payment to each of them a sum of 5*s*., by the dean and chapter [L.1777–1789, f. 65].

Robert Gutch, gent., grant for 40 years in consideration of a fine of 20*l*., made on 1st October 1779 [EB 1771–1780 (DD/CC 110009), p. 281; L.1777–1789, f. 67; A.1777–1792, p. 49; Docs. V/63, V/64, ADD/4128, 4175].

George Daubeney, of Bristol, was legally entitled to the premises in 1794 [EB 1780–1798 (DD/CC 110010), p. 165; cf. Docs. ADD/4197].

John Helyar Rocke, gent., grant on surr. for 40 years made on 8th December 1796 [L.1790–1807, f. 266; A.1792–1817, p. 85; Docs. V/68].

Edward Parfitt, gent., grant (together with a doorway or entrance leading into the premises from Penniless porch [A.1832–1840, p. 208]) on surr. for 40 years on 1st April 1808, [L.1808–1813, p. 7; A.1792–1817, p. 85; Docs. V/70, V/71]; regrant on surr. for 40 years, on 2nd January 1822 [Docs. V/74 (endorsed, 'renewed in 1836'), V/75, V/78; A.1817–1832, p. 95]; regrant for 40 years in consideration of a fine of £58, on 8th July 1850 [R.2, p. 285; DD/CC 114080^2, p. 31] – stipulation in this grant: no rooms facing the cathedral green to be used as a hotel or inn.

The occupant during the period 1827–1834 was Mr (Dr) Nicholls,[15] and in 1835, Miss Jeffrey. From 1836 the premises were used as the offices of the West of England bank, to which they were sublet. In 1856 a new bank manager was appointed whose wife, Emma Marshall was a well known literary figure in her day;[16] she based many of her novels on Wells and the surrounding country. Mr. Marshall moved to Exeter in 1869. The bank, now the Wilts and Dorset bank, terminated its tenancy of the garden of the choristers' house in 1887, and on 1st July 1887 the chapter was informed of this, and also that 16 Market place, with Penniless porch, would shortly fall in hand (M.1886–1892, p. 66) On 3rd December 1887 Edward Parfitt offered to surrender his tenancy provided all claims for dilapidations were waived (M.1886–1892, p. 80). The chapter accepted this offer.

Thomas Dehany Bernard, chancellor of the cathedral, took a lease of this property for two years and a quarter at a rent of £45 [M.1886–1892, pp. 90, 107]

Arthur Jefferay Mawer, solicitor and registrar of the county court of Somerset held in Wells, grant for 21 years at a rent of £45 on 1st October 1908 [A.1900–1923, p. 75]. On 1st January 1931 it was decided to renew the lease for either 7 or 14 years at a rent of £65 [A.1900–1923, p. 75].

Notes

1. See Appendix I, p. 211–8.
2. See below, Article 76, pp. 182–5.
3. A.1683–1704, f. 24.
4. It is not known by what authority Mr. Clynton appropriated this little plot of ground.
5. A.1683–1704, f. 64; L.1681–1701, f. 53; DD/CC 112056; Cal. ii, p. 457.
6. Docs. V,74, 75; A.1817–1832, p. 95.
7. M.1831–1837, p. 5.
8. It is not explained how an additional watercourse under the garden would have reduced the risk of flooding in the houses.
9. There is no evidence of a lease by the dean and chapter to the Misses Parfitt; the tenant, as will be seen from the subjoined list of tenants, was Edward Parfitt, and these ladies must have been his subtenants.
10. M.1919–1928, p. 271; A.1924–1954, p. 81.
11. M.1938–1952, p. 102.
12. Ibid, p. 219.
13. SB 1629–1637, p. 3.
14. There is no trace of a lease of the property to Mr Clynton.
15. Probably the surgeon who took a lease of 3 The Liberty on 20th September 1858, see CHW, Article 1, p. 26.
16. See Beatrice Marshall, *Emma Marshall, a Biographical Sketch* (London, 2nd ed. 1901).

18

Property No. 25
The Camery

The Camery,[1] or the Church Camery – to distinguish it from the bishop's camery, is the churchyard situated on the south side of the south transept, the quire, and the Lady chapel, and on the east side of the east cloister. In Saxon times a portion of the north west corner of the Camery was used as a lay cemetery,[2] and in mediaeval times part of it served as a burial ground for vicars choral, who were to be interred to the east of the chapel of St Mary (the so-called Lady chapel by the cloister).[3] In recent time the place reserved for vicars choral has been used for the burial of persons closely associated with the cathedral, but no new burials are now allowed in the Camery. On the site of the Lady chapel by the cloister bishop Stillington caused to be built his chantry chapel,[4] a magnificent and much larger building. This chapel was completed in 1488, but was demolished in 1552 by Sir John Gate, the king's collector of lead.[5] Gate was under contract to clear the site, but he left some stone, which proved a useful quarry for the repair and construction of capitular houses of residence.[6] By a decree of 25th May 1586[7] the chapter attempted to exercise some control over the use of this stone; it was ordered that 'no more stones be given or sold out of the Camery and that they be used only for repairs to the cathedral and the canonical houses, and that by general consent of the whole chapter on a general chapter day.'[8]

On 21st May 1433[9] bishop John Stafford granted to the dean and chapter a gate newly constructed in the wall extending southward from the east cloister door, with free ingress and egress through it, and the right to move into the Camery by means of this gate and by means of his park and palace gates and entries[10] all manner of building materials for the repair of the church, churchyard, and cloisters. The gate mentioned in this grant, commonly called the 'Camery gate',[11] is that which now gives entrance to the masons' yard; by means of it, use of the east cloister by workmen was avoided.

Between the present masons' yard and the south transept of Stillington's chapel stood two masons' workshops,[12] each divided into two rooms. These workshops were probably used by the masons who built the chapel. The northernmost workshop was demolished at the same time as the chapel. The southernmost is the 'work howse' specified in a grant made on 20th March 1542[13] to Walter Cretyng, archdeacon of Bath. This lease was for life at an annual rent of 6s. 8d. payable to the master of the fabric. The premises let to Dr Cretyng consisted of the western part or room of the remaining (southermost) workshop; it is described as a 'rome of two coples'[14] . . . conteyning by estimacion xvi foote of lengthe.'[15] The lease included 'the whole lofte over all the saide workehowse, with a litle orchard there lyeng and the herbage of the . . . Camery'. Archdeacon Cretyng intended to use the premises as a stable; at this time he was living in the canonical house now known as 'The Rib',[16] so that the disused worshop when converted into a stable would lie conveniently at hand, while the Camery would afford useful grazing for his horses. This lease reserved to the dean and chapter 'a pentyse howse'[17] . . . at the west end of the workehowse', and also to the master of the fabric free ingress and egress to and from the Camery 'for thaccustomd worke there to be don concernynge the reparacion of the . . . Churche.'

To a later occupant of Dr Cretyng's house, Dr Gerard Wood, archdeacon of Wells, a grant was made on 1st July 1616[18] of *cameram et stabulum* adjoining the cathedral – literally a room and a stable, from which it would appear that Dr Wood had both the stable leased by Dr Cretyng and the adjoining eastern room, which it seems that he converted into a wash house, as we learn from the following incident.

In 1635 archbishop Laud asked bishop Peirs to report upon a complaint made by dean Warburton against Dr Wood. The bishop informed Laud on 18th April[19] that the dean had charged Dr Wood with creating a stable and wash house on consecrated ground' on the place called the Camerie'. Peirs explained that an ancient stable stood on the spot, and because it was ruinous Dr Wood had taken it down and had built a new stable; there was no wash house, however;[20] nor was the spot in question consecrated ground. The bishop seems to have been misinformed that the stable did not stand on consecrated ground, for the workshop which Dr Cretyng had converted into a stable had been erected on part of the Camery used as a burial place for vicars choral.[21]

In the survey made in 1649 it is recorded that Dr Wood was in possession of a stable and the close adjoining thereunto, called the Cambrey, but no mention is made of the eastern room of the workshop – the wash house.[22] Dr Wood also claimed an estate for life in a grove, more or less one acre in area, belonging to the Camery, called 'the

Withybeds'. This grove was then in the occupation of Humphrey Marsh[23] at a rent of 15s. Dr. Wood asserted that he had a grant of 'Withybeds' from the dean and chapter, but no evidence of such grant can be found; Marsh was doubtless a subtenant.

On 28th May 1650[24] Dr Cornelius Burges, the presbyterian minister of the cathedral during part of the Interregnum, purchased the Camery for the sum of 18l. 6s. 8d. At the Restoration, the dean and chapter recovered the Camery, and on 11th April 1661[25] leased it for 40 years to Alexander Jett, notary, chapter clerk, and bishop's registrar. No mention is made in this grant of the stable, which may explain the reduction of the rent from 6s. 8d. to 1s. 8d. However, on 3rd April 1682, a grant for 40 years was made of the Camery with a stable built therein, to Nicholas Dowthwaite, clerk of the courts of the dean and chapter, 'only in trust to and for the use and behoof of . . . William Peirs . . . his executors, administrators, and assigns'.[26] The premises had been assigned to Dr William Peirs, archdeacon of Taunton, on 1st May 1661, for 40 years at a rent of 1s. 8d.[27] On 21st January 1682 Dr Peirs signified his desire to surrender his interest with a view to a new lease for 40 years to either himself or to such persons as he should nominate.[28] The document is endorsed 'lease . . . of the little Camery', but it is not known why the premises were so designated.

According to a survey of the manor made in 1703,[29] the Camery was then in the tenure of William Coward, serjeant at law, at a rent of 10s. On 14th March 1705[30] a grant for 40 years of the Camery and the stable was made to Guydo Clynton, chapter clerk, who undertook to maintain the stable, and not to keep any horse or other beast in the Camery or in the stable which might annoy the way or outlet of the bishop lying before and leading to the great gate of the Camery, without the previous consent of the bishop. Free access was also secured for the master of the fabric, his servants and workmen, and also liberty for the tenants of the houses in the New Works,[31] and their workmen, at all times to inspect and repair pipes and water courses. This last mentioned provision related to the subterranean water course from St Andrew's well to the houses in the New Works, which passed beneath the Camery, and for the repair and maintenance of which the tenants of those houses were responsible and bound to bear a proportion of the cost.

On 1st July 1720,[32] a regrant on surrender[33] for 40 years was made to Mr Clynton on the same conditions as those in his first lease, and at the same annual rent of 10s., 6s. 8d. of which was allocated to the fabric fund, and 3s. 4d. to the master of the fabric. The next tenant was Andrew Cross of Broomfield to whom was made a grant for 40 years on

11th Janurary 1741,[34] and whose lease was renewed for a fine of 6*l.* on 7th December 1756.[35]

William Simes's plan of Wells (1735) depicts the Camery with trees and intersecting walks.[36] This is typical of Simes's conventional and formal style, and cannot be taken as an exact representation of the Camery at that time. The next lease, made for 40 years on 1st October 1774[37] to Francis Willes of Westminster (after surrender) contained a reservation to the chapter of timber trees and other trees, suggesting that the Camery had been planted with trees, but not in the formal manner depicted by Simes.

On 2nd January 1789[38] a grant for 40 years was made to Edward Parfitt, deputy registrar of the diocese of Bath and Wells. This grant was of the Camery, there being no reference to the stable; but in other grants made on 6th December 1804 (40 years)[39] and on 2nd January 1822[40] to Parfitt's widow, Ann, both the Camery and the stable are specified. It appears that the tenancy passed from Mrs. Parfitt to the Misses Parfitt (presumably her daughters) who applied for a renewal of the lease. A minute of a chapter meeting on 6th July 1833[41] runs: 'it appeared that the chapter had some years ago come to a resolution that the Camery . . . should not again be leased; and it was deemed altogether advisable to adhere to that resolution.' At another chapter meeting on 7th December 1858[42] it was noted that the Misses Parfitt had asked, through their agent, for possession for a short time longer, as their lease had expired; the chapter acceded to this request. On 14th May 1859,[43] the chapter noted that the Misses Parfitt still held the stable and the Camery.

The chapter's surveyor was asked at this time to report on the possibility of removing the ladder house situated near the chapter house, and on the practicability of making the stable and its yard available for the purpose of a ladder house. There seems to have been a garden in the Camery in the tenure of the Misses Parfitt; this garden was probably adjacent to the stable. On 27th October 1860[44] the chapter remitted to a committee of three the question of the improvement of this garden. On 10th September 1861[45] chancellor Beadon was asked to report on some suitable site in the immediate vicinity of the cathedral for erecting a place where ladders, scaffold poles, planks, and similar equipment could be stored. Finally on 23rd April 1862[46] the dean was empowered to take steps, with the aid of the chapter clerk, to make a place for storing ladders in the building now standing in the garden lately belonging to Miss Parfitt – this building, presumably, was the stable.[47]

In the arrangements for the commutation of the manor in 1866 the Camery was reserved to the dean and chapter. On 17th May 1867[48] the chapter decided to improve the Camery by building a wall, presumably on the south side, and on 24th April 1868[49] to order sufficient grass seed for laying down the ground of the Camery to lawn, and also so much gravel as was necessary to make the walks. At the present time there are no walks; presumably they were not made. Ladders and building equipment are not stored within the Camery, but in the masons' yard on the south.

Notes

1. The meaning and origin of this name are not known. It appears to be related to *camera*, and may denote simply an enclosed space – a close.
2. See Warwick Rodwell, *Wells Cathedral, Excavations and Discoveries*, Wells (The Friends of Wells Cathedral, 2nd ed., 1980 (cited hereafter as WR1980 to distinguish it from the 1st ed. – cited as WR1979), plans 6B and 6C.
3. Cal. i, p. 74 (R.I, f. 64d); another burying place for vicars choral lay in the south west corner of the Camery, see WR1980, plan 4 and WR1979, plan 3.
4. See WR1980, plan 5.
5. Ch. 773 (Cal. ii, p. 705) where Stillington's chapel is confusingly designated 'the Lady chapel in the cloister'; see also WR1980, p. 12.
6. See CHW, Article 10 (the dean's house), p. 107 and Article 9 (25 The Liberty), p. 96.
7. Cal. ii, p. 309.
8. On general chapter days, see D.S.Bailey *SRS* 72, p. xix.
9. Cal. i, pp. 465–466.
10. The 'gates and entries' probably referred to the 'bishop's eye' and the road therefrom to the 'camery gate'.
11. See Cal. ii, p. 309.
12. See WR1980, plan 5, and WR1979, illustration 8.
13. L.1535–1545, f. 4; Cal. ii, p. 254; Ch. 763 (Cal. ii, p. 703).
14. A cople (couple) was a pair of rafters meeting at a point and joined at the base by a tie, thus forming a triangular member. The room in question would have had two such couples supporting its roof.
15. The plan in WR1980 (plan 5) suggests that the length was in fact 17 feet.
16. See *CHW*, Article 15, pp. 137–138.
17. 'pentyse howse' means a pent house or lean-to.
18. A.1608–1622, f. 115.
19. *State Papers (Domestic)*, 1635, p. 33.
20. Drains discovered on the site, however, would appear to confirm the existence of the wash house.
21. See above, p. 55 and note 3 above. There is no evidence of the secularization of the south western part of the Camery used as a burial ground.
22. S1649, p. 23.

23. Humphrey Marsh lived in the house on the north eastern side of the undercroft, see below Article 78, p. 188.
24. D. Underdown, 'A Case concerning Bishops' Lands', in *Eng. Hist. Rev.*, LXXVIII, Jan. 1965, p. 27.
25. Ch.830 (Cal. ii, p. 714).
26. Docs. V/25.
27. Docs. ADD/4017.
28. Docs. ADD/4054.
29. S1703, p. 179.
30. Docs. V/25; the fine was 10*l.*, and was received by the master of the fabric (Cal. ii, p. 487).
31. See Appendix I.
32. L.1701–1739, p. 159; A.1705–1725, f. 152d.
33. Docs. V/41; L.1701–1739, f. 37.
34. Docs. V/52; L.1740–1760, f. 84; Cal. ii, p. 539; A.1725–1744, f. 228d.
35. EB 1756–1762 (DD/CC 110007), p. 49; L.1740–1760, p. 500; A.1743–1760, p. 242; Docs. ADD/4090, 4091.
36. This, John Carter's plan of 1794, and references in the Dean & Chapter Order Book to 'Mrs. Parfitt's garden' explain the statement in WR1980, p. 17, that in the 18th century the Camery became a 'formal garden'.
37. L.1761–1777, f. 446; A.1761–1777, p. 337; EB 1771–1780 (DD/CC 110009), p. 117; Docs. ADD/4107, 4110, 4161a, 4161b.
38. L.1777–1789, f. 494; A.1777–1792, p. 271; Docs. ADD/4159.
39. Docs. ADD/4218a.
40. A.1817–1832, p. 95; Docs. ADD/4216 (fine 10*l.* 10*s.*), 4246.
41. M.1831–1837, p. 64.
42. M.1849–1859, p. 311.
43. Ibid, p. 342.
44. M.1860–1872, p. 28.
45. Ibid, p. 77.
46. Ibid, p. 108.
47. No plan or other details accompany the minute, and it is not clear precisely what was intended.
48. M.1860–1872, p. 276.
49. Ibid, p. 290.

19

Property no. 26
25, Market Place, and 1a, Cathedral Green

This house[1] was traditionally designated 'the first house from the east end of the New Works', and originally yielded a rent of 33*s.* 4*d.* In the mid-17th century, one tenant (Mary Baber) held[2] by indenture[3] a coal-house in the churchyard [*repositorium carbonum in cemeterio*],[4] which may have been annexed to the property, though it is not mentioned in any previous grant, nor can any separate lease of it be traced. Adjoining this property was the gate built by bishop Bekynton, generally known as Penniless porch. From 1668 for the next three centuries the 'gate or porch commonly called pennylesse porch or bench', and two chambers over the gate, were included in grants of the property, so that the gate and chambers became part and parcel of the tenement.

The house numbered 1a, Cathedral Green, was built on the back of 25, Market place in the late 18th century: on 2nd January 1770[5] the chapter decreed that the tenant of the property, Benjamin Andrews, 'may have full liberty and authority to take from the churchyard at the north east corner of the house (25, Market place) seven feet or thereabouts for the purpose of building thereon, which said ground shall be hereafter considered as part of [property no. 26], and be held accordingly'.

During the latter years of the reign of Henry VIII, the property was let to a physician, Richard Rosemonde, *alias* Martyn, who also dwelt in the house. When he renewed his lease on 21st January 1545,[6] the chapter substantially reduced the annual rent to 4*d*., in recognition of 'the profounde knowledge he hath in the arte of Phisicke and his great diligence and painestaking in thadministracion of the same to sundrie and diverse of us in our sickenes and for other causes and consideracions'. This renewed lease was for three lives, one of whom was the physician's son Robert; but it was provided that should the latter survive his parents, the rent would revert to the customary 33*s*. 4*d*. Evidently Robert inherited the tenancy and also survived his parents, for he paid the full rent for the period C1559/60–C1562/3. Subsequent tenants were:

John Bysshope, yeoman, grant for 40 years on 1st April 1575 [L.1571–1624, f24]. For C1587/8 rent was received from Bartholomew Chaple, who may have been an assignee.

Thomas Maicock, grant for 40 years on 10th October 1572 [A.1571–1599, f. 84d]; regrant for 40 years on 13th February 1593 [L.1571–1624, f. 137]; paid rent for C1602/3; regrant for 40 years on 1st July 1614 [A.1608–1622, ff. 88, 94]; further regrant for 40 years on 1st July 1624 at a reduced rent of 10*s*.[7] [A.1621–1635, f. 37d].

Mary Maicock, to whom the tenancy may have been assigned or devised by Thomas Maicock, whose wife she probably was, paid rent (33*s*. 4*d*.) for C1634/5.

John Baber (recorder of Wells) paid rent for C1636/7; c.1636 the chapter's steward noted that the property was then in the tenure of Mary Baber, which suggests that Mary Maicock had become John Baber's wife.

Mary Baber, grant for 11 years[8] for a fine of 4*l*. on 28th December 1636 [S1649, p. 5; A.1635-1645, f. 16 – lessee described as 'of Tormarton'].

John Baber, or his assignee, named as tenant in the survey of 1649; the rent was stated to be 26*s*. 8*d*. but there is no record of its being increased; in the view of the surveyor the rent ought to be improved to 7*l*. 13*s*. 4*d*. [S1649, p. 5]

William Andrews, mercer, grant after surr. for 40 years on 5th October 1650 (or 1661) [DD/CC 112338; L.1624-1681, p. 615; SRS 72, p. 16; Docs. ADD/4018]

Bridget Andrews, relict of William Andrews, grant on surr. for 40 years on 23rd October 1690 [DD/CC 112351; L.1681-1701, f. 125; Cal.ii, p. 168; S1703, p. 173].

George Andrews, son of Bridget Andrews, mercer, grant on surr. for 40 years on 8th July 1710 [DD/CC 112362; L.1701-1739, f. 59].

James Yorke, grant on surr. on 9th July 1724 [DD/CC 112403; L.1701-1739, f. 266; A.1705-1725, f. 205d]. On 12th April 1729, the chapter declared 'that Mr York [hath] not any pretence of right or claime to any part of the ground lately taken in, railed and inclosed out of the churchyard by Mr chancellor Pope,[9] and that the said Mr York shall be forbid the hanging any cloths on the rails or pales there erected by the said Mr Pope or his family'.[10] This business seems to have been settled satisfactorily, and Yorke to have remained an acceptable tenant, for he received a regrant of his lease for 40 years on 8th January 1741 [DD/CC 112371; L.1740-1760, p. 34; A.1743-1760, p. 229].

James Yorke jun., surr. with a view to a new lease for 40 years on 7th April 1755 [EB1745-1755 (DD/CC 110006), p. 317]; grant in consideration of a fine of 9*l*. 9*s*. made on 1st October 1755 [DD/CC 112234; L.1740-1760, f. 466; A.1743-1760, p. 229]; regrant on surr. on 2nd January 1770 [EB 1762-1771 (DD/CC 110008), p. 357; DD/CC 112235; L.1761-1777, p. 266; A.1761-1777, p. 242].

Benjamin Andrews, steward of the dean and chapter, grant on surr. on 1st July 1790 (premises then in possession of Robert Graves as tenant[11] [DD/CC 112236; L.1790-1807, f. 10; A.1777-1792, p. 287; Docs. ADD/4164].

John Andrews, nephew of Benjamin Andrews, occupied the newly built house, 1a, Cathedral Green, until the death of the latter in 1803. John Andrews himself died in 1804; thereafter property no. 26 came into the lawful possession of

Thomas Andrews, of Bradford Abbas, Dorset, and Richard Andrews, of Yetminster, Dorset, to whom a grant on surr for 40 years was made on 2nd January 1805 of the house 'enclosed by permission of the dean and chapter on the north and east parts from the churchyard with iron palisades', and also of 25, Market place together with Penniless porch and the two rooms over, and in addition, of the garden (property no. 49) hitherto annexed to property no. 48 (3, Market place, and two stables in the New Works garden,[12] lately held by the lessee of property no. 30 (21, Market place), but which had been purchased by Benjamin or John Andrews.

The lease of these various properties was purchased by a banker, Daniel Beaumont Payne, to whom a grant was made on 12th October 1805 [DD/CC 112239].

For consideration of £1,300, Payne assigned all the properties on 5th January 1815 to another banker, Henry Hope (DD/CC 112240], to whom, on surrender, a regrant for 40 years was made on 2nd January 1819 [DD/CC 112241, 112242; A.1817–1832, p. 32].

Henry Hope and D.B. Payne, with one George Hulbert Hope, were partners in business as bankers, dealers, and chapmen. A commission of bankruptcy was issued against them on 31st May 1831 [DD/CC 112243], and for the benefit of their creditors the commission sold all the properties held jointly or severally by them to Henry Brookes. Brookes in turn sold the tenancies of the properties leased to Henry Hope by the dean and chapter to Robert Bartlett Coles and William Parfitt.

On 1st November 1831, at the Swan hotel, Coles and Parfitt sold certain parts of the real estate and chattles which had belonged to the bankrupts. Lot 1, which probably included property no. 26, Penniless porch with the two rooms over, and the garden, was purchased by a surgeon Henry Jones Bernard, acting for Sarah Hope of Bristol. The price paid for lot 1 was £1,070, and those items held under the dean and chapter were valued at £990. On 2nd January 1834 property no. 26, Penniless porch, and the two rooms over, the garden and stable, were granted for 40 years to Sarah Hope [A.1832–1840, p. 70; cf. DD/CC 112243, 112244]; it appears that Henry Hope continued in residence at 1a, Cathedral Green until 1838.

On 8th October 1835 Sarah Hope assigned all the premises to Cam Gyde Heaven of Bristol, as security for a mortgage of £408. 10s. [DD/CC 112245], and on 2nd April 1839, Miss Hope and Mr Heaven jointly assigned them for 40 years to Benjamin Hope, who, on the following day assigned them to Thomas Barnes as security for a loan of £1000 at 5% interest [DD/CC 112246, 112248].

On the 4th February 1841 Barnes gave Hope three months notice of his intention to sell the tenancy of the premises to a schoolmaster, John Vickery [DD/CC 112247]. This was done for a consideration of £600; on 15th June 1848 Vickery surrendered his interest [DD/CC 112249], and on the following day was granted a new lease for 40 years in consideration of a fine of £70. The garden (property no. 27) was excluded from the lease and the rent was reduced to £1 yearly [DD/CC 112250; R.2, p. 207). Finally the premises were regranted for 40 years to Vickery on 1st April 1862. From 1845 to 1857 the house was occupied by Messrs Davies and Foster, and from 1858 to 1865 by Mr Foster. Vickery died in 1864 and by his will devised the premises to his son in law, Orlando Say, who in 1866 conveyed a fourth part of the premises to Thomas Jones.

Notes

1. Now used as offices by Messrs King, Miles & Co.
2. SB 1640, n.p. Mary Baber sought a renewal of the lease for a further 40 years; this was granted in consideration of a fine of 5s.
3. The date of this indenture, which was for 40 years is not stated.
4. It is curious that such a building should have been permitted, when the chapter exercised a strict contol over the churchyard, see Appendix I.
5. A.1777–1792, p. 288.
6. L.1635–1645, f. 6.
7. No explanation is given for this reduction in rent; Maicock, however, was chapter clerk, and it was possibly felt that he merited some concession.
8. To make up the term to 40 years.
9. The Revd John Pope, prebendary of Timberscombe, was chancellor of the diocese of Bath and Wells, and tenant of the adjoining properties no. 28 and no 30.
10. A.1725–1744, f. 59d.
11. Probably a subtenant of Yorke.
12. See Appendix I, p. 216.

20

Property No. 28
23, Market Place

This property, now the eastern part of Mr Edward Nowell's antiques shop, originally carried a rent of 26s. 8d. annually; this was thought to be too low by the parliamentary surveyor in 1649, who proposed an increase to 4l. 13s. 4d..,[1] though after the Restoration the customary rent remained unchanged. From 1702 this property was let with the adjoining premises on the west, property no. 30, now 21, Market place, both properties forming a single tenement. The record of tenants begins in 1545:

Robert Beckham [C1545/6].
William Mathewe, linen draper, grant for two lives on 8th October 1551 (Mathewe was then in occupation of the premises) [L.1546–1565, f. 60d]. The premises were vacant in C1559/60.
William Northfolke [C1560/1, C1561/2 (Norfolke)].
Christopher Webster [C1562/3 (4th quarter), C1563/4].
Thomas Zayer, yeoman grant for 40 years made on 1st October 1576 (Zayer then in occupation) [L.1571–1624, f. 36d; C1587/8].
John Grenestret, assignment from Zayer for a fine of 14l. on 1st July 1592 [Ch. 810 (Cal. ii, p. 711)]; grant for 40 years on 13th February 1593 [L.1571–1624, f. 136d; A.1571–1599, f. 84d].
Widow Clark, '*modo* Robert Owen' [C1602/3].
Nicholas Willowby, grant for 40 years in consideration of a fine of 40 marks, on 1st October 1625 [A.1621–1635, f. 44d]; regrant on surr. for 40 years (to Nicholas Willughby), on 9th October 1625 [L.1624–1681, p. 31; A.1621–1635, f. 46d; C1627/8].
Frances Owen, widow [C1625/6; C1634/5; Docs. ADD/4008].
Frances Willughby,[2] ([1636/7].
James Huish, named as tenant in the survey of 1649, the lease of 9th October 1625 (to Nicholas Willughby) being cited as evidence of title[3] [S1649, p. 5]; grant for 40 years on 5th October 1660 [DD/CC 112391].
William Westley, chapter clerk, grant on surr. for 40 years on 4th

October 1682 [DD/CC 112342; A.1683–1704, f. 64]. By a decree of the chapter on 21st January 1688, Westley was given leave 'to set up some more rails in the churchyard, 6 feet from the wall against his own house, and at such convenient length as he shall see fit, from the rails already set up'. [Cal. ii, p. 463]. Regrant for 40 years on 2nd February 1702 (with property no 30[4]) [DD/CC 112356; L.1701–1739, f. 2d; A.1683–1704, f. 310].

Notes

1. S.1649, p. 5.
2. This may be an error for Owen.
3. Huish was probably an assignee of Willughby.
4. For an account of property no. 28 after 1702, see below Article 21.

21

Property No. 30
21, Market Place

This property, traditionally designated the third house from the east end of the New Works, now forms the western part of the premises of Mr Edward Nowell. It anciently carried a rent of 33*s*. 4*d*. plus a charge of 2*s*. (later increased to 3*s*.) for a door into the churchyard. After 1702 this property and the adjoining property no. 28 on the east side were always let as a single holding with the gardens pertaining to them, but there is no evidence that the premises were united until recent time. The following tenants can be traced:

John Rokysbye, skinner [C1545/6].[1]
David Saunders [C1559/60, C1560/1, C1561/2, C1562/3, C1563/4].
Alice Saunders, widow of David Saunders, grant for three lives on 31st March 1565 [L.1546 – 1565, f. 149].
William Norton (Nurton), yeoman, claimed to hold in right of his wife Alice[2] for her life by virtue of the lease made in 1565[3] [S1570, f.8]; grant for 40 years on 25th March 1574 [L.1571–1624, f. 14; C1587/8].

David Sarney,[4] grant for 40 years on 24th June 1599 (Sarney then in occupation) [L.1571–1624, f. 165].
Christabella Bowring, 'modo Mark Tabor' [C1602/3].
Mark Tabor, grant for 40 years, in consideration of a fine of 24*l.*, on 1st July 1623 [A.1608–1622, f. 153; cf. S1649, p. 9; C.1625/6, C1626/7, C1627/8, C1634/5, C1636/7]; in possession in June/July 1649 [S1649, p. 9[5]].
Sarah Tabor, widow and executrix of Mark Tabor [DD/CC 112390].
Jane Keene, daughter of Mark and Sarah Tabor, grant on surr. for 40 years, on 12th April 1661 [DD/CC 112390]; grant on surr. for 40 years on 12th April 1681 [DD/CC 112341; L.1624 – 1681, p. 716; SRS 72, p. 87].
William Westley, chapter clerk, grant for 40 years (including property no. 28, and a parcel of ground on the east side of the New Works gardens[6]), on 2nd February 1702 [DD/CC 112356; L.1701–1739, f. 2d; A.1683–1704, f. 310].
John Pope, prebendary of Timberscombe, chancellor of the diocese of Bath and Wells, grant (including property no. 28[7]) for 40 years, on 1st July 1720 [DD/CC 112399; L.1701–1739, p. 167; A.1705–1725, f. 152].
Margaret Pope, widow of John Pope, grant on surr. for 40 years on 11th December 1734 [DD/CC 112409; L.1701–1739, p. 636; A.1725–1744, f. 138]; regrant for 40 years in consideration of a fine of 16*l.*, on 14th December 1748 [EB 1745–1755 (DD/CC 110006), p. 102; L.1740–1760, f. 285; A.1743–1760, p. 98].
Andrew Crosse, of Broomfield, Somerset, and Catherine Westley, widow, grant[8] on surr. for 40 years in consideration of a fine of 16*l.*, on 20th June 1763 [EB 1762–1771 (DD/CC 110008), p. 36; DD/CC 112273; L.1761–1777, f. 48; A.1744–1760, p. 71].
George Layng, grant on surr, for 40 years, in consideration of a fine of 20*l.*, on 2nd January 1777 [EB 1771–1780 (DD/CC 110009), p. 209; DD/CC 112274; L.1761–1777, f. 534; A.1761–1777, p. 377; Docs. ADD/4119].
William Jeboult, organist, his wife Ann, and Margaret Layng, the legal tenants, surr. on 1st January 1791, with a view to a new lease in favour of Peter Layng at a fine of 37*l.* [EB 1771–1790 (DD/CC 110010), p. 39[9]; DD/CC 112276[10]; Docs. ADD/4169].
Peter Layng, grant for 40 years, on 3rd January 1791 (DD/CC 112277; L.1790–1807, f. 35; A.1771–1792, p. 302]; regrant on surr. for 40 years, on 15th January 1805 [DD/CC 112278; L.1790–1807, f. 522; A.1792–1807, p. 306]; regrant on surr. for 40 years on 2nd January 1821 [DD/CC 112279; A.1817–1832, p. 72].

John Bergreen Matthews, premises assigned by Layng as security for a mortgage of £1,300 with interest, on 19th March 1824 [DD/CC 112280].

John Drew, assignee under a further mortgage for £419. 10*s*. [DD/CC 112280]. Layng having defaulted in payments of interest to one of his creditors, the parties concerned caused the tenancy to be sold by auction at the Somerset hotel, Wells, on 8th July 1826 [DD/CC 112280]. Layng became insolvent, and was imprisoned in the Fleet. He applied on 5th January 1828 to the court for relief as an insolvent debtor, and eventually obtained his discharge by act of Parliament. Thereupon a proper assignment of all his estate was made to Henry Dance, the provisional assignee of the court, trustees were appointed and sanctioned the sale of the tenancies. On payment of £800 to J.B. Matthews, property no. 30 (with property no. 28) by common consent of those interested, was assigned to:

Charles Binning, linen draper, who surr. on 24th December 1834 [DD/CC 112281]; grant for 40 years made on 2nd January 1835[11] [DD/CC 112282; A.1832–1840, p. 121].

George Adams, assignee under a mortgage for £700 on 3rd February 1841 [DD/CC 112283].

Sarah Louisa Cruttwell, on payment to G. Adams of £700, took over his interest in the premises. On 1st June 1849 C. Binning discharged his mortgage to Miss Cruttwell. She and Binning jointly surr. the tenancy with a view to a new lease.

Charles Binning, grant for 40 years on 2nd June 1849 [DD/CC 112284; R.2, p. 242] Binning having died intestate on 18th March 1853, his widow, Elizabeth sold the tenancies of property no. 28 and property no. 30 to:

John Willmott, linen draper, properties assigned on 27th December 1854 [DD/CC 112287]; regrant on surr. on 7th March 1864 [DD/CC 112288, 112289; R.4, p. 73].

Notes

1. Rokysbye also held the property (no. 32) on the west.
2. Apparently Alice Saunders remarried.
3. The date of the lease is shown as 21st May, not 31st March.
4. Sarney is described in the lease of 1599 as 'notary public', but he was also a vicar choral, see R.D. Reid, 'The New Works at Wells', WNH&A Soc. *Report*, 1930, p. 31.
5. The surveyor recommended an increase in rent by 6*l*. 6*s*. 8*d*..

6. See below, Article 83.
7. In all subsequent leases of property no. 30, property no. 28 is included.
8. On the death of Margaret Pope.
9. In this entry, George and Peter Layng are confused.
10. Surrender of property no. 28; a corresponding deed of surrender of property no. 30, appears not to have survived.
11. With liberty to enclose the tenements facing the churchyard with iron palisades, parallel to those belonging to the adjoining property no. 26, in the direction from east to west – the dean and chapter reserving the right to remove the palisades.

22

Property No. 32
19, Market Place

Tenants:

John Roksbye,[1] skinner [C1545/6].

Henry Cornyshe, tailor, grant for three lives on 7th July 1546 [L.1546–1565, f. 1d; C1559/60, C1560/1, C1561/2, C1562/3, C1563/4].

Peter Lane, Yeoman, grant for 40 years on 1st April 1575 [L.1571–1624, f. 23; C1587/8]; regrant for 40 years on 24th June 1599 [L. 1571–1624, f. 167; C1602/3].

Thomas Maicock, notary and chapter clerk, grant for 40 years on 1st July 1624 [A.1622–1635, f. 33d]; regrant for 40 years on 1st October 1625 [A.1622–1635, f. 44d; C1625/6, C1626/7, C1627/8, C1634/5].

Tristram Towse, deputy chapter clerk, registrar of the peculiars of the dean and chapter, registrar of the archdeaconry of Bath, grant for 40 years on 2nd January 1637 [SB 1629–1637, p. 126]; in possession, June/July 1649 [S1649, p. 9^2].

John Standish and Robert Hole, grant on 27th October 1654 (fine 115*l*. 10*s*.) from the excrs: of Tristram Towse [Docs. ADD/4012].

John Standish, surr. and grant for 40 years on 11th January 1661 [L.1624–1681, p. 363].

Francis Standish, vicar choral, grant for 40 years on 12th January 1672 [SRS 72, p. 37].

Nicholas Neblett, notary [S1703, p. 182].

Sarah, Mary, and Edith Neblett, daughters of Nicholas Neblett (lately deceased), to whom the tenancy had passed by various assignments, surr. on 3rd November 1699 with a view to a new lease to be made to John Day [EB 1698–1699 (DD/CC 110005), p. 69].

John Day, grant for 40 years on surr., in consideration of a fine of 10*l*., made on 7th December 1699 [EB 1698–1699 (DD/CC 110005), p. 69; L.1681–1701, f. 227; A.1683–1704, f. 290; S1703, p. 182].

John Day, son of the last tenant, devisee of the tenancy on the death of his father.

Joseph Keene, apocathecary, of St James's Middlesex, grant (on the death of John Day, jun.) on surr. for 40 years, on 17th August 1715 [DD/CC 112367; L.1701–1739, p. 109; A.1705–1725, f. 104].

William Watt, apocathecary, grant on surr. for 40 years, made on 21st October 1767 [DD/CC 112181; L.1761–1777, f. 168]; regrant on surr. for 40 years on 5th December 1786 [DD/CC 112182; L.1777–1789, f. 384; A.1760–1777, p. 233; Docs. ADD/4152].

Ann Parfitt, widow, grant on surr. for 40 years, on 1st April 1801 (fine 30*l*. [DD/CC 112183; L.1794–1807, f. 391; A.1792–1812, p. 190; Docs. ADD/4202]. regrant for 40 years on 2nd January 1817 [DD/CC 112184; A.1792–1817, p. 562; Docs. ADD/4239]. Occupant in 1827, William Parfitt [DD/CC 114080/1].

The Misses Ann, Mary, Elizabeth Granville, and Catherine Parfitt, acquired the tenancy on the death of Mrs Ann Parfitt; grant on surr. for 40 years, on 21st September 1829 [DD/CC 112181; A.1817–1832, p. 465]. Occupant, 1830–1842, Edward Parfitt [DD/CC 114080/2]

The Misses Elizabeth Granville and Catherine Parfitt, grant for 40 years on 31st July 1843 [DD/CC 112185; R.2, p. 7]. Occupant 1843–1845, George Milton [DD/CC 114080/1, 2].

John Wilmott, draper, assignee on purchase of the tenancy, 29th September 1848 [DD/CC 112185]; grant for 40 years in consideration of a fine of £50, on 2nd May 1857 [DD/CC 112186; R.3, p. 114; Docs. ADD/4260]. Occupants 1849–1855, Messrs Gilling and Bernard.

Notes

1. See also Article 21 above on the adjacent property no. 30.
2. The surveyor for the Parliament recommended an improvement of the rent from the customary 26*s*. 8*d*. to 8*l*..

23

Property No. 34
17, Market Place

Tenants:

Thomas Dorset, linen draper [C1545/6]; grant for three lives made on 6th February 1551 [L.1546–1565, f. 51].
William Dorset, son of Thomas Dorset [C1559/60, C1560/1, C1562/3, and C1563/4].
Henry Browne, of Ho....ill,[1] Herts, grant for 40 years on 25th March 1574[2] [L.1571–1624, f. 12].
David Sarney, vicar choral, and William Clark, grant[3] on 1st October 1597 [A.1571–1599, f. 112]; regrant for 40 years on 2nd January 1598, in consideration of a fine of 6*l*. 17*s*. 4*d*. [A.1571–1599, f. 113].
Richard Crosse [C1602/3][4].
William Clark, LL.B., in 1617 held the tenancy with 24 years to run [SB 1615–1617, n.p.]; new lease proposed but not proceeded with.
Robert Powell, grant for 40 years on 4th April 1621[5] [DD/CC 112378; L.1571–1624, f. 237a; A.1608–1622, f. 170].
Valentine Powell [C1625/6, C1626/7, C1627/8], grant for 40 years in consideration of a fine of 5*l*., on 1st October 1640 [SB 1637–1640, p. 66; S1649, p. 11; C1634/5, and 1636/7]. Power of attorney was given on 5th January 1669 to four officers of the dean and chapter to demand arrears of rent [Cal. ii, p. 716].
John Prickman, notary public, in possession June/July 1649 [S1649, p. 11[6]]; lease sealed on 6th October 1673 [Cal. ii, p. 50].
—— Penny, occurs as tenant in 1703 [S1703, p. 188].
Ann Penny, widow, grant on surr. for 40 years on 1st April 1704 [DD/CC 112360; L.1701–1739, f. 15d; A.1683–1704, f. 334].
Charles Penny, goldsmith, son of Ann Penny, grant on surr. for 40 years, made on 16th November 1732 [DD/CC 112408; L.1701–1739, p. 553; A.1725–1742, f. 102d].
James Penny, goldsmith, son of Charles Penny, grant on surr. for 40 years made on 7th April 1752 [EB 1745–1755 (DD/CC 110006), p. 205; DD/CC 112170; L.1740–1760, f. 378; A.1743–1760, p. 157];

regrant for 40 years on surr. in consideration of a fine of 12*l*. 12*s*., on 2nd January 1768[7] [EB 1762–1771 (DD/CC 110008), p. 271; L.1761–1777, f. 196; DD/CC 112171]; regrant for 40 years on surr. on 30th June 1784 [DD/CC 112172; L.1777–1789, f. 291; A.1777–1792, p. 177; Docs. ADD/4145].

George Penny, goldsmith, son of James Penny, grant for 40 years on surr. made on 2nd December 1801 [DD/CC 112173; L.1790–1807, f. 414; A.1792–1817, p. 211; cf. Docs. ADD/4186, 4203a, 4203b] regrant for 40 years on surr., on 2nd January 1817 [DD/CC 112174; A.1792–1817, p. 161; cf. Docs. ADD/4238?].

Vincent Stuckey of Langport Eastover, Somerset, assignee of George Penny, the tenancy having been assigned as security for 'a considerable sum of money'. Penny died intestate, and power of administration of his estate was granted to his sole next of kin, John Wills of Bristol. Wills and Stuckey surr. on 1st November 1826 [DD/CC 112175].

William Perkins, gent., grant for 40 years on 7th December 1826 [A.1817–1832, p. 253; DD/CC 112175].

'Mr Knight' occurs as lessee and occupant, 1827–1829 [DD/CC 114080/1].

'Mrs Knight' occurs as lessee and occupant, 1830–1831 [DD/CC 114080/1].

John Voysey, lessee, 1832–1839 (occupant, 1833–1839, Mrs Willmott) [DD/CC 114080/1].

John Willmott, linen draper, grant for 40 years of the premises 'sometime since in the possession of William Perkins, afterwards of William Knight, since of John Voysey, and now of John Willmott', made on 14th December 1840 [DD/CC 112177; R.1, p. 309]; regrant for 40 years on 17th February 1855, in consideration of a fine of £60 [DD/CC 112178; R.3, p. 3; Docs. ADD/4259].

Notes

1. Illegible, ?Hockerill.
2. Before this grant was made, Richard Anstice, deceased, had dwelt in the house, L.1571–1624, f. 12.
3. This grant was made to make up the years which Sarney and Clark had in the premises, from which it would appear that they were joint subtenants of Browne.
4. There is no trace or mention of a lease; Crosse was probably a subtenant or an assignee.
5. Powell was dwelling in the house at this time, probably as a subtenant.

6. The surveyor for the Parliament recommended that the rent be raised from 26s. 8d. to 6l.
7. This grant included a provision that the occupants of the houses adjoining on either side might enter upon the premises at convenient times for the purpose of executing repairs to such houses when occasion required.

24

Property No. 36
15, Market Place

The tenants of this house, generally described as the sixth from the east end of the New Works, were:

Thomas Lewes (Lewys), goldsmith, grant for three lives on 28th January 1545[1] [L.1535–1545, f. 106; C1545/6].
Richard Furneye[2] [C1559/60, C1560/1, C1561/2, C1562/3, and C1563/4].
William Dotherell, mercer, grant for 40 years on 20th November 1562 [L.1546–1565, f. 144d].
Thomas Goodier, yeoman, claimed in 1570 to hold the tenancy by assignment from William Dothewell (sic) [S1570, f. 7d]; grant for 40 years on 1st April 1575 [L.1571–1624, f. 21d].
Bridget Goodier [C1587/8].
William Clarck, notary public, grant for 40 years on 24th June 1599 [L.1571–1624, f. 164d][3].
Robert Powell, grant (on the death of W. Clarck) for 40 years on 9th October 1622 [DD/CC 112380; A.1622–1625, f. 12d; L.1571–1624, f. 239[4]; C1625/6, C1626/7, and C1634/5]; regrant for 13½ years to extend the current term to 40 years, on 10th October 1637 [SB 1629–1637, p. 102; S1649, p. 10].
'Mrs Powell', widow of Robert Powell, in possession, June/July 1649 [S1649. p. 10[5]].
Thomas Pierce, grant on surr. for 40 years on 4th October 1662 [DD/CC 112393; rental temp. Charles II, DD/CC 111736, 21/33].
Francis Cary [DD/CC 112344].
John Paine, notary public, registrar to the dean and chapter, grant on surr, for 40 years, on 7th January 1687[6] [DD/CC 112344; L.1681–1701, p. 58; A.1683–1704, f. 334]; regrant for 40 years on 1st April 1704 [DD/CC 112361; L.1701–1739, f. 14d; A.1683–1704,

f. 334]; further regrant for 40 years on 25th May 1721 [DD/CC 112402; SRO.DD/FS, box 27; L.1701–1739, p. 200; A.1705–1725, f. 162d].

John Paine, prebendary of Barton St David and canon residentiary, son of John Paine, grant on surr. for 40 years on 16th June 1737 [L.1701–1739, p. 703; A.1725–1740, f. 174d]; regrant for 40 years on 1st April 1766[7] (fine 27*l.*) [EB1762–1771 (DD/CC 110008), p. 170].

Simon Witherell [DD/CC 112256].

Mary Witherell, widow of S. Witherell, John Witherell, of Bridgwater, and John Brock, the three devisees under the will of Simon Witherell, grant for 40 years on 1st April 1785[8] [DD/CC 112256, 112257; L.1777–1789, f. 324; A.1777–1792, p. 195; Docs. ADD/4150].

Peter Layng, grant on surr. for 40 years on 15th January 1805[9] [DD/CC 112259; L.1790–1807, f. 520; A.1792–1817, p. 307; Docs. ADD/4205].

Joseph Lax, assignee of the tenancy on 12th December 1808, as security for a loan of £550 [DD/CC 112260].

Francis Besly, druggist, purchased the tenancy for the remaining years to run, on 21st April 1810 [DD/CC 112262]; grant on surr. for 40 years on 1st July 1819]DD/CC 112264; A.1817–1832, p. 42]; according to this grant, Miss Hook had lately dwelt in the house. During Besly's tenancy the following are recorded as occupants: 1828–1831, Messrs Besly and Voisey; 1836–1837, Messrs England and Powell; 1838–1840, Messrs England and Berryman; 1841–1837, Mrssrs Purnell and Berryman [DD/CC 114080/1]; regrant for 40 years on 2nd January 1834 [DD/CC 112270; A.1832–1840, p. 65].

Francis Besly, devisee of his uncle Francis Besley (died 15th December 1844).

Frederick Every, of Exeter, assignee of this and other tenancies as security for a mortgage of £430 plus interest; the assignment was dated 25th September 1849 [DD/CC 112271].

William Henry Besley, surgeon, of Bradninch, Devon, and Francis Besley, surgeon of Shebbear, Devon, grant for 40 years (fine £140) on 15th October 1849[10] [DD/CC 112272; Docs. ADD/4254].

William Charles Berryman jun., wine and spirit merchant, to whom the tenancy was assigned for £750 on 14th September 1855 [DD/CC 206765].

Notes

1. John Mullens was then living in the house.
2. There is no trace of a grant; Furneye may have been an assignee.
3. Clarck was then dwelling in the house.
4. Most of the transcription of this grant is missing, several pages between July 1621 and October 25th 1623 having been cut out of the ledger.
5. The surveyor recommended an increase in rent from 26s. 8d. to 6l.
6. On 7th July 1687 Mr. Paine was given leave to put up rails in front of his door into the churchyard, as other tenants of houses in the New Works had done, Cal. ii, p. 462.
7. At this time Ralph Sutton was dwelling in the house.
8. At this time Benjamin Andrews was living in the house.
9. Miss Hook was then dwelling in the house.
10. This grant included the adjacent property (no. 38) on the west side.

25

Property No. 38
13, Market Place

This property, recently the Anchor restaurant, was known as the Anchor inn during the period 1850–1930.[1] It is curious that such use was permitted by the dean and chapter while the premises were part of its manor,[2] for in a lease of 19, Market place, made on 31st July 1843,[3] a stipulation was inserted that the premises must not be used for *inter alia* an inn or tavern.

On 8th October 1546[4] this house was granted to Richard Evans, a tailor, for the lives of himself, his wife Elinor, and their daughter Mary. It was provided that the lives nominated should successively inhabit the tenement unless released from this obligation by the lords. The tenants were also required to make suit to the court of the dean and chapter held in Canon Barn on 'the Lawdaie'. The tenants after Mr Evans were:

Elinor Evans, widow of Richard Evans [C1559/60–C1563/4]; in 1570 she claimed to hold the tenancy by virtue of the grant made to her husband in 1546 [S1570, f. 8; cf also C1587/8 and C1602/3].
Walter Brick, woollen draper, grant on surr. for 40 years, on 3rd January 1623 (fine 10l.) [A.1622–1635, ff. 12, 16; DD/CC 112379]; extension of 17 years granted on 20th January 1640 (fine, 20 nobles) [S1649, p. 10; SB 1637–1640, p. 57].

75

Ezekiel Nash, assignee of Walter Brick, in possession in June/July 1649 [S1649, p. 10⁵].

John Davidge, mercer [terrier *temp*. Charles II, *c*. 1665 ?, DD/CC 111736, 25/31]; grant on surr. for 40 years, on 11th January 1687 [DD/CC 112345; L.1681–1701, f. 59; A.1683–1704, f. 98d]; regrant on surr. for 40 years, on 2nd January 1703 [DD/CC 112357; L.1701–1739, f. 9; A.1683–1704, f. 318; S1703, p. 181].

Thomas Baron, mercer, grant on surr, for 40 years, on 16th December 1728 [DD/CC 112405; L.1701–1739, p. 399].

Ann Baron and Katherine Giles (formerly Baron), wife of Henry Giles [L.1740–1760, f. 137].

Ann Baron, spinster, and John Mosse, grant on surr. for 40 years, on 7th December 1743 [L.1740–1760, f. 137; A.1725-1744, f. 354d].

Ann Baron, grant on surr. (John Mosse having died), for 40 years (fine 15*l*.), on 4th December 1765 [EB 1762–771 (DD/CC 110008), p. 125; DD/CC 112254; L.1761–1777, f. 132; A.1761–1777, p. 146; Docs. ADD/4093].

Simon Witherell.

Mary Witherell, John Witherell, of Bridgwater, and John Brock, devisees under the will of S. Witherell, deceased, grant for 40 years on surr., on 1st April 1785 (fine 14*l*. 14*s*. [DD/CC 112258; L.1777–1789, p. 321; A.1777–1792, p. 195; Docs. ADD/4149].

Mark Spicer, grant for 40 years on surr., on 3rd April 1810 (fine 36*l*.) [DD/CC 112261; L.1808–1813, p. 69; A.1792–1817, p. 424; Docs. ADD/4193].

Thomas Robins, legally entitled to the premises in 1819 [DD/CC 112267].

Francis Besly I, purchased the tenancy at auction for £315 on 4th September 1819 [DD/CC 112267]; tenancy assigned on 26th October 1819 [DD/CC 112267].

Francis Besly I and William Melliar, in whom the tenancy became vested 'by virtue of certain legally valid assignments' [DD/CC 112268].

Francis Besly I, grant on surr. for 40 years, on 30th September 1824 [DD/CC 112269; A.1817–1832, p. 159]; grant for 40 years on 2nd January 1834⁶ [DD/CC 112270; A.1832–1840, p. 65].

Francis Besly II, devisee under the will of his uncle Francis Besly I (died 15th December 1844) [DD/CC 112271].

Frederick Every of Exeter, assignee of the premises as security for a mortgage of £430 plus interest [DD/CC 112271].

Francis Besly II, Frederick Every, and William Henry Besly (joint executors of the will of Francis Besly I, deceased), grant for 40 years on 15th October 1849 [DD/CC 112271].

William Henry Besly, surgeon, of Dunmore house, Bradninch, Devon, and Francis Besly II, surgeon, of Shebbear, Devon, (joint executors of the will of Francis Besly I, deceased), grant for 40 years on 15th October 1849 (fine £140) [DD/CC 112272, 206764; R.2, p. 258].

William Chester Berryman jun., wine and spirit merchant, assignment in consideration of the payment of £750 on 24th September 1855 [DD/CC 206765].

On 25th November 1833,[7] the chapter decreed that Francis Besly I's renewal of his lease must be deferred on account of an impediment arising from the assignment of the garden formerly belonging to the house. There is no record of this assignment, but it seems that Besly recovered possession of the garden to the satisfaction of the chapter, for his lease was renewed on 2nd January 1834.[8] It is possible that the unnamed assignee was William Melliar with whom Besly jointly held the house, for having obtained his renewal, Besly proceeded to restore the situation by assigning the garden with a stable and outbuildings, to Melliar on 1st February 1834.[9] Five years later, on 26th March 1839, Melliar himself assigned the garden to a carpenter, Cornelius Peddle.[10] These transactions were irregular; although the garden and 13, Market place were counted as separate properties of the manor, they were always united as a single tenement for the purpose of letting. In the view of the chapter it was not open to a tenant to sever them in order to make a separate assignment of the garden, as Besly had done. His attention must have been drawn to this anomaly, and possibly in return for some comsideration, Peddle was persuaded to rectify the irregularity by an assignment of the garden to Besly on 15th June 1841.[11]

Notes

1. R.D. Reid, 'The New Works at Wells', WNH&A Soc., *Report*, 1930, p. 34.
2. The New Works properties were taken over by the Ecclesiastical Commissioners at the commutation of the capitular estates in 1866.
3. See above, Article 22, p. 68, and R.2, p. 7 (cf. R2, p. 207). See also p. 53 above.
4. L.1546–1565, f. 1.
5. The surveyor recommended an increase in rent from 26*s*. 8*d*. to 6*l*. At the time of this survey, the garden in the New Works gardens annexed to this house was in the hands of the widow of Robert Powell, for whom, see Article 23, p. 71.

6. This and all subsequent leases include the adjacent property no. 36-15, Market place, see above, Article 24.
7. M.1831-1837, p. 75.
8. DD/CC 112270; A.1832-1840, p. 65.
9. DD/CC 112271.
10. Ibid.
11. Ibid.

26

Property No. 40
11, Market Place

Tenants:

Thomas Mylys, linen draper, renewal of lease (fine 40s.) for three lives, on 8th October 1552 [SB 1545, f. 33d; L.1546-1565, f. 58].
Isabell Miles (or Millis) [C1559/60-C1562/3].
Elizabeth Myles, wife of Thomas Mylys [C1563/4].
Elizabeth Miles, widow, and Alice Miles, daughter of the late Thomas Mylys and his wife Elizabeth,[1] claimed on 12th December 1570 to hold the tenancy by indenture dated 8th October 1552 [S1570, f. 8].
Philip Welch [C1587/8].
Philip Welch *modo* Edward Huyshe [C1602/3].
James Huishe, notary public, grant on surr. for 40 years, on 10th January 1625 (fine 20*l.*) [L.1624-1681, p. 2; A.1622-1635, f. 36; DD/CC 112397]; regrant on surr for 40 years, on 3rd January 1638 (fine, 20 nobles) [L.1624-1681, p. 266; SB 1629-1637, p. 158; C1636/7].
Edward Huishe [C1625/6[2]].
Edward Huishe *modo* James Huishe [C1626/7, C1627/8].
John Prickman, in June/July 1649 claimed to hold the property in right of his wife[3] by virtue of the lease dated 3rd January 1638 [S1649, p. 9[4]; DD/CC 111736, 25/33].
Sarah Huish, spinster, grant on surr. for 40 years, on 29th July 1674 [L.1624-1681, p. 685; DD/CC 112395].
Mary Broderwick, widow, grant on surr. for 40 years, on 4th August 1697[5] [DD/CC 112354; L.1681-1701, f. 204; A.1683-1704, f. 272].
Robert Kingston, tenant in 1703 [S1703, p. 185].

Francis Day, grant on surr. for 40 years, on 1st March 1718 [DD/CC 112368; L.1701–1739, p. 129; A.1705–1725, f. 128].

Francis Day, mercer. Elizabeth and Mary Day, spinsters, son and daughters of Francis Day, deceased, grant on surr. for 40 years, on 10th June 1737 [DD/CC 112369; L.1701–1739, p. 696; A.1725–1744, f. 175d]; regrant for 40 years on surr., on 20th May 1758 [DD/CC 112304; L.1740–1760, p. 371; EB 1756–1762 (DD/CC 110007), p. 102].

Elizabeth and Mary Day, tenants following the death of their brother Francis Day [EB 1771–1780 (DD/CC 110009), p. 242]; surr. in favour of a new lease for 40 years [Docs. ADD/4105].

Mary Dawson, in whom the tenancy was vested after the deaths of the Misses E. and M. Day, grant on surr. for 40 years (fine 20l.), on 1st October 1778 [EB 1771–1780 (DD/CC 110009), p. 242; DD/CC 112305; L.1777–1789, f. 44; A1777–1792, p. 22; Docs. ADD/4121, 4122].

Jacob Mogg, of High Littleton, grant on surr. for 40 years, on 3rd January 1803 [DD/CC 112306; A.1792–1817, p. 252; L.1790–1807, f. 456; Docs. ADD/42086].

Decima and Maria Withers, spinsters, grant for 40 years, on 2nd January 1821 [DD/CC 112307, 112308; A.1817–1832, p. 73]. During this tenancy the occupants of the house were: Robert Burden, 1827–1828; and James Cox, 1829–1835 [DD/CC 114080/1].

After the death of Maria Withers, various assignments under mortgage were made: to James Cox, surveyor and auctioneer [DD/CC 112309, 112315]; to John Clitsome Warren, of Taunton [DD/CC 112310, 112311]; to John Daniel Delancey[6] [DD/CC 112311, 112316]; to Thomas Young, broker [DD/CC 112313]; to Charles Grist, confectioner [DD/CC 112317]; to Sarah Louise Cruttwell, of Bath [DD/CC 112318]; to Lucy Chester Ann Sturgess, of Camberwell, Surrey [DD/CC 112314]. The following leases were also made by the dean and chapter:

John Daniel Delancey, writer, grant on surr. for 40 years, on 1st July 1836 [DD/CC 112312].

Sarah Willmott, spinster, grant on surr. for 40 years, on 21st April 1851 (fine, £45) [R.2, p. 328; DD/CC 112319, 112320; Docs. ADD/4257].

Notes

1. Elizabeth and Alice Miles were the surviving lives of those named in the grant of 8th October 1552.
2. This payment should have been credited to James Huishe.
3. Sarah, daughter of James Huishe.
4. The surveyor recommended an increase in the rent from 26s. 8d. to 7l. 15s.
5. It is evident that Mrs Broderwick's tenancy had begun earlier, for on 7th October 1680, she was permitted 'to have a doore out of her backside into the church yard', at a rent of 2s. [SRS 72, p. 80].
6. This assignee later became a lessee, see below.

27

Property No. 42
9, Market Place

This house,[1] designated the fourth from the west end of the New Works, had the following tenants:

Robert Canway, *alias* White [C1545/6].
Nicholas Prymet, grant probably for three lives,[2] on 18th June 1552 [S1570, f. 8d].
Julyan Prin (Prinn) [C1559/60, C1560/1].
John Crosse [C1561/2, C1562/3].
Leonard Crosse [C1563/4, C1587/8, C1602/3].
Juliana Prymet, 'once wife of Nicholas Prymet', and Anthony their son, claim to hold the tenancy by virtue of the grant made on 18th June 1552 [S1570, f. 8].
Thomas Shattock, late Edward Lea [C1525/6, C1526/7, C1527/8].
Thomas Shattock, haberdasher, grant on surr. for 40 years, on 1st April 1628 [L.1624–1681, p. 211]; regrant on surr. for 40 years, on 1st April 1634 [L.1624–1681, p. 261; A.1621–1635, f. 158; C1634/5, C1636/7].
Richard Hickes, assignee of Thomas Shattock, in possession, June/July 1649 [S1649, p. 11[3]]; regrant on surr. for 40 years, on 11th January 1660 [DD/CC 112334; L.1624–1681, p. 345]; tenant in 1665 [DD/CC 111736, 25/33], and in 1671 [DD/CC 111740, p. 12].
Anne Hickes, widow, grant on surr. for 40 years, on 6th May 1679 [DD/CC 112339].
Richard Hickes, of Dinder, son of Anne Hickes, grant on surr. for 40 years, on 15th April 1695 [DD/CC 112353; L.1681–1701, f. 184].

Henry Jeanes, mercer, tenant in 1703 [S1703, p. 184]; regrant on surr. for 40 years, on 7th July 1715 [DD/CC 112366; L.1701–1739, f. 88d; A.1705–1725, f. 103].

John Mosse, grant on surr. for 40 years, on 10th April 1729 [DD/CC 112406; L.1701–1739, p. 429; A.1725–1744, f. 59d]; regrant on surr. for 40 years, on 30th September 1743[4] [L.1740–1760, f. 123; DD/CC 112372; A.1725–1744, f. 249d].

Elizabeth Truman, widow, grant for 40 years, on 14th May 1755[5] [DD/CC 112191]; grant on surr. for 40 years, on 2nd January 1772[6] (fine 9*l*. 13*s*.) [DD/CC 112293; EB 1771–1780 (DD/CC 110009), p. 14; L.1761–L.1777, f. 333; A.1761–1777, p. 277; Docs. ADD/4098].

Elizabeth Salmon, spinster, grant on surr. (Miss Salmon being legally possessed of the tenancy on the death of Mrs Truman) for 40 years, on 9th December 1790 (fine 26*l*. 15*s*.[7]) [EB 1780–1798 (DD/CC 110010), p. 33; DD/CC 112292; L.1790–1807, p. 25; A.1777–1792, p. 298; Docs. ADD/4168].

Elizabeth Abraham, of Bathwick, widow, being legally possessed of the tenancy, surr. on 1st December 1807 [DD/CC 112295].

George Lax, grant for 40 years on 3rd December 1807[8] [L.1790–1807, f. 611; A.1792–1817, p. 378; DD/CC 112296]; regrant on surr. for 40 years, on 2nd January 1822 [DD/CC 112297; A.1817–1832, p. 94]; regrant for 40 years, on 1st July 1836 [A.1832–1840, p. 204; DD/CC 112298]; regrant for 40 years, on 21st April 1851 (fine £54) [DD/CC 112299; R.2, p. 325; Docs. ADD/4256].

Fanny Lax, spinster, of Monmouth house, Burnham, Somerset, grant on surr. for 40 years, on 28th July 1865 (fine £60)[9] [DD/CC 112300, 112301, R.4, p. 149].

Notes

1. Now in the occupation of Barclays bank.
2. Prymet himself, his wife Juliana, and their son Anthony, see below.
3. The surveyor recommended an increase in rent from 26*s*. 8*d*. to 8*l*.
4. This grant contained a prohibition against hanging or placing 'linnen, linnen cloaths or other things whatsoever upon the rails or pallisadoes belonging to (the) garden lately enclosed and situated at the backward side of the . . . tenement'. In the event of infringement of this prohibition, the dean and chapter, its agents or servants might lawfully take away or pull down the offending objects 'without interruption, let, hindrance, suit, or denyal of . . . John Mosse.'
5. The premises are described as 'where John Sutton, gent., lately dwelt', but there is no record of a grant; he may have been a subtenant or an assignee.

6. At this time, Miss Elizabeth Salmon was dwelling in the house.
7. Initially a fine of 30*l*. was set and agreed [Docs. ADD/4168].
8. At the time of this grant, Lax was living in the house.
9. The property had been let to a subtenant, John Woodward, and after the death of George Lax on 26th January 1853 had been held in trust for Miss Lax until she attained her majority [DD/CC 112300].

28

Property No.44
7, Market Place

Unlike other houses in the New Works, this house had traditionally two designations: it was variously termed the third from the west end, and the tenth from the east end. There seems to be no reason why it alone should have been described with reference to both ends of the New Works. The tenants were as follows:

Agnes James, widow, grant for three lives[1] on 24th January 1545 [L.1535–1545, f. 106d; C1545/6].

Thomas Fulwell[2], [C1559/60–1563/4].

Christable Fulwell, widow, grant for three lives, on 25th August 1565 [L.1546–1565, f. 154, C1563/4].

Richard Anstie, grant on surr. for three lives, on 2nd January 1585 [A.1681–1701, f. 28d, f. 30].

Henry Wells [C1587/8].

Mary, wife of Henry Wells, grant for four lives on 1st July 1572[3] [L.1571–1624, f. 132; Ch. 811, Cal.ii, p. 711 (abbr.)].

Henry Wells, *modo Johannes Bull*[4] [C1602/3].

Elizabeth Wells, widow, grant for three lives, on 2nd January 1624 [A.1622–1625, f. 31d].

John Bradford, grant for 40 years on 10th January 1625 (fine 50*l*.) [DD/CC 112381; L.1624–1681, p. 4; A.1622–1635, f. 37d]; renewal for 11 years (to make up the term to 40 years) on 2nd January 1636 (fine 4*l*.) [SB 1629–1637, p. 92; A.1635–1645, f. 16]; named as tenant in June/July 1649 [S1649, p. 11[5]; C1625/6–C1627/8, C1634/5. C1636/7].

Matthew and George Irish, of Banwell, grant for 40 years, on 12th January 1664 [DD/CC 112336].

Richard Cupper, apothecary, grant on surr. 40 years, on 20th October 1686 [DD/CC 112346; L.1683–1704, f. 91d]; named as tenant in 1703, p. 180]; regrant on surr. for 40 years on 4th January 1714 [DD/CC 112363; A.1705–1725, f. 88d; L.1701–1739, f. 79]; regrant for 40 years, on 2nd October 1732 [DD/CC 112407; L.1701–1739, p. 537; A.1725–1744, f. 101d].

Edith and William Fricker, devisees under the will of Richard Cupper (who died on 21st January 1739) [SRO, DD/WM 17].

William Keate, apothecary, purchased the tenancy for 180*l.*; assignment by E. and W. Fricker on 14th February 1744 [SRO, DD/WM 17]; grant on surr. for 40 years, on 1st April 1748 (fine 15*l.*) [EB 1745–1755 (DD/CC 110006), p. 78; L.1740–1760, p. 86; DD/CC 112217; regrant for 40 years on surr. (fine 15*l.* 10*s.*), on 2nd February 1770 [EB 1762–1771 (DD/CC 110008), p. 358; DD/CC 112218; L.1761–1777, f. 268; A.1761–1777, p. 242].

Revd William Keate and Thomas Keate, surgeon, in whom the tenancy was legally vested on the death of William Keate [EB 1780–1798 (DD/CC 110010), p. 40].

William Porch, glover, grant for 40 years on surr. (fine 38*l.*), on 1st April 1791 [EB 1780–1798 (DD/CC 110010), p. 40; DD/CC 112219, 112220, L.1790–1807, f. 43; A.1777–1792, p. 307; Docs. ADD/4170]. regrant for 40 years on surr., on 22nd April 1806 [L.1790–1807, f. 570; A.1792–1817, p. 351; DD/CC 112221].

Richard Dix, saddler, assignee of William Porch, on 29th September 1810 [DD/CC 112222].

William Porch, glover, assignee of Richard Dix, under a mortgage of £200 [DD/CC 112224].

Richard Dix, grant for 40 years on surr.,[6] on 2nd January 1821 [A.1817–1872, p. 74; DD/CC 112224, 112225].

William Porch, assignee under a mortgage of £300, on 2nd April [DD/CC 112226].

Richard Dix, grant for 40 years, on 11th May 1833 [A.1832–1840, p. 40; DD/CC 112227].

Revd John East of Bath, assignee under a mortgage of £300 plus interest, on 13th May 1833 [DD/CC 112228].

Richard Dix (II), son of Richard Dix, devisee under the will of the latter, who died on 30th August 1838 [DD/CC 112231].

William Inman Welsh, grant for 40 years on surr. (fine £77), on 10th February 1853 [DD/CC 112232, 112233; R.2, p. 408[7] Docs. ADD/4258]. Richard Dix continued in occupation, probably as a subtenant, until at least 1865 [DD/CC 114080/2].

Notes

1. Agnes James, Thomas Fulwell, and his wife Christable.
2. The tenancy reverted to Fulwell, as the second named life, on the death of Agnes James.
3. The house is described as 'where Henry Wells now lives'.
4. From this entry, it would appear that John Bull had succeeded Wells in the tenancy on the latter's death.
5. The surveyor proposed an increase in rent from 26s. 8d. to 8l.
6. Presumably the tenancy had reverted to Dix on the discharge of the mortgage.
7. Prior to this grant, several assignments under mortgage were made, which are detailed in DD/CC 112231.

29

Property No. 46
5, Market Place

This property was charged with a rent of 33s. 4d. annually, whereas the standard rent for the properties in the New Works was 26s. 8s. The higher rent seems to have been to this house having a cellar, a fact which is specifically mentioned in many leases. The following tenants have been traced:

John Gye [C1545/6].
John Lane, grant for three lives,[1] on 9th July 1551 [L.1546–1565, f. 56d; C1559/60–C1563/4].
Christopher Pollerde, yeoman, grant for 40 years, on 1st October 1576[2] [L.1571–1624, f. 37].
Peter Archer [C1587/8].
Fortuna Archer [C1602/3].
John Lane, late Fortuna Archer [C1625/6–C1627/8; C1634/5, C1636/7].
John Lane, held the tenancy by indenture (date not stated) for 30 years, the residue of a 40 year term, and sought (date unknown) an extension to 40 years. This was granted for a fine of 30l. No new lease can be traced, and it would appear that John Lane was not the person of that name to whom a grant was made in 1551[3] [SB 1637–1640, p. 20; SB 1640–1644 (DD/CC 110004), p. 47 (and loose leaf) — fine proposed 10l.].

William Derricke, shown as tenant in June/July 1649 [S1649, p. 1⁴].
Arthur Alderley, vicar choral, grant for 40 years, on 2nd January 1660 [DD/CC 112333; L.1624–1681, p. 365⁵]; *c.* 1671, he 'hath assigned his interest to Stephen Dorset . . . and Stephen Dorset hath assigned his interest to Richard Trant' [DD/CC 111740, p. 11].
Elizabeth Trant(er), widow, grant on surr. for 40 years, on 5th June 1686 [L.1681–1701, p. 49; A.1683–1704, f. 84d].
Thomas Marchant, haberdasher of hats, grant on surr. for 40 years, on 2nd January 1703 [DD/CC 112358; L.1701–1739, f. 10; S1703, p. 187; A.1683–1704, f. 318d; DD/CC 112401]; further grant on surr. for 40 years, on 25th May 1721 [L.1701–1739, f. 194; A.1705–1725, f. 163].
Anne Browne, widow, grant on surr. for 40 years, on 3rd January 1741 [DD/CC 112370; L.1740–1760, f. 36; A.1725–1744, f. 214d].
Ann, Martha, and Ekizabeth Browne, spinsters, grant on surr. (following the death of Mrs. Anne Browne) for 40 years, on 3rd January 1758 [A.1743–1760, p. 244; DD/CC 112187; EB 1756–1762 (DD/CC 110007), p. 58].
Ann Browne, spinster, grant for 40 years on surr. (Martha and Elizabeth Browne having died), on 13th December 1774 (fine 12*l.*) [A.1761–1777, p. 340; L.1761–1777, f. 486; EB 1771–1780 (DD/CC 110009), p. 87; DD/CC 112188; Docs. ADD/4198].
Ann Walker, of East Harptree, Edmund Broderip, and John Richards, of Axbridge, in whom the tenancy was vested 'by virtue of divers legal assignments', surr. on 1st September 1790 [DD/CC 112275; L.1790–1807, p. 15]
William Parsons, collar maker, grant on surr. for 40 years, on 14th September 1790 (fine 20*l.* 10*s.*) [EB 1780–1798 (DD/CC 110010), p. 22; L.1790–1807, f. 17; A.1777–1792, p. 292; DD/CC 112789].
Hugh Trenchard, clothier of Chard, assignee under a mortgage for 300*l.*, on 20th June 1793 [DD/CC 112790].
James Lane, saddler, assignee under a mortgage for £225 on 25th March 1794 (DD/CC 112790).
Solomon Pain, of Axbridge, assignee under a mortgage for £550 on 27th December 1794 [DD/CC 112790].
John Garrod, grocer, grant on surr. for 40 years, on 1st July 1805 (fine £75) [L.1790–1807, f. 542; A.1792–1817, p. 320; DD/CC 112191; DD/CC 112790; Docs. ADD/4225]; regrant for 40 years on surr., on 2nd April 1821 [DD/CC 112192; A.1817–1832, p. 79].
John Garrod, grant for 40 years on surr., on 12th November 1832 [DD/CC 112193, 112194; A.1832–1840, p. 16]; regrant on surr. for

40 years, on 18th September 1848 (fine £70) [DD/CC 112195; R.2, p. 218]; regrant on surr. for 40 years, on 17th November 1863 (fine £70) [DD/CC 112196, R.4, p. 42].

Notes

1. John Lane, Elizabeth his wife, and Richard Gye, her son; it appears that John Gye had died, and that Lane had married his widow.
2. Pollerde was then living in the house, possibly as an assignee.
3. This John Lane may have been the son of the grantee in 1551.
4. As in the case of other New Works houses the surveyor proposed an improvement in the rent to 6*l*.
5. Here, the house is described as 'where Stephen Dorset now lives'.

30

Property No. 48
3, Market Place

Tenants:

William Bulman, weaver [C1545/6, C1559/60, C1561/2, C1562/3].
William Smith, tailor, grant for three lives,[1] on 27th March 1561 (fine 40*s*.) [L.1546–1565, f. 149d; S1570, f. 9].
John Smith, son of William Smith [C1587/8].
Anne Smith, widow, grant for three lives,[2] on 1st July 1588 [L.1571–1624, f. 105d].
Edmund Bower [C1602/3].
John Smith, of Badgeworth, clerk, grant for three lives, on 1st October 1625 (fine 10*l*.) [A.1621–1635, f. 44d]
Adryan Bower, grant on surr. for three lives, on payment of a 'competent sum', on 9th October 1625 [L.1624–1681, p. 29[3]; A.1621–1635, f. 99; DD/CC 112329; A.1621–1635, f. 46d]; rent received from George Bull, David[4] Tuttle and Edmund Bower [C1625/6–C1627/8, C1634/5].
Tristram Towse, notary, grant for 40 years on surr., on 1st July 1630 (fine 6*l*. 'to be paid in six accounts') [A.1621–1635, f. 99; SB 1629–1631, p. 22; A.1635–1645, f. 16].

Robert Phippen, in whom the tenancy was legally vested, died and bequeathed the sum of 80*l*. to his son West Phippen. In order to discharge this legacy, Robert Phippen's widow and executrix, Martha, assigned the tenancy to her father William West for a sum (not stated) sufficient to enable her to pay the 80*l*. to her son. William West having died, and the deed of assignment entitling him to the tenancy having been lost or mislaid, Martha Phippen married Raulf Conyers who was willing to settle the tenancy upon West Phippen [DD/CC 112119].

James Clutterbuck and Katherine West, assignees to hold and employ the tenancy for the benefit of West Phippen [DD/CC 112119].

Robert Chicke, in June/July 1649, held the tenancy in right of his wife (unnamed), and claimed an estate by virtue of a grant from the dean and chapter, but could produce no evidence in confirmation [S1649, p. 26[5]].

Robert[6] Thomas, woollen draper, grant for 40 years, on 4th April 1672[7] [DD/CC 112396; SRS 72, p. 38].

John Irish, mercer, grant on surr. for 40 years, on 2nd April 1688[8] [DD/CC 112349; L.1681–1701, f. 85; A.1683–1704, f. 125d; S1703, p. 185].

Elizabeth Irish, widow, grant on surr. for 40 years, on 8th February 1714[9] [A.1705–1725, f. 90d; DD/CC 112364; L.1701–1739, p. 413]; regrant on surr. for 40 years, on 16th December 1728 [A.1725–1744, f. 54d; L.1701–1739, p. 80; DD/CC 112404]; regrant on surr. for 40 years, on 19th November 1744 [DD/CC 112373; A.1743–1760, p. 23].

Hester Baron, spinster, grant on surr. for 40 years, on 12th December 1758 (fine 12*l*.) [EB 1756–1762 [DD/CC 110007], p. 121; DCR VIII, p. 9; L.1744–1760, f. 538; A.1743–1760, p. 280; DD/CC 112200].

Rebecca Miller, spinster, surr. with a view to a lease for 31 years (portion of the lease surr. unexpired) [EB 1780–1798 (DD/CC 110010), p. 6[10]].

Benjamin Andrews, grant on surr. for 40 years, on 2nd January 1790 [DD/CC 112201; L.1790–1807, f. 3].

John Brown, haberdasher, assignee on 24th March 1801 (having purchased the tenancy from Benjamin Andrews for £472. 10*s*. for the remainder of the term of the lease of 1790 [DD/CC 112202]; mortgage of premises by Andrews for £300 on 24th March 1801 [DD/CC 112203].

Thomas Andrews, of Bradford Abbas, Dorset, yeoman, and John Brown, shopkeeper, being legally entitled to the premises on the death of Benjamin Andrews, surr. on 1st January 1805 [DD/CC 112204].

Thomas Andrews, grant on surr. for 40 years of premises occupied by John Brown, on 2nd January 1805 [DD/CC 112205; L.1790–1807, ff. 512, 515[11] A.1792–1817, p. 305].

John Vickery, schoolmaster, grant on surr. for 40 years, on 2nd January 1819 [DD/CC 112206; A.1817–1832, p. 33].

Edward Say, druggist, assignee for the residue of the last lease (1819), on 25th March 1829 [DD/CC 112207].

John Wookey, yeoman, assignee under a mortgage for £500 on 25th April 1829 [DD/CC 112208].

William Hardisty, of Darshill, Shepton Mallet, crape manufacturer, grant for 40 years, on 4th December 1832 [DD/CC 112209, 112210].

Elizabeth Pearce, spinster, assignee under a mortgage for £500 on 19th July 1837 [DD/CC 112211].

Mary Hardisty, spinster, daughter of William Hardisty, assignee on 30th December 1842 [DD/CC 112212]; grant on surr. for 40 years on 1st July 1865 (fine £233) [R.4, p. 141; DD/CC 112213, 112214; DD/CC 250758].

Notes

1. William Smith, Ann Smith his wife, and John their son.
2. Anne Smith and her sons, Bartholomew and John.
3. The premises are described here as 'where Daniel Tuthill lately dwelt, and where George Bull now dwells'.
4. In DD/CC 112329, Daniel — and see n.3 above.
5. The surveyor advised an increase in rent from 26s. 8d. to 6l.
6. Richard (incorrectly) in DD/CC 112396.
7. John Greene was then said to be dwelling in the house.
8. The premises were described as 'late in the tenure of John Greene'.
9. On the strength of documents found on the premises, Dr R.D. Reid concludes that four years before this grant (c. 1710) this house was occupied by one Hugh Brown, bookseller and scrivener. There is no trace of any grant or assignment to any one so named. See WNH&A Soc., *Report*, 1951–1952, pp. 4f.
10. A fine of 50l. was fixed, but there is no evidence of a grant to Miss Miller.
11. The lessee, elsewhere described as 'yeoman' is here described as 'apothecary'.

31

Property No. 50
1, Market Place (East Part).

The plot of land on which bishop Bekynton built his 'New Works' is described in the grant which he made to two feoffees on 27th September 1459[1] as abutting westward upon the tenement wherein David Taillour then dwelt. Since the property which is the subject of this article adjoins, on the east, the westernmost house in the New Works, the site of property no. 50 and that of Taillour's tenement must be identical, though nothing is known of that tenement, nor of David Taillour. His name does not occur in the escheator's account rolls, in which are recorded the names of the early tenants from whom the annual rent of 22s. was received. The premises now form the eastern portion of the offices of the Midland Bank, and were often described as standing opposite the high cross of Wells;[2] from a lease made of an adjoining property in 1704[3] we learn that at that time the premises were known as 'the coffee house'. On 11th October 1861,[4] the chapter considered an application from the lessee (Mr W.I. Welsh) 'to allow the surveyor of the local board to inspect the map of Canon grange with a view to identify and make alterations in the premises numbered 50': he also suggested that 'a new plan of the premises should be made, and that the expense of making it should be borne equally by himself and the dean and chapter'. It is not stated what alterations were visualized, and the chapter resolved 'that the chapter clerk act in this matter as his judgement shall dictate, bearing in mind that the dean and chapter decline incurring any expense in reference to the new plan in question'. The following tenants can be traced:

John Gosinhill [E1558/9].
Joan Mullins, widow, [E1559/60, E1560/1, E1564/5, E1584/5, E1586/7].
Philip Jeffries [E1587/8].
John Ashe [E1588/9, E1589/90]
William Evans [E1590/1–E1594/5].
Robert Thomas [E1600/1].

Daniel Tuthill, in 1629, held the premises[5] for life [SB 1629–1637, p. 2].

Robert Thomas, grant for three lives[6] on 20th December 1630 (fine 10*l.*) [SB 1629–1637, p. 2; S1649, p. 18[7]].

Richard Thomas, grant on surr. for 40 years, on 4th April 1672 [DD/CC 112394; SRS 72, p. 38].

'Mr Cordwent' [E1685/6–E1691/2].

Edward Middlecroft, of Warminster, Wilts., grant on surr. for 40 years, on 5th January 1691 [DD/CC 112507]; further grant for 40 years, on 5th January 1695 [A.1683–1704, f. 200d;[8] L.1681–1701, f. 134[8]].

John Brown, haberdasher of hats, grant on surr. for 40 years, on 3rd November 1711 [L.1701–1739, f. 68d; DD/CC 112501; A.1705–1725, f. 66; L.1701–1739, p. 622]; regrant on surr. for 40 years, on 30th September 1734 [DD/CC 112505; L.1701–1739, p. 622].

Thomas Bartlett, hatter [L.1761–1777, f. 55].

Robert Jeannour and his wife Jane, in possession in 1763 [EB 1762–1771 (DD/CC 110008), p. 45].

Francis Day, mercer, grant on surr. for 40 years, on 8th October 1763 (fine 15*l.*) [EB 1762–1777 (DD/CC 110008), p. 45; L.1761–1777, f. 55; A.1761–1777, p. 78].

Mary Dawson, spinster, in whom the tenancy was vested in 1777, grant on surr. for 40 years, on 1st October 1778 (fine 10*l.*) [EB 1771–1780 (DD/CC 110009), p. 243; L.1777–1789, f. 46; A.1777–1792, p. 22].

Jacob Mogg, of High Littleton, grant on surr. for 40 years, on 3rd January 1803 [L.1790–1807, f. 455; A.1792–1817, p. 251].

Thomas Jenkyns, of Stowey, cordwainer, grant for 40 years, on 1st July 1825 [A.1817–1832, p. 179].

John Dix [R.2, p. 115].

William Inman Welsh, grant for 40 years (fine £50), on 21st April 1846 [R.2, p. 115]; further grant for 40 years, on 30th January 1861[9] (fine £33) [R.3, p. 371].

Notes

1. Cal. i, p. 435.
2. This cross stood on the east of the conduit in the Market place, (see Simes's map of Wells, 1735).
3. L.1701–1739, f. 17; DD/CC 112359.
4. M.1866–1872, p. 92.

5. Described as a house or tenement in Sadler street.
6. Robert Thomas himself, Agnes his wife, and William their son, 'successively according to the custom of the manor', i.e., the property, on the death of the lessee, passed to the first life and then to the life next named, and so on, in order, provided no variation had been made in subsequent grants.
7. The surveyor advised an increase in rent from 22s. to 7l.
8. Here the lessee's name is shown as 'Middlecot'.
9. The premises are described as late in the occupation of Robert Stewart, cf. DD/CC 114080/2, p. 134.

32

Property No. 51
1, Market Place (West Part)

This property now forms the western portion of the offices of the Midland Bank. In 1380 it was described as a 'corner tenement with cellar and shops near St. Andrew's churchyard'.[1] Later, like the adjoining property no. 50 on the west,[2] it was often described with reference to the high cross of Wells, either as *ex opposito alta cruce* or as *iuxta altam crucem*. In 1415[3] it is described as a shop with a solar above and half a cellar, on the corner opposite the high cross in the north (*sic*) part of Sadler street, and in 1417[4] as a *cellarium* (cellar or storeroom) with shops, solars, houses and chambers built above, situated in Sadler street in the south corner of the churchyard, opposite the high cross, and in 1418[5] as a burgage with cellar, shops, solars, and chambers built thereupon, situated at the south end of Sadler street opposite the high cross called *La Condyt* in the south. The cellar seems to have been an important feature of the premises, for in E1543/4 they are termed *unum tenementum vocatum* the Celler, and in 1561[6] a tenement at the end of Sadler street, called 'the Seller'. In the middle of the 17th century the premises appear to have been divided, for there are grants of two tenements,[7] which were rebuilt and converted into one house early in the 18th century.[8] The record of tenants begins at the end of the 14th century:

Thomas Tanner, burgess, and Isabel his wife named as feoffees; release dated 25th April 1380 [Ch. 411, Cal. ii, p. 636 (abbr.)].
John Parker *alias* Barbour, burgess, lease for three lives made by

Isabel, widow of Thomas Tanner, on 20th January 1415 [Ch. 535, Cal. ii, p. 658 (abbr.)]
John Alhampton and Thomas Attewode, chaplains, to whom the premises had been donated by Isabel Tanner [Ch. 513, Cal. ii, p. 654 (abbr)].
Isabel Tanner, widow, grant by John Alhampton and Thomas Attewode, on 2nd December 1417 [Ch. 513, Cal. ii, p. 654 (abbr.)].
Richard Mylton *alias* Tayllour, burgess, and his wife Margery, grant by Isabel Tanner of reversion after her death, on 7th April 1418 [Ch. 552, Cal. ii, p. 662 (abbr.)]. The escheator's accounts for the last part of the 15th, and the first part of the 16th centuries record receipts of rents and payments for repairs in respect of this property, with the names of its 'inhabitants', but it is not always clear whether these were tenants under the dean and chapter, or simply assignees or subtenants:
John Winter and John Watkyn are named together in E1490/1, E1494/5, E1503/4[9]; likewise William Aleyn (Alun, Alen) *alias* Taylor, and Ludovicus Taylor, in E1505/6, E1508/9, E1509/10, E1511/2, E1513/4, E1515/6.

It appears that dean Gunthorpe granted this property to certain vicars choral and clerics, possibly acting as feoffees, and that it was then granted on 1st July 1495 to six other vicars choral by John Menyman, canon residentiary and Richard Huchons, vicar choral [Ch.723, Cal.ii, p. 695], and afterwards by Menyman to three other clerics [Ch.726, Cal.ii, p. 696]. Ralph Huchyns, tailor, paid rent for E1518/9, E1520/1, E1524/5, and defaulted in E1529/30. The record of tenants continues with:

William Pynner [E1543/4].
William Sprott [E1558/9], then in the tenure of John Gosynhill.
Margaret Sprat [E1559/60, E1560/1].
Assignees of William Sprat, grant for 40 years made on 20th September 1542 [E1564/5].
William Smythe, draper, grant for 40 years, on 16th April 1561[10] [L1571–1624, f. 9; E1584/5, E1586/7–E1590/1].
Edward Smith [E1591/2, E1593/4, E1594/5, E1600/1].
John Beaumond, apothecary, grant for 40 years, on 1st October 1633 [L1624–1681, p. 197; E1633/4].
Thomas Beaumont, vicar choral, grant for 40 years, on 1st January 1634 [S1649, p. 8], in possession June/July 1649 [S1649, p. 8[11]];

regrant on surr. for 40 years, on lst January 1660 [DD/CC 112482: E1660/1, E1668/9, E1670/1, E1672/3, E1691/2].

'Mr Cordwent' [E1692/3–E1697/8].

Thomas Marchant, haberdasher of hats, grant for 40 years, on 1st April 1704 [DD/CC 112359; A.1683–1704, f. 334; L.1701–1739, f. 17; E1704/5–E1708/9]; further grant on surr. for 40 years, on 25th May 1721[12] [L.1701–1739, p. 196; A.1705–1725, ff. 162d, 163].

Thomas Pearce, barber [DD/CC 112063; E1708/9–E1742/3].

Henry Hillard (Holland), apothecary, grant on surr. for 40 years, on 1st March 1735 [DD/CC 112063; L.1701–1739, p. 671; A.1725–1744, f. 153].

Dodington Sherston, grant on surr. for 40 years, on 4th December 1750 (fine 10*l.*) [EB 1745–1755 (DD/CC 110006), p. 162; DD/CC 112507, 112069; L.1740–1760, p. 343; E1742/3–E1759/60].

Moses Garland, yeoman, and Osborne Thomas Templeman, yeoman, in whom the premises were legally vested [EB 1771–1780 (DD/CC 110009), p. 250], surr. on 1st January 1778 [DD/CC 112070; L.1777–1789, f. 25].

Osborne Thomas Templeman, yeoman, grant on surr. for 40 years, on 2nd January 1778 (fine 38*l.*) [L.1777–1789, f. 26; A.1777–1792, p. 15; Cal.ii, p. 544; DD/CC 112071; E1760/1–E1761/2; Docs. ADD/4123, 4172 a/b].

Osborne Thomas Templeman, yeoman, and Robert Lax, gent., in whom the premises were legally vested [DD/CC 112072].

John Evill, bookseller, grant on surr. for 40 years, on 21st December 1791 [EB 1780–1798 (DD/CC 110010), p. 83; DD/CC 112072; Docs. ADD/4172a, 4172b] regrant on surr. for 40 years, on 20th February 1792 [DD/CC 112073; L.1790–1807, p. 80; A.1777–1792, p. 337] regrant for 40 years, on 12th April 1813 [A.1792–1817, p. 498; DD/CC 112074]; regrant for 40 years, on 2nd January 1828 [SR0, DD/FS, box 27; DD/CC 112075; A.1817–1832, p. 334a].

John Evill Lewis, of Evercreech, devisee under the will of John Evill [SRO, DD/FS, box 27].

John Godfrey, of Shepton Mallet, linen draper, grant by J.E. Lewis for 21 years, with power of determination by either party at 7 or 14 years at a rent of £36, on 21st December 1838 [SRO, DD/FS, box 8].

Robert Keen, linen draper, grant by J.E. Lewis for 21 years, with power of determination by either party at 7 or 14 years, on 25th June 1840 [SRO, DD/FS, box 8].

James Badman, of Evercreech, devisee under the will of J.E. Lewis [SRO, DD/FS, box 27].

Henry Wookey, of Shipham, shopkeeper, grant by J. Badman for 15 years at a rent of £40 on 24th June 1844 [SRO, DD/FS, box 8].

Trustees of Ann Badman, wife of James Badman [SRO, DD/FS, box 27].

Thomas Tucker Boyce, brush manufacturer, purchased the tenancy from Mrs Badman's trustees for £100, on 11th October 1860 [SRO, DD/FS, box 27].

Notes

1. Ch. 411, Cal.ii, p. 636.
2. See Article 31, p. 89.
3. Ch. 535, Cal.ii, p. 658 (abbr.).
4. Ch.513, Cal.ii, p. 654 (abbr.).
5. Ch. 552, Cal.ii, p. 662 (abbr.).
6. L.1571–1624, f. 9.
7. L.1624–1681, p. 167, DD/CC 112482, 112359.
8. L.1701–1739, p. 196; the documents do not make it clear whether properties nos. 51 and 50 were customarily let as a single tenement, and eventually united into a single house; or whether property no. 51 was divided into two houses which, a little more than a century later were united, thus restoring it to its original condition.
9. Above the names of Winter and Watkyn in this roll is written: *Willielmus Taylor et Ludowicus Taylor.*
10. The premises were then in the tenure of Margaret Mullyns.
11. The surveyor recommended an increase in rent from 32s. 8d. to 8l.
12. This grant reveals that the two tenements conveyed by previous grants had lately been rebuilt by Marchant, and converted into one house.

33

Property No. 52
A House in Sadler Street

This house was situated on the east side of Sadler street, on part of the small garden opposite the Swan hotel. It appears to have been built between 1573 and 1600 on a piece of ground belonging to the bishop's manor.[1] It was erected against the ancient wall which enclosed the churchyard, and according to the map of Canon Grange drawn about 1825 it had then an 'L' shape, with the shorter arm of the 'L' abutting on to the street.[2] The house was demolished about 1850 in order to open a view of the cathedral from the Swan hotel.[3] It is not known how the freehold passed to the dean and chapter in the 16th century or when and to whom it was sold. From certain grants of the adjoining property on the north made in the early years of the 18th century, it appears that this was for a short time a coffee house,[4] and that the premises were later occupied by a baker, who constructed under the churchyard an ash pit, the removal of which the chapter ordered on 16th March 1843,[5] having declined to accept a rent for it. Very few documents pertaining to this house have survived, but it is possible to trace its tenants and occupants (or subtenants) from the descriptions in grants of the adjoining property no. 53. From these and other sources the following list has been compiled:

John Streate, dwelling in the house on 1st January 1601 [L.1571–1624, f. 170].

Richard Cox, on 2nd July 1619, then or recently an inhabitant [L.1571–1624, f. 229].

Robert Downton, on 1st October 1636, then or lately dwelt there [L.1624–1681, p. 263; DD/CC 112476; S1649, p. 6[6]

Margaret Trym, widow, named as tenant on 4th July 1664, the house being described as where John Hobbs, vicar choral, now lives [DD/CC 112488].

Jane Taylor, widow, living in the house on 24th March 1701 [L.1701–1739, f. 6d; SRO, DD/SAS (c/151(2/1)].

William Moore, shoemaker, named as tenant on 20th August 1727 [DD/CC 112503, L.1701–1739, p. 232; L.1740–1760, f. 168].

John Lovell, grant on surr. for 40 years, on 9th[7] December 1760 [L.1740–1760, f. 610; A.1743–1760, p. 313]. Proposal for surr. with a view to a new lease for 40 years on 13th December 1775 (fine 14*l.*) [Docs. ADD/4114]; regrant from 3rd December 1795 (fine 55*l.* 10*s.*) [Docs. ADD/4182].

Revd Thomas Gyllet and Thomas Burnell, yeoman, assignees of J. Lovell, on 8th March 1826 [Docs. V/76, ADD/4231] (certain parts of the premises – a bakehouse, staircase, and kitchen, with rooms over –being vested in Thomas Burnell).

Thomas Burnell, surr. on 9th October 1826 of those parts of the premises vested in him, with a view to a grant to himself only [Docs. V/76[8]; A.1817–1832, p. 252].

Thomas Burnell, baker, grant for 40 years of the back or eastern part of the premises at a rent of 5*s.* plus 2*s.* for a private pathway 3 feet broad from the back door of the premises to the western gravel walk of the churchyard, on 7th July 1827 [DD/CC 110057; Docs V/77; ADD/4245a, 4245b].

Revd William Wheeler and James Brewin, grant for 40 years on 16th July 1842 [R.1, p. 408].

The survey of the manor made for the Ecclesiastical Commissioners in 1875 reveals that the premises were then in the occupation of a Mr. Thompson [Ch.C. file 51807, pt 1].

Notes

1. L.1571–1624, ff. 16d, 75; DD/CC 112472.
2. Within the angle of the 'L' of the house there still remained a piece of land which continued to belong to the see; cf. the inset plan on the map of Canon Grange.
3. See E.A. Freeman, *History of the Cathedral Church of Wells* (London, 1870], p. 143; the demolition of the house involved the destruction of the wall, which professor Freeman condemned in characteristic manner as the wanton obliteration of part of the city's history.
4. See L.1701–1739, f. 6d (1701)–'now called the coffee house'; SRO, SAS (c/151), 2/1 (1701); DD/CC 112503 (1722) – 'lately used to a coffee house'; L.1740–1760, f. 610.
5. M.1817–1849, p. 164.
6. It is curious that this house is not specifically included in the survey made of the properties of the dean and chapter in June/July 1649.
7. 3rd. in Docs. V/76 and ADD/4231.
8. Endorsed: 'reversion sold upon special terms'.

34

Property No. 53
18, Sadler Street

This house is situated on the east side of Sadler street, and its rear portion extended southward behind a garden belonging to the bishop's manor.[1] On this garden the house, now 16, Sadler street, was built. 18, Sadler street was probably built outside or against the western boundary wall of the churchyard, for in 1634 the tenant, one Mrs Addams, asked leave of the chapter to make a door in the wall in order that she might have a way into the churchyard from her house. Permission was granted on 1st April 1634,[2] so long as she lived in the house. One of the residentiaries would not give an unqualified assent, however; Dr Gerard Wood, archdeacon of Wells, consented only *ad rem, sed non ad actum faciendum*, while Dr Paul Godwyn dissented *tam ad rem quam ad actum*. It is not clear to what the two Doctors objected, and the grounds of their objections are not stated. On 1st July 1720 another tenant, John Browne was allowed 'to make a way and door into the churchyard from a little house situated in the west end of the churchyard and lying north of the house[3] where William Moore now lives'.[4] An acknowledgement of 2s. annually was required for this privilege.

As in the case of certain houses in the New Works, the lessee, under a grant made in 1842[5] was forbidden to keep beasts of various kinds on the premises, to erect stabling, and to hang out washing in the churchyard; furthermore, he was required to paint the exterior of the house in imitation of free stone. This lease and the copy in the record book of the dean and chapter are particularly interesting because both have an inserted drawing which shows not only the ground plan of the premises, but also the western elevation as seen from Sadler street. Here we see the appearance of the building in the middle of the 19th century. This has changed little during the last hundred years, save that the first floor sash window has been converted into a bay window.

Under the commutation of the estates of the dean and chapter in 1866 this property passed to the Ecclesiastical Commissioners. In the survey made for them in 1875[6] it is described as a dwelling house and offices, the kitchen and adjoining offices being part of the house then held by lease from the see.[7] The following tenants have been traced:

Robert Myllyamont, *alias* Cobet, grant for three lives at a rent of 20s., on 13th August 1545[8] [SB (temp. Gye), f. 31d].
William Gibbons, cutler, grant[9] for three lives, on 24th August 1553[10] [L.1546–1565, f. 75].
Andrew Peers,[11] yeoman, grant for three lives, on 30th June 1574 [DD/CC 112472; L.1571–1624, f. 16d].
William Nurton [C 1587/8].
Humphrey Willis, grant for 40 years on 1st January 1601 [L.1571–1624, f. 170; C1602/3 (widow Norton *modo* Humphrey Willis)].
Martha Willis, widow of Humphrey Willis [died 2nd October 1618[12]), grant for 40 years, on 2nd January 1619 [fine 20*l*.) [A.1608–1622, f. 153]; regrant for 40 years, on 2nd July 1619 [L.1571–1624, f. 229]; regrant for 40 years, on 3rd July 1620 [DD/CC 112475]; 'Martha Willis *modo* Thomas Ashman' [C1625/6].
Thomas Ashman, late Martha Willis [C1626/7, C1627/8].
Mrs. Addams [C1634/5; Cal.ii, p. 407]

Eleanor Bull, widow, grant on surr. for 40 years on 1st October 1636 (fine 10*l*.) [L.1624–1681, p. 263; SB 1629–1637, p. 90; C1636/7].
Sebastian Smith, precentor, grant on 3rd October 1636 [A.1635–1645, p. 14].
Eleanor Bull, widow, grant on surr. for 40 years, on 1st October 1638 [DD/CC 112476]; named as tenant in June/July 1649 [S1649, p. 6[13]].
Henry Bull, of Midsomer Norton, son of Eleanor Bull, grant on surr, for 40 years, on 4th July 1664 (fine 25*l*.) [A.1664–1666, f. 10d; DD/CC 112488].
John Browne, haberdasher of hats, grant on surr. for 40 years, on 24th March 1701 [L.1701–1739, f. 6d; SRO, DD/SAS [c/151), 2/1; S1703, p. 176[14]]; regrant on surr. for 40 years, on 20th August 1722 [DD/CC 112503; L.1701–1739, p. 232; A.1705–1725, f. 178d]; regrant for 40 years, on 30th September 1734 [A.1725–1744, f. 135; cf. Cal.ii, p. 543].
George Moore and Joseph Lovell, bakers, grant on surr. for 40 years, on 1st April 1745 [L.1740–1760, f. 168; A.1743–1760, p. 28].
Joseph Lovell, baker, grant on surr, for 40 years, on 9th December 1760 [DD/CC 112419; L.1740–1760, p. 610; A.1743–1760, p. 313]; regrant on surr. for 40 years, on 2nd January 1775 [L.1761–1777, f. 489; A.1761–1777, p. 350; EB 1756–1762 (DD/CC 110007) p. 199; DD/CC 112420]; regrant on surr. for 40 years, on 3rd December 1795 [L.1790–1807, f. 209; A.1792–1817, p. 60; DD/CC 112421; cf. ? EB 1780–1798 [DD/CC 110010], p. 232].
John Lovell, grant on surr. for 40 years, on 3rd December 1795 [L.1790–1807, f. 209; A.1792–1817, p. 60].
George Lovell, of Bristol, gent., in whom the tenancy was legally vested, surr. on 28th September 1812 [DD/CC 112422].
George Lovell, of Bristol, and George Biggs Lax, grant on surr. for 40 years, on 1st October 1812 [L.1808–1813, p. 169;[15] DD/CC 112423].
John Spencer, of Oakhill, Maurice Davies, and Edmund Broderip, grant for 40 years, on 3rd June 1829 (fine £56) [A.1817–1832, p. 421; DD/CC 112424; cf. DD/CC 114080[1], p. 41].
Revd William Wheeler and James Brewin, trustees for Thomas Francis Lovell, brother of Arabella Frances Wheeler, wife of William Wheeler, grant for 40 years, on 16th July 1842 [DD/CC 112425]; T.F. Lovell died unmarried and intestate in February 1850; James Brewin died in 1845. Revd and Mrs. W. Wheeler contracted with John Vickery to sell the tenancy for £230. The sale was concluded on 23rd October 1850 [DD/CC 112426].

John Vickery, grant for 40 years on 11th February 1856 (fine £37) [R.3, p. 50; DD/CC 112428].[16]

Notes

1. L.1546–1565, f. 75.
2. Cal.ii, p. 407.
3. See property no. 52–Article 33, above.
4. Cal.ii, p. 503.
5. DD/CC 112425; R.1, p. 408.
6. Ch.C. file 51807, pt 1, leasehold property no. 32.
7. The house (now 16, Sadler street) is shown on the ground plan and elevation (coloured blue) in the lease of 1842, DD/CC 112425; R.1, p. 408.
8. The premises were then in the tenure of Thomas Yonge *alias* Soly.
9. This grant requires that subtenants must be approved by the dean and chapter.
10. The description specifies, on the south, a garden ground pertaining to the bishop.
11. Peers had married Gibbons's widow, Margaret.
12. On Humphrey and Martha Willis, see A.J. Jewers, *Wells Cathedral, its monumental Inscriptions and Heraldry* (London, 1892), pp. 72 and 73.
13. The surveyor considered that the rent of 20s. should be increased to 8l.
14. In this survey the tenant's name is incorrectly entered as James Browne.
15. In this lease the following stipulation appears: the lessee 'shall not hang out or place or cause to be hung out or placed in the churchyard adjoining (the premises) any manner of cloths for drying or otherwise, nor place or permit to be placed any Publish (*sic*, for rubbish?) whatsoever'.
16. The bishop also granted to Mr Vickery the dwelling house now 16, Sadler street, consisting of an entrance passage, with a room or kitchen, and two bedrooms over [DD/CC 112427].

35

Property No. 54
20–22, Sadler Street

This property[1] consisted originally of two separate tenements under one roof. It passed into the hands of the Ecclesiastical Commissioners at the commutation of the estates of the dean and chapter in 1866, and from the survey made in 1875 for the Commissioners it appears that at some time during the 19th century the two tenements had been thrown into one.[2] In the 18th century this property was designated 'the Mitre', or 'the Mitre tavern'.[3] The tenancy of Brown's gate, a separate tenement on the north, was frequently joined with that of this property. The record of tenants begins with Richard Brown, a shoemaker from whom it is generally supposed that Brown's gate took the name by which it has traditionally been known, though the gate was never in Brown's tenure.

Richard Brown, shoemaker,[4] grant for two lives of the two houses in which he then lived, on 19th May 1542 (fine 12*d*.), at a rent of 28*s*. 8*d*. [SB 1542, f. 37].

William Doderell, grant for three lives, on 8th April 1568[5] [L.1571–1624, f. 56].

Gyles Wallis, pewterer, grant (including Brown's gate and a house in New street[6]) for 40 years, on 1st July 1580 (fine 16*l*.) [Cal.ii, p. 302].

Edmonde Bower, grant (including Brown's gate and a house in New street), for 40 years, on 1st July 1586 [L.1571–1624, f. 74d; DD/CC 112474; C1587/8, C1602/3].[7]

William Bowre, grant (including a house in New street), for 40 years, in October[8] 1608 [Ch.818 (Cal.ii, p. 712)]

William Clutterbooke, grant (including a house in New street) on surr., for 40 years, on 1st October 1625 [L.1624–1681, p. 33]; named as tenant in June/July 1649 [S1649, p. 6[9]; C1625/6 (William Bower *modo* William Clutterbuck), C1626/7, C1627/8, C1634/5]. Surr. agreed in view of a new lease for 40 years[10] for a fine of 10*l*. [SB1637–1640, p. 39)]

James Clutterbooke [C1636/7].

John Edmonds [L.1681–1701, p. 146].

Jane Edmonds, surr. on 6th December 1692 [DD/CC 112496; L.1681–1701, p. 146].

Robert Warmall, grant (including Brown's gate) on surr. for 40 years, on 6th December 1692 [L.1681–1701, p. 146; A.1683–1704, f. 217].

Mary Warmall, widow, named as tenant in 1703 [S1703, p. 193]; grant (including Brown's gate) on surr. for 40 years, on 4th January 1714 [L.1701–1739, f. 73; DD/CC 112502; A.1705–1725, f. 88d].

Frances Browne, spinster, grant (including Brown's gate) on surr. for 40 years, on 1st July 1752 (fine 20*l*.) [L.1740–1760, f. 383; EB 1745–1755 [DD/CC 110006], p. 211].

Ann and Elizabeth Brown, spinsters, executrices of the will of Frances Brown, sold the tenancy on 14th March 1754 to Thomas Maynard, 'tyler and plaisterer', and surr. on 29th March 1765 [DD/CC 112508].

Joseph Lovell, grant (including Brown's gate), on surr. for 40 years, on 1st April 1765 (fine 10*l.*) [EB 1762–1771 [DD/CC 110008], p. 137; A.1761–1777, p. 124; L.1761–1777, p. 115; L.1777–1789, f. 187].
John Lovell [L.1790–1807, f. 359].
John Conway, grant (including Brown's gate) on surr. for 40 years, on 1st October 1800 [L.1790–1807, f. 359; A.1792–1817, p. 180].
Sarah Conway, widow, grant (including Brown's gate) on surr., on 21st September 1829 [A.1817–1832, p. 467].
Edward Parfitt, grant (including Brown's gate) on surr. for 40 years, on 15th December 1845[11] [R.2, p. 100; Docs ADD/4250].
John James Rocke, of Glastonbury, grant on surr. for 40 years, on 17th September 1859[12] (fine £44) [R.3, p. 317; DD/CC 114080/2[13], p. 105].

Notes

1. Now the Ancient Gatehouse Hotel.
2. Ch.C. file 51807, pt 1, lease no. 28.
3. Cf. A.1683–1704, f. 217 [1692: 'the Mitre tavern']; L.1790–1807, p. 209 (1795: 'late called the Mitre'); during the 18th century there are many references to this property as 'the Mitre'.
4. Cf. L.1546–1565, f. 75.
5. This lease provided that if the rent was allowed to fall 21 days in arrears, steps might be taken to recover the amount due; a memorandum of 4th August 1580 [L.1571–1624, f. 56] records that five quarters rent being in arrears on 25th March 1580, the chapter's officers entered the premises accordingly, and that thereafter the lease was determined.
6. See Article 1, p. 3.
7. According to a lease of 1st January 1600 [L.1571–1624, f. 170], the southernmost of the two tenements (now 20 Sadler street), was inhabited at that time by John Martine.
8. No day is given in the sources.
9. The surveyor considered that the property was worth a rent of 9*l.* 18*s.* (not 18*s.* 8*d.*).
10. No new grant seems to have been made.
11. The lease prohibits the keeping of poultry in the churchyard, and use of the premises as a post office, excise office, auctioneer's sale rooms, or shop; it requires the exterior to be painted in imitation of freestone.
12. For a plan of the premises see Docs. ADD/4273(10).
13. Occupants: 1850–1855, R. Thorley; 1856–1865, Mrs Fry [DD/CC 114080/2].

36

Property No. 55
A house in Sadler Street

This small house stood on the west side of Sadler street, on the south of, and contiguous to the property now known as the White Hart hotel; it was pulled down almost a hundred years ago to make space for the yard and outbuildings on the south side of the hotel. Traditionally the house was known as 'Cary's house', but the origin of this designation is nowhere explained.[1] Originally it had been in the possession of Ralph de Lullyngton,[2] a canon of Wells who, for the benefit of his soul made provision by his will for the rent from the house, 16s., to be paid to the communar and applied by him to the welfare of the poor.[3] Later the house was in the tenure of Nicholas Bath.[4] The rent of 16s. was entered by the communar in the Barlynch[5] section of his account. In 1364,[6] because of the ruinous condition of the building, and the cost of repairing and in great part rebuilding it, the rent was reduced to 10s., payable quarterly. This was a special concession to the tenants, Hugh and Maud Remyngton, for their lifetimes only; nevertheless in C1392/3 the rent was further reduced to 6s. 8d. For this and the following sixteen years the accounts show that a sum of 10s. was devoted annually to the poor from the rent issuing from Bath's house, which implies that Lullyngton's charity was being subsidized by the common fund. Apparently in order to adjust matters, the rent was increased by 6s. in C1414/5 bringing it to 16s. in accordance with the old account rolls. In C1430/1 the rent was again raised, this time to 22s., but the amount devoted to charity was not increased; in C.1455/6 the rent was reduced to 16s. at which figure it remained until C1498/9, when Bath's house and the adjoining Hart's Head[7] were let as a single tenement at a rent of 58s. 8d. This arrangement continued for roughly two hundred years; after about 1700 the two properties were usually let separately.

Bath's (or Cary's) house passed into the possession of the Ecclesiastical Commissioners in 1866 at the commutation of the estates of the dean and chapter, and in the survey made for the Commissioners in 1875 it is described as a beer house known as the Nag's Head, containing a bar parlour and kitchen with three bedrooms over and a small attic in the roof. There was also a tiled shed in the yard, and the premises were said to be very old and in bad repair.[8]

After Ralph de Lullyngton and Nicholas Bath the record of tenants continues with:

Hugh Remyngton and Maud his wife, indenture granting a reduction in rent, on 21st September 1364 [Cal. i, p. 267 (R.I, f. 252)].
Hugh Baylyf, held for his life and that of his wife Matilda [C1392/3, C1393/4].
James Mores, *nunc inhabitat* [C1437/8].
Thomas Nabbe *modo tenet* [C1445/6, C1446/7, C1448/9, C1449/50, C1455/6, C1461/2].
Isabella, *nuper uxor Thome Nabbe nuper inhabitat* [C1470/1, C1473/4].
John Nabbe, *modo tenet* [C1478/9].
Henry Cornysshe *modo inhabitat* [C1504/5].
Joan Wylles *modo uxor Thome Wylles modo tenet* [C1537/8].
Thomas Willis, tailor [C1547/8].
William Jones, official of the archdeacon of Wells [C1568/9, C1587/8 ?].
Thomas Attwell *alias* Wills, tailor, grant (including the Hart's Head), for 40 years, on 1st January 1578 [L.1571–1624, f. 43d; DD/CC 112473; C1549/50, C1550/1, C1553/4, C1557/8, C1561/2, C1568/9].
Sir Thomas Hughes, grant (including the Hart's Head), for 40 years, on 30th September 1625 [A.1622–1635, f. 44; cf. C1625/6–C1627/8].
Lady Frances Hughes, widow, grant (including the Hart's Head) for 40 years, on 5th October 1625[9] [DD/CC 111945].
Augustine Jefferies, pewterer, held this house[10] by assignment from Sir Thomas Hughes; sought renewal of his tenancy from the dean and chapter, this was approved on 1st April 1642, subject to a fine of 5*l*.[11] [SB1637–1640, p. 73; C1634/5, C1636/7].
Hercules Whiting, tenant in right of his wife,[12] the widow of Augustine Jefferies, sought renewal of the lease with the term extended to 40 years [SB1640–1644, f. 49d].[13]
Lady Frances Hughes, shown as tenant on the strength of the lease of 1st October 1625, in June/July 1649 [S1649, p. 6][14].
Robert Baylie, cutler, grant for 40 years, on 31st October 1690 [DD/CC112495; DD/CC114086].
Jonathan Parfitt, founder, grant on surr. for 40 years, on 24th January 1703 [DD/CC112499; A1683–1704, f. 327d].
Sarah Caines, widow, grant on surr. for 40 years, on 14th December 1737 [L.1701–1739 p. 739; DD/CC112506; Cal. ii, p. 534].
Isaac White, grocer, grant on surr. for 40 years, on 7th April 1752 (fine

2*l*.) [EB1745–1755 (DD/CC110006), p. 203; L.1740–1760, f. 375; A.1743–1760, p. 156; L.1761–1777, f. 142[15]].

John Millard (L.1777–1789, f. 232; A.1817–1832, p. 251][16].

William Burge, tailor, grant on surr. for 40 years, on 7th April 1752 (fine 5*l*.) [EB1762–1771 (DD/CC110008), p. 196]; regrant on surr., on 2nd January 1783 (fine 10*l*.) [L.1777–1789, f. 232; A.1777–1792, p. 144; Docs. ADD/4142], regrant on surr. for 40 years, on 1st April 1799 (fine 16*s*. 10*d*.) [EB1798–1815 (DD/CC110011, p. 52; L.1790–1807, f. 325; A.1792–1817, p. 136; Docs. ADD/4189], regrant on surr. for 40 years, on 8th December 1814 [A. 1792–1817, p. 527].

Lucy Thorley, widow, grant for 40 years, on 7th December 1826 [A.1817–1832, p. 251][17].

John Walker, grant (on Surr. ?) for 40 years[18] [R.1, p. 260]; renewal of lease in 1839 for a fine of £40 [DD/CC114080/1, p. 137].

George Williamson, retailer of beer, grant for 40 years, on 19th December 1860 (fine £58) [R.3, p. 354].

Notes

1. The designation first occurs in 1578, L.1571–1624, f. 43d; DD/CC112473.
2. Occurs 1260–1263.
3. Cal. i, p. 267 (R.I, 252d).
4. Occurs 1316–1381; he may have been the fourth prior of Bath (Cal. i, p. 266).
5. In the Barlynch account was entered a pension paid to the dean and chapter by the prior of Barlynch, from which the costs of certain obits were met, Cal. ii, p. x.
6. Cal. i, p. 267 (R.I, f. 252); from this indenture we learn that Bath's house was situated 'by the western steps in the churchyard', these must have been on the east side of Sadler street, possibly between properties nos. 53 and 54.
7. See below Article 37, p. 105.
8. Ch. C. file 51807 pt. 1, lease no. 42.
9. Cary's house was then in the occupation of Augustine Jefferies.
10. Described as 'a house called Barlynch, formerly granted together with the horse head [*sic* for Hart's Head]
11. No grant can be traced; possibly Lady Hughes did not wish to surrender.
12. Eleanor Jefferies married Hercales [Hercules] Whiting of Shepton Mallet on 7th February 1643 in St Cuthbert's church, Wells; Jefferies died on 22nd July 1642.
13. It appears that renewal was not approved.
14. No mention is made in the survey of Whiting; the premises are described as abutting on the Hart's Head on the north and on the Flower de Luce (on the south); the surveyor considered that the current rent of 6*s*. 8*d*. ought to be increased to 5*l*.
15. According to this entry, the premises were in the occupation of James Bonsall.
16. There is no trace of a grant.

17. According to this entry the premises were in the occupation of Joseph Oxley as [sub]tenant.
18. No date is given; the grant was probably made in 1830. The occupant was James Hardwich, undertenant to John Walker.

37

Property No. 56
The White Hart Hotel, Sadler Street

This property originally belonged to the bishop's manor, as appears from a grant by bishop John Harewell on 14th August 1382[1] to John and Agnes Hayward for their lives of a tenement on the north of Nicholas Bath's house,[2] which latter lay on the south of property no. 56. It is not known how or when this property came into the possession of the dean and chapter, but at the end of the 15th century the communar was receiving the rent of 58s. 8d. with which the property was charged. In C1497/8 an entry for this amount was made in error in the Barlynch section of the communar's account,[3] *de domibus quondam Nicholai Bath*... This was subsequently deleted, and at the beginning of the roll was inserted under *nova recepta* the same amount, *de reditu de la Harteshed in Sadler strete cum duobus messuagiis in eodem*, while a note against the incorrect Barlynch entry made by the communar warns his successor to take care next year to avoid confusing Bath's house with the Hart's Head.

This is the first explicit reference in the records of the dean and chapter to the Hart's Head or the White Hart, as it was later designated. There is a gap in the record of tenants after John and Agnes Hayward, until we come to:

Henry Cornysshe [C1504/5], already named in the C1497/8 entry mentioned above.

Thomas Attwell *alias* Wills, tailor, grant (including Cary's house[4]) for 40 years, on 1st January 1578 [DD/CC 112473; L.1571–1624, f. 43d; C1534/5, C1537/8, C1547/8, C1549/50, C1550/1, C1553/4, C1557/8, C1559/60, C1560/1, C1561/2, C1568/9.

William Jones (C1587/8).

Sir Thomas Hughes [cf. DD/CC 111945; C1602/3, C1625/6, C1626/7, C1627/8].

Lady Frances Hughes, widow of Sir Thomas Hughes, grant (including Cary's house) on surr. for 40 years, on 5th October 1625[5] [L.1624–1681, p. 28; DD/CC111945].

Matthew Peck [notary public], [C1634/5, C1636/7; cf. SB 1637–1640, p. 78].

Anne Peck, held by indenture in 1642 [SB 1640– ?, n.p. – renewal sought for 40 years; approved for a fine of 10*l.* on 1st April 1642]; Mrs. Pecke, widow, named as tenant (producing the lease of 1625) in June/July 1649 [S1649, p.6[6]].

Robert Phippen, linen draper, grant on surr. for 40 years at a rent of 50*s.*, on 1st April 1642[7] [SB1640–? n.p. (see under date given): DD/CC112479].

James Clutterbooke, trustee for Elinor Phippen (daughter of Robert Phippen and his first wife Martha), grant for 40 years, on 7th January 1664 [EB1698–1699 (DD/CC 110005), p. 117; cf Ch. 856 (Cal. ii, p. 717[8]), cf. A.1683–1704, f. 16d].

John Humphrey, innholder, grant on surr. for 40 years, on 13th July 1700 (fine 28*l.* 15*s.*, on condition that security be given to the laying out of 60*l.* on the reparation of the premises in four years time) [L.1681–1701, f. 229[9]; Docs. ADD/4071; EB 1698–1699 (DD/CC 110005), p. 117; A.1683–1700, f. 293]; named as tenant in 1703 [S1703, p. 184].

William Seller, yeoman of Pill, grant on surr. for 40 years, on 16th November 1732[10] [L.1701–1739, p. 551; A.1725–1744, f. 102d; DD/CC 112504].

William Melliar of Glastonbury, grant for 40 years, on 6th December 1757 (fine 31*l.* 10*s.* [A.1743–1760, p. 261[11]; DCR VIII, p. 7; EB 1756–1762 (DD/CC 110007), p. 69]; regrant on surr. for 40 years, on 7th December 1757[12] [L.1740–1760, f. 529; DD/CC 112462].

Priscilla Melliar, of Castle Cary, spinster, grant on surr. for 40 years, on 2nd December 1772 (fine 21*l.*) [EB1771–1780 (DD/CC 110009), p. 22; DD/CC 112463; L.1761–1777, f. 362; A.1761–1777, p. 286, Docs. ADD/4099a, 4099b].

Joseph Coles, paper maker, and Margaret Bartlett, spinster, both of Wookey Hole, grant on surr. for 40 years, on 1st July 1788 [A.1777–1792, p. 263; DD/CC 112464 (surr.); DD/CC 112465; L.1777–1789, ff. 473, 474]; regrant on surr. for 40 years, on 2nd January 1805 [A.1792–1817, p. 303, cf. Docs. V/83; L.1790–1807, f. 371[13]; DD/CC 112466, 112467]; tenancy sold on 30th June 1819 to Cornelius Palmer for £510 [DD/CC 112468].

Cornelius Palmer, grant for 40 years, on 1st July 1819 [A.1817–1832, p. 43; DD/CC 112469].

Charles James Thorley, grant for 40 years from Cornelius Palmer, on 17th November 1818[14] [SRO, DD/WM 17].

Robert Green, occupant as tenant of the dean and chapter [DD/CC 114080/2, p. 91; Docs. ADD/4261].

William Bennet Taylor, brewer, grant for 40 years, on 1st July 1858[15] (fine £102) [R.3, p. 182; DD/CC 112470]. Before this grant was made the chapter resolved to sell the White Hart by auction, and was informed on 25th May 1858 that it had been sold for £192 (M.1849–1859, pp. 237, 270, 272, 283].

Notes

1. Cal. i, p. 291.
2. See above Article 36, p. 102.
3. See above Article 36, p. 102.
4. Cary's house (see Article 36), formerly Nicholas Bath's house, was generally granted together with the White Hart, until about 1700.
5. The Hart's Head was then in the occupation of Anne Nories (or Morris, cf. L.1624–1681, p. 28), widow.
6. The surveyor considered that the property was worth an increase in rent from 50s. to 16l.
7. The premises were then or had been lately in the occupation of Ann Peck, widow.
8. The date of the lease is here shown incorrectly as 17th January 1635.
9. Premises stated to have been late in the possession of Edward Slape (Slade ?) dec.
10. In this lease there is a similar repair clause to that in the lease of 13th July 1700, with this addition: 'such further and necessary reparations for amending and repairing the street against the house, and in paving and pitching, as need shall require'.
11. The premises are described as the Hart's Head, now the White Hart.
12. The lessee is here described as of Castle Cary, and the premises as late in the possession (i.e. occupation) of William Coward, innholder.
13. Then 'in possession (i.e. occupation) of Cornelius Palmer,'
14. This grant also included four stables and a yard belonging to the dwelling house adjacent to the White Hart; the exact location of this house is not given.
15. For a plan of the premises, see Docs. ADD/4273(46).

38

Property No. 57
3, New Street.[1]

It is not known how or when this property came into the possession of the dean and chapter; it passed to the Ecclesiastical Commissioners at the commutation of the capitular estates in 1866.

Bartholomew Haggat, notary public and sometime communar, grant on 22nd April 1568 at a rent of 13*s*. 4*d*. [S1570, f.7][2].

Isabella Haggat, widow, and Martha and John, children of Bartholomew Haggat, claimed to hold the tenancy by copy of the grant made in 1568 [S1570, f. 7].

Bartholomew Haggat[3] [C1587/8].

Thomas Mawndrill, grant on surr. for three lives, on 2nd January 1596 [L.1681–1701, f. 104; C1602/3].

Maurice Robinson, 'late Wm. Vowles' [C1625/6–C1627/8].

Nicholas Niblett, notary public [DD/CC 111778].

Sarah Hall, *alias* Niblett [DD/CC 111778].

William Saunders (July 1667) [L.1624–1681, p. 54].

William Cross (1682) [L.1681–1701, f. 19].

James Parfitt, joiner, grant on surr. for three lives, on 1st April 1730 [DD/CC 111778; L.1701–1739, p. 506; A.1725–1744, f. 85d].

Mary Gardner, widow, and George Gardner her son, goldsmith, of Bristol, grant on surr. for three lives, on 8th December 1742 [DD/CC 111782; L.1740–1760, f. 105; A.1725–1744, f. 238].

George Gardner, of Appledorry, North Wales, jeweller, and James Haynes,[4] stocking maker, grant on surr. for three lives, on 2nd January 1783 [DD/CC 111834; DD/CC 111836; EB 1762–1771 (DD/CC 110008), p. 103].

John Haines, stocking maker, and George Gardner, of Appledory, North Wales, jeweller, grant on surr. for three lives, on 5th December 1764 [L.1761–1777, f. 109; A.1761–1777, p. 120]; regrant on surr. for three lives, on 2nd January 1783 [A1777–1792, p. 144; L.1777–1789, ff. 224, 226; Docs. ADD/4143].

James Haynes, grant on surr. [L.1777–1789, f. 307], for three lives, on

1st October 1784 (fine 14*l.*) [L.1777–1789, p. 314; DD/CC 111838; A1777–1792, p. 187; Docs. ADD/4147].

George Lax.

Trustees under the marriage settlement of George and Elizabeth Lax, grant on surr. for three lives, on 6th December 1804 [A.1792–1817, p. 300; L.1790–1807, f. 508; DD/CC 111839].

Thomas Bath, of Glastonbury, trustee for Edmund William and Elizabeth Clift, of Bourton, Somerset; Norman and Eleanor Uniake, of Mount Uniake, Cork; John and Caroline Farthing, of Backwell, Somerset; and John Henry and Susan Augusta Fitzgerald, of Castle Maityi, Cork, grant on surr., on 18th November 1839[5] [DD/CC 111840; R.1, p. 257; DD/CC 111841].

Robert Phippen, of Bristol, and others (to whom T. Bath's trusteeship passed at his death on 16th February 1858), grant on surr. for six lives, on 24th May 1859[6] (fine £32) [R.3, p. 296; DD/CC 111842; DD/CC 114080[2], p. 105; DD/CC 111843].

Notes

1. From 1596 to 1859 this property is described as being situated in Chamberlain street.
2. In A.1571–99/Cal. ii, p. 303) it is noted that ten wayne loads of freestone from the Camery, probably from the ruins of Stillington's chapel there, were given to Bartholomew Haggat. This entry of 1581/2 cannot refer to the tenant listed, who was dead when the survey of 1570 was made (see next entry in list of tenants). It is not stated whether this stone was for the repair of this property or for some other use.
3. Haggat's name here may simply be shorthand for '(rent from) the house late of Bartholomew Haggat', unless, in addition to John, Haggat had another son who bore his name – cf. n.2 above.
4. James Haynes married Mary Gardner.
5. At this time the house was the residence of Stephen Davies, the Wells postmaster.
6. At this time the house was the residence of Miss Charlotte Messelbrook.

39

Property No. 58
1, New Street.[1]

This property is now in the occupation of E.W. Heath, dispensing optician. Having been part of the manor of Canon Grange since at least the 16th century, when it was charged with a rent of 12s., it passed into the possession of the Ecclesiastical Commissioners under the arrangements for the commutation of the estates of the dean and chapter in 1866. The record of tenants begins late in the 16th century:

Agnes Brewton, widow [C1587/8].
Richard Bowrne [C1602/3].
John Bradford [C1625/6–C1627/8].
John Prickman, merchant, of the parish of All Hallows on the Wall, city of London, grant (including 1 acre of pasture in Wells east field) for 40 years, on 1st April 1629 (fine 5l.) [L.1624–1681, p. 67; A.1621–1635, f. 84d].
Michael Hunt [C1634/5, C1636/7].
Marshall (? Michael) Hunt, named as tenant, June/July 1649 [S1649, p. 8[2]].
Edward Slade, sen., yeoman, grant (including ground in Wells east field) on surr. for 40 years, on 9th July 1667 (fine 20l.) [L.1624–1681, p. 561]; regrant for 40 years, on 6th October 1682 [L.1681–1701, f. 19; SRS 72, p. 100]; regrant (including a former copyhold tenement in Chamberlain street, in addition to the ground in Wells east field) for 40 years, on 11th January 1687 [L.1681–1701, f. 74; A.1683–1704, f. 98d; S1703, p. 190].
Edward Slade jun., grocer and tallow chandler, grant (including ground in Wells east field and a copyhold tenement in Chamberlain street) on surr. for 40 years, on 2nd October 1703 [L.1701–1739, f. 12; A.1683–1704, f. 325]; regrant on surr. for 40 years, on 21st July 1719 [Cal. ii, p. 143; L.1701–1739, p. 149]; regrant on surr. for 40 years, on 13th September 1734 (fine 8l.) [DD/CC 111779; EB 1745–1755 (DD/CC 110006), p. 126; A.1725–1744, f. 135; L.1701–1739, p. 620].
Anne Slade, widow of Edward Slade sen., grant (including ground in Wells east field and a copyhold tenement in Chamberlain street) on surr. for 40 years, on 2nd October 1749 [DD/CC 111785; L.1740–1760, p. 298; A.1743–1760, p. 118]; regrant on surr. for 40 years, on 29th October 1763 (fine 10l.) [EB 1762–1771 (DD/CC 110008), p. 62; A.1761–1777, p. 80].
Edward Slade jun. grant by Anne Slade for the residue of the term of her lease in 1763, on 9th May 1769 [SRO, DD/WM 14].
Sarah Jenkyns, spinster, assignee of Edward Slade under a mortgage for 100l. plus interest, on 21st December 1769 [EB 1771–1780 (DD/CC 110009), p. 249; SRO DD/WM 14].
Richard Jenkyns, assignee of Edward Slade, on 30th June 1772[3].

William Rood, goldsmith, purchased the tenancy for 155*l*., 125*l*. being due to Sarah Jenkyns [SRO, DD/WM 14; EB 1771–1780 (DD/CC 110009), p. 249].

George Lax, grant (including the copyhold tenement in Chamberlain street) on surr. for 40 years, on 1st October 1778[4] (fine 10*l*.) [L.1777–1789, f. 30; A.1777–1792, p. 20; EB 1771–1780 (DD/CC 110009), p. 249].

Trustees under the marriage settlement of George and Elizabeth Lax (Revd Wadham Pigott, Cary Bayley, and Robert Lax), grant (including a copyhold tenement in Chamberlain street), on surr. for 40 years, on 1st October 1794 (fine 21*l*.) [EB 1780–1798 (DD/CC 110010), p. 163; L.1790–1807, f. 166].

Revd Wadham Pigott and Robert Lax (the third trustee, Cary Bayley having died), grant on surr. for 40 years, on 1st April 1809 [A.1792–1817, p. 403].

George Biggs Lax, grant (including the copyhold tenement in Chamberlain street) for 40 years, on 2nd January 1822 [A.1817–1832, p. 94].

John Robert Lax, grant for three lives, on 2nd April 1832[5] [A.1832–1840, p. 235].

Thomas Bath, of Glastonbury (trustee for Elizabeth Clift, widow, of Exmouth, Devon; Norman Uniake, of Mount Uniake, co, Cork; John and Caroline (formerly Lax) Farthing, of Backwell, Somerset; and John and Susannah Augusta (formerly Lax) Fitzgerald of Killeagh co. Cork), grant for 40 years, on 21st April 1851[6] (fine £60) [R.2, p. 323; DD/CC 114080[2], p. 39 and p. 115].

Notes

1. Up to 1851 this property is described as situated in Chamberlain street.
2. The surveyor considered that the rent for the property, including the ground in Wells east field was worth 3*l*. 3*s*. in addition to the rent charged, 17*s*. (house 12*s*., ground 5*s*.).
3. This assignment presumably superseded that to Sarah Jenkyns.
4. At this time the premises were in the occupation of Henry Matthews, undertenant to George Lax.
5. J.R. Lax was in occupation of the house at this time.
6. The premises were then in the occupation of Henry Jones Bernard, surgeon.

40

Property No. 59
2, Chamberlain Street

This small property was formerly united with 4, Chamberlain street, to form a large tenement – the *magnum hospicium*[1] which, in C1490/1 was called the Antelope inn, the recorded history of which begins early in the 15th century. By 1683 the name of the inn had been changed; it was then the King's Arms, a name which it bore until, at the end of the 18th century, it ceased to be an inn. At this time also the small house, 2, Chamberlain street, became a separate property; this probably happened as a result of certain transactions recorded in a document of 12th July 1781.[2] Thereafter the dean and chapter appears to have lost possession of 4, Chamberlain street, while the adjoining 2, Chamberlain street remained among the properties of the manor, finally passing into the hands of the Ecclesiastical Commissioners as a result of the commutation of the capitular estates in 1866.

The Antelope Inn

The building which originally stood on the site of the Antelope inn seems to have been part of a block of properties, including shops, which at the end of the 14th century belonged to Agnes Mogge, the widow of John Mogge, a citizen of Wells. In his account for 1407/8 the communar entered a receipt of 40s. *pro redditu magni hospicii domorum quondam Agnetis Mogge*, and also a transfer to the escheator's account of 8s. *de domibus quondam Agnetis Mogge* for the obit of John Hoo, vicar choral. These meagre details serve to identify the house which later became known as the Antelope with a house which was the subject of certain transactions at the beginning of the 14th century.

Originally Agnes Mogge's property was in the tenure of David de Welweton,[3] who demised it by his will to his wife Isabel.[4] She granted it to her son, Richard de Welweton, on 5th December 1338,[5] subject to an annual payment of 8s. to John de Hoo, vicar choral. Richard de Welweton granted this property for life to Nicholas de Plecy, vicar choral,[6] who, on 3rd December 1301[7] disclaimed all interest in it, in favour of another vicar choral, Maurice de Ash, to whom on 3rd December 1301,[9] Richard de Welweton made a grant of the property for a fine of 45 marks, with the provision that Plecy should continue to pay the rent for the rest of his life while Ash should be responsible for the annual payment of 8s. at Midsummer to Hoo. In this grant the premises are described as a tenement with house, garden and croft in Chamberlaynestrete, between the tenements of Hugh le Rus, vicar choral, on the east, and John de la Pole (on the west), extending from the street northward to the field (*campus* – Monday's meadow).

It appears that Richard Mogge of Tickenham, Somerset, then acquired an interest in this property, from whom it passed to his son and heir, John Mogge, who granted it to a burgess of Wells, Hugh le Barbor, for life and four years longer.[10] John Mogge afterwards wished to repossess the premises, and having secured Barbor's consent and release dated 29th November 1333, undertook to pay him in acknowledgement a sum of 100s. in the cathedral.[11] Barbor's grant and quitclaim to Mogge were made on 24th March 1334.[12] The business was concluded by a quitclaim to Mogge from Richard[13] de Welweton on 20th September 1333,[14] and, after Richard's death by a quitclaim from his widow Cristina to Mogge on 27th September 1334.[15]

In respect of this property the communar annually charged his account from this time with a transfer to the escheator of 8s. for John Hoo's obit, and with 12d. paid to the bishop,[16] noting that both payments were made out of the revenue issuing from the property once belonging to Agnes Mogge; this property eventually came into the possession of the cathedral, probably by donation from John Mogge.[17]

After John (or Agnes) Mogge, the following tenants are recorded:

Stephen de Hulle,[18] prebendary of Combe X, grant for life on 2nd May 1354 [Ch. 332 (Cal. ii, p. 620(abbr.))].
John Hull [C1407/8].
Reginald Bryt [C1418/9[19], C1421/2, C1428/9, C1430/1][20].
William Gascoign [C1437/8].
John Wyn [C1445/6].
Edward Osteler [C1446/7].
John Bettys *alias* Smith, grant for 40 years in 1448–1449 [C1448/9, C1449/50, C1455/6, C1461/2, C1470/1, C1472/3].
Alice Betts [C1478/9].
David Peynter *nuper inhabitabat* [C1490/1], *nuper tenuit* [C1497/8].

113

Thomas Cornish, chancellor, and John Lugwardyn, succentor, grant[21] for 80 years, at a rent of 4s.[22], on 1st October 1501[23] [Cal. ii, p. 165][24].

Walter Stryde and Alice his wife, Edmund Tynte and Joan his wife, devisees under Cornish's will (31st March 1513) [SRS. 19, p. 168].

Walter Stryde, burgess, and his wife Alice, devisees of Cornish and Lugwardyn, grant on 20th April 1526 (including 1 acre of pasture [Ch. 744 (Cal. ii, p. 699)[25]].

Thomas Weston and John Godarde, vicars choral, grantees for the commemoration of Stryde, Cornish and Lugwardine in Cokeham's chapel in the south churchyard of the cathedral, on 20th April 1526 [Ch. 744 (Cal. ii, p. 699)].

Blanche Ronyon, widow of Walter Strowde (Stryde)[26] and wife of Thomas Ronyon [C1534/5, C1537/8].

Thomas Ronyon *tenet* [C1547/8, C1557/8, C1559/60].

Richard Brewton *modo tenet* [C1560/1, C1561/2].

John Totterdale, carpenter, grant of 'the house known by the name of the sign of the Antelope'[27] for three lives at a rent of 13s. 4d., on 2nd January 1604 [L.1571–1624, f. 191].

William Vowles, grant for three lives,[28] on 26th June 1615[29] (fine 20l.) [A.1608–1622, f. 106].

Maurice Robinson, grant for three lives, on 2nd October 1622 [A.1622–1635, f. 12d].

Adrian Bower, grant on surr. for three lives, on 1st October 1624[30] [L.1624–1681, p. 8; A.1622–1635, ff. 33d, 35d; Docs. ADD/4009].

Edmund Bower, named as tenant in the survey of June/July 1649 (Adrian Bower having died [S1649, p. 14[31]].

Richard Thomas, woollen draper, grant on surr. [Cal. ii, p. 450] for three lives, on 2nd August 1683 [A.1683–1704, f. 295]; regrant on surr. for three lives, on 5th August 1700 (fine 24l.) [L.1681–1701, p. 231[32]; EB 1698–1699 (DD/CC 110005), p. 116; A.1683–1704, f. 295d; S1703, p. 192].

Martha Bartlett, widow [see L.1701–1739, p. 320].

Richard Comes and Thomas Millard, grant on surr. for three lives at a rent of 13s. 4d., on 13th April 1726 [L.1701–1739, pp. 318, 320; DD/CC 111774; A.1725–1744, f. 9].

James Helmes, innholder, and Samuel Helmes his brother, grant on surr. for three lives, on 1st July 1737 [L.1701–1739, p. 715[33]; A.1725–1744, f. 175d; DD/CC 111781].

James Helmes, innholder, purchased Samuel Helmes's interest for 80l., on 23rd February 1739 [SRO, DD/WM, 14]; lease for three lives on surr. on 2nd January 1754 (fine 15*l.* 15*s.*) [A.1743–1760, p. 191; L.1740–1760, f. 444; EB 1745–1755 (DD/CC 110006), p. 266].

Clement Tudway, assignee of James Helmes for three lives under a mortgage for 170*l.*, on 20th June 1754 [SRO, DD/WM, 14].

Clement Tudway and Elizabeth Helmes, widow, legal possessors of the tenancy in 1776 [EB 1771–1780 (DD/CC 110009), p. 189].

George Lax, grant on surr. for three lives, on 1st October 1776 (fine 40*l.*) [L.1761–1777, pp. 515, 552; EB 1771–1780 (DD/CC 110009, p. 189; A.1761–1777, p. 374; Docs. ADD/4116].

Trustees (Revd Wadham Piggott, Carey Bayly, Robert Lax) under the marriage settlement of George and Mary Lax, grant for 40 years sealed 1st October 1794 [A.1792–1817, p. 42; cf. Docs. ADD/4124 ?, cf. 4223a,? 4223b ?] Tenancy vested in Revd Wadham Pigott, and Robert Lax (Carey Bayly having died); proposal for surr. and new grant from 1st October 1806 (fine £70) [Docs. ADD/4226].

2, Chamberlain Street

The following transactions appear to have preceded the separation as properties of 2 and 4 Chamberlain street:

On 1st July 1778 the tenant of the former Antelope inn, George Lax, surrendered to the dean and chapter a little backside to the premises on which he had built a brewhouse and stable; he also surrendered a small garden [L.1780–1807, p. 28[34]].

Robert Michell (or Mitchell) purchased for 300*l.* the tenancy, excluding the premises surrendered to the dean and chapter in 1778; grant by G. Lax for three lives, on 12th July 1781 [SRO, DD/WM, 14].

Tenants of 2, Chamberlain street:

Richard Hawkes, surgeon, grant for three lives, on 3rd November 1846[35] [R.2, p. 148].

Mary Ann Gibbs, widow, grant for three lives on 1st August 1860[36] (fine £66) [R.3, p. 342].

Notes

1. C.1407/8.
2. SRO, DD/WM 14.
3. Welton, Somerset.

4. Ch. 261 (Cal. ii, p. 605).
5. Ibid.
6. Ch. 158 (Cal. ii, p. 581); Cal. i, pp. 509 (entry 5), 511 (entry 1).
7. Ch. 158 (Cal. ii, p. 581): 1st Sunday in Advent, 30 Edw.I.
9. Cal. i, p. 510 (entry 5).
10. Cal. i, p. 510 (entry 2).
11. Ibid.
12. Ibid.
13. The text of the charter copy in *Liber Albus ii* (R.III, f. 433, cf. Cal.i, p. 510 (entry 3) has *Raðus*, consequently the Calendar gives the grantor's name as Ralph de Welweton, ignoring a marginal note by the registrar: *Relaxacio Ricardi de Welweton ad Johannem Mogge.*
14. Cal. i, p. 510 (entry 3).
15. Cal. i, p. 510 (entry 1).
16. This was probably a chief rent.
17. Ralph Canon, residentiary, claimed 12s. for expenses incurred on his visit to London on the business of the chapter, particularly in connexion with a licence in mortmain relating to two properties: Lymington's house (see CHW, Article 9, p. 86.), and the properties *quondam Agnetis Mogge* (C1400/1 (Cal. ii, p. 36)); Agnes Mogge probably enjoyed a life interest, but documentary evidence of this is lacking.
18. Otherwise Stephen Martin of Hull, see *Fasti 1300 – 1541*, p. 32.
19. In this year payments were made for the retiling of the hall and one room: wages for 2 tilers (6 days work), 3s. 11d., tiles 6s. 8d. laths 16d., fencing, laths, tiles, pins, lime and sand, 21d. oak timber 12½d.
20. Reginald Bryt is shown as inhabitant in C1437/8, C1445/6, and C1446/7.
21. Of a tenement called the *hospicium de la Antilope;* the name occurs first in C1490/1.
22. The rent had been 40s., see n.6.
23. Provided that the lessees rebuild the tenement *de novo* and maintain it at their own expense – hence, presumably, the reduction in rent, see n.5.
24. Cornish was granted permission on 28th February 1504 to have celebrated annually for 99 years the office of the dead for the obits of bishop Oliver King, John Lugwardyn, and himself, for which he granted a sum of 30s. yearly issuing from the rents of the Antelope and of certain closes and meadows (Cal. ii, p. 176).
25. No term is stated.
26. Strowde's wife Alice had died, and Blanche was his second wife.
27. On the west, a house 'commonly called the sign of the Angel'.
28. One of the lives was Vowles's wife, Anne Totterdale, one of the lives named in the previous lease,
29. On 1st July 1613 the chapter decreed to lease the Antelope to someone named Cook for a fine of 20*l*. This does not appear to have been proceeded with (A.1608–1622, f. 69d.).
30. On the west a house 'called the sign of the Beare', but afterwards the Angel.
31. On the west of the Antelope, according to the survey, was 'the house commonly called the Beare, but now the sign of the Angel'. The surveyor suggested an increase in the rent of the Antelope from 13s. 4d. to 12*l*.
32. The premises are now called 'by the name of the sign of the King's Arms (late, the Antelope), with the Angel (formerly the Beare) on the west.'
33. The premises are described as The King's Arms, heretofore the Antelope.

34. For details, see SRO. DD/WM, 14.
35. Then in the occupation of George Pitman Gibbs.
36. Then in the occupation of the lessee.

41

Property No. 60
11/13, New Street

On the map of Canon Grange c. 1825 this property is shown as an irregular area with a frontage to the street of about 140 feet and extending backward from the street at most 150 feet, containing some 2,000 square yards. This area was divided into two unequal portions, the southern having at its south eastern corner a building, now 11, New street. This building was originally an inn, known as the Three Horse Loaves[1] until about 1667, when the name was changed to the Globe. 13, New street was newly built during the first decade of the 19th century, incorporating from the Globe inn a hall or kitchen, and one room over, and including in its grounds the inn's yards, garden, and stables.[2] Both these houses, with the land pertaining to them, were sold in 1821 and 1825.[3] The following tenants of the properties have been traced:

11, New Street (the Three Horse Loaves, later the Globe)

Joan Gallington, wife of John Gallington, yeoman, grant for three lives, on 1st April 1575 [L.1571–1624, f. 136;[4] C1587/8, rent 30s.]
William Godwine, grant for 40 years, on 10th October 1592[5] [A.1571–1599, f.85]; grant on 1st October 1594[6] (fine 20l.) [L.1571–1624, f.143d; C1602/3; A.1671–1599, f. 99d].
Robert Crees[7] [sadler[8]], grant for 40 years, on 1st October 1622 (fine 20l.) [A.1622–1635, ff. 12d, 30]; further grant on surr. for 40 years, on 2nd January 1624 (fine 20l.) [L.1571–1624, f. 240d; DD/CC 112114; C1625/6, C1627/8, C1634/5].
Francis James,[9] D.C.L., assignee of Robert Cross [L.1571–1624, f. 240d; DD/CC 112144].
Walter Brick, yeoman, held by indenture in 1639; grant for 40 years, on 2nd January 1640 [SB 1637–1640, p. 57; S1649, p. 3; C1634/5, C1636/7].

Ezekiel Nash, named as tenant in June/July 1649 [S1649, p. 3[10]].

John Curtis, named as late tenant [DD/CC 112154].

Thomas Stephens, innholder, assignee of John Curtis [DD/CC 112154]; grant on surr. for 40 years, on 26th October 1667, rent 30s. [L.1624–1681, p. 590; A.1664–1666, p. 55 (Cal. ii, pp. 440–441); further grant on surr. for 40 years, on 26th October 1680 [DD/CC 112154].

John Yarbury, innholder, grant[11] on surr. for 40 years, on 7th October 1692 [L.1681–1701, f. 142; DD/CC 112156; A.1683–1704, f. 215d; S1703, p. 197].

Anne Creswick, spinster, of Clifton, Glos., grant on surr. for 40 years, on 14th August 1719 [DD/CC 112161; A.1705–1725, f. 143d].

John Wilcox, grant on surr. for 40 years, on 5th September 1733 [DD/CC 112164; L.1701–1739, p. 582; A.1725–1744, f. 113].

William West, of Wookey, yeoman, grant on surr. for 40 years, on 18th January 1752 (fine 30*l*. [EB 1745–1755 (DD/CC 110006), p. 212; DD/CC 112168; DD/CC 112125; L.1740–1760, p. 374; A. 1743–1760, p. 154].

Richard West, of Bristol, yeoman, son of William West, grant on surr. for 40 years, on 16th February 1770 (fine 30*l*.) [EB 1762–1771 (DD/CC 110008), p. 378; DD/CC 112126; A.1761–1777, p. 244; L.1761–1777, f. 271].

Edmund Read, of Brisstol, assignee of R. West under a mortgage of 120*l*., on 24th March 1770 [DD/CC 112127].

Mark Spicer, innholder, assignee of R. West in consideration of 93*l*. 14s. and 125*l*. 5s. to be paid, on 10th May 1771 [DD/CC 112128]; assignee of William Hucklebridge, of Bristol, executor of the will of Edmund Read, deceased, in consideration of 129*l*. 19s. 6d., on 10th February 1774 [DD/CC 112129]; grant on surr. for 40 years, on 1st July 1788 [EB 1798–1815 (DD/CC 110011), p. 150; A.1777–1792, p. 263; L. 1777–1789, f. 476; DD/CC 112130; Docs. ADD/4158].

George Say, innholder, grant on surr. for 40 years, on 2nd December 1801 [DD/CC 112132; L.1790–1807, f. 416; A. 1792–1817, p. 211; cf. Docs. ADD/4204[12]].

Thomas Shearston, innholder, grant (excluding the hall or kitchen and a room over, also a yard, garden, and stable, lately incorporated into a newly built house) for a consideration of £260, on 25th March 1805 [SRO, DD/FS box 33 (c/648)].

Edmund Broderip, purchaser on 1st April 1809 under the Land Tax Redemption acts, from the dean and chapter for the remainder of the term of the lease granted to T. Shearston [A.1792–1817, p. 404].

Trustees under the will of T. Shearston.

Edmund Broderip, purchaser from the trustees of T. Shearston for £330, on 20th September 1825 [SRO, DD/FS box 33 (c/643).

13, New Street

This house, incorporating from the Globe inn, a hall or kitchen and a room over, and also a yard, a garden and a stable, was newly built by George Say, who died on 4th June 1805, devising the tenancy to trustees.[13] Tenants thereafter were:

Clement Tudway, grant on surr. for 40 years (rent 15s.), on 1st October 1813 [DD/CC 112133; A.1792–1817, p. 513].
Thomas Porch, 'occupant as tenant' [A.1817–1832, p. 66].
Trustees of the real estate of the late Clement Tudway (Revd Edward Foster and Revd Richard Thomas Whalley), grant on surr. for 40 years, on 30th September 1820 [A.1817–1832, p. 66; SRO, DD/SAS (c/238), 54]; purchasers for £162 9s. (paid to the Land Tax Commissioners), on 2nd January 1821 [SRO, DD/SAS (c/238), 54].

Notes

1. 'Horse loaves' were 'a kind of bread formerly given to horses. It was anciently a common proverb to say that a diminutive person was no higher than three horse loaves. A phrase still current says that such a one must stand on three penny loaves to look over the back of a goat, or sometimes, a duck', J.O. Halliwell, *Dictionary of Archaeic and Provincial Words*, 2 vols (London 1901), i, p. 460. By the beginning of the 19th century the meaning of the name had obviously been forgotten, for in a lease of 1801 it is changed to the commoner 'Three Horse Shoes' [A.1792–1817, p. 211; L.1780–1807, f. 416].
2. See DD/CC 112169.
3. SRO, DD/SAS (c/238), 54; DD/FS box 33 (c/643).
4. After surr. on 13th May 1591 by Robert Brinscombe, of London, barber surgeon, one of the lives named in the lease of 1575.
5. This grant was not sealed, and was therefore of no effect, because the lessee withheld the sealing fee of 53s. 4d.; it was paid two years later, and a new grant was made, see 1st October 1594.
6. Premises described as late in the tenure of Joane Gallingtonn and John Gallington; the chapter dec reed that 'for the twoo yeares gayned by hym [Godwine] in the lease since the graunt thereof [he] shall pay xiiis. iiiid. [A. 1571–1599, f. 99d].
7. This appears to be an error for 'Cross'.
8. A.1622–1635, f. 30.
9. Deceased by 1624.

10. The surveyor recommended that the rent of 30s. should be improved to 14l.
11. The premises are described as formerly the Three Horse Loaves, now the Globe.
12. In this proposal the premises are referred to as 'the Three Horse Shoes. [sic], late called The Globe, and now called the White Lyon'.
13. The occupant after G. Say was his widow, Elizabeth Say [DD/CC 112169]; the house was also in the possession of James Cannings, and after his death, of the Revd William Hunt. Both the last named were probably subtenants.

42

Property No.61
15, New Street

This property, situated at the southern corner of the junction of Milton lane with New street, was donated by Walter Hornyngton[1], probably at the end of the 14th century, to the dean and chapter in order that the rent of 5s. issuing therefrom might be used to provide for his obit. Some time before E1408/9 the house was totally destroyed by fire; nevertheless throughout the 15th century the property was continuously in tenure, and in the middle of the 16th it appears that the house itself was rebuilt by Peter Carsleygh[2]. In a grant of 1576 the property is described as 'the tenement or house commonly called or known as the Dunghill[3]'. No explanation can be found for this opprobrious designation, which occurs as late as 1810; it may have originated from the derelict condition of the property after the destruction of Hornyngton's house, or even from the fact that the derelict site had been regarded as waste ground, and had actually been used as a dunghill. At the time of the commutation of the estates of the dean and chapter (1866) the property passed into the hands of the Ecclesiastical Commissioners. After Hornyngton the tenants were:

John Frankelayne [E1408/9, E1417/8, E1423/4].
Sir Roger Wodehill (Wodehele), [E1424/5, E1433/4].
John Lychfeld (? prebendary of Dinder), [E1438/9: *modo in manu Johannis Lychfeld*, E1439/40, E1445/6, E1458/9, E1461/2, E1469/70, E1472/3, E1480/1, E1490/1, E1494/5, E1503/4, E1508/9, E1509/10, E1511/2, E1513/4].
Dr Peter Carsleygh, prebendary of Shalford, grant for 60 years in 1513 or 1514[4] [E1515/6, E1518/9, E1520/1, E1524/5, E1529/30, E1543/4[5]].

Stephen Carslighe, purchaser of this[6] and other properties of Peter Carsleygh, on 19th May 1542 [SRS, 51, p. 9, no.18].

Thomas Bricke, grant for three lives, on 30th September 1576[7] (L.1571–1624, f. 38, E.1584/5, E1586/7–E1589/90, E1591–2].

Joan Bricke, wife of Thomas Bricke, grant for three lives, on 1st April 1584 [L1571–1624, f. 67; widow Bricke – E1592/3–E1594/5, E1600/1; DD/CC 112140].

Joan Brick, widow, and John Raynold, *alias* Knowell, of Litton, grant for their two lives, on 2nd January 1603 [L.1571–1624, f. 192].

Walter Brick, grant for 40 years, on 2nd January 1640 (fine 5*l.*) [S1649, p. 3; SB 1637–1640, p. 58; E1633/4 ?].

Ezekiel Nash, named as tenant in June/July 1649 [S1649, p. 3[8]].

William Perfect, named as tenant in a rental *c.* 1665 [DD/CC 111736, 25/33].

Leonard Parfitt [E1660/1].

Widow Parfitt [E1668/9].

John Parfitt [E1670/1].

Richard Brock [E1671/2].

James Browne, baker, grant on surr. for 40 years, on 10th October 1676 [DD/CC 112150; E1672/3, E1674/5, E1675/6–E1685/6].

Samuel Phelps, grant for 40 years, on 4th January 1683 [DD/CC 112157; A.1683–1704, f. 231; L.1681–1701, f. 169; E1686/7–E1694/5].

Widow Phelps [E1695/6, E1699–E1708/9].

Mr. Fry, shown as paying rent [E1709/10].

John West, grant on surr. for 40 years, on 7th August 1714 [L.1701–1739, f. 82; A1705–1725, f. 96d;[9] E1711/2–E1728/9; DD/CC 112160].

William Goldfinch, grant on surr. for 40 years, on 27th August 1730 [DD/CC 112163; A.1725–1744, f. 78d.; L.1701–1739, p. 469; E1729/30–E1756/7, E1762/3–E1766/7]; grant on surr. for 40 years, on 14th December 1748 (fine 10*l.* 10*s.*) [DD/CC 112166; A.1743–1760, p. 98; L.1743–1760, p. 98; L.1740–1760, f. 284; EB 1745–1755 (DD/CC 110006), p. 104].

Elizabeth Goldfinch, widow of William Goldfinch, grant on surr. for 40 years, on 3rd January 1763 [A.1761–1777, p. 64; L.1765–1777, f. 32; E1757/8–E1761/2; E1767/8–E1768/9].

Sir John Elliott, bart., of Cecil street, St Clement Danes parish, city of London, grant on surr. for 40 years (fine 6*l.* 6*s.*), on 1st April 1777 [L.1777–1789, f. 3; EB 1771–1780 (DD/CC 110009), p. 211; A.1761–1777, p. 380; Docs. ADD/4120].

Robert Robertson, doctor of physic, of Howard street, St. Clement Danes parish, city of London, grant on surr. for 40 years, on 1st July 1793 (fine 20*l.*) [EB 1780–1798 (DD/CC 110010), p. 123; L.1790–1807, f. 129; E1769/70 (Mrs. Robertson); E1770/1 (Mr Robertson); E1771/2–E1795/6 (Dr Robertson); E1790/1–E1798/9 (Mrs Robertson)].

Trustees of the Revd Thomas Abraham Salmon and his wife Frances (Clement Tudway and Revd Dr Thomas Eyre), grant for 40 years on surr., on 1st August 1810[10] (fine £48 [EB 1798–1815 (DD/CC 110011), n.p.; A.1792–1817, p. 431; L.1808–1813, pp. 82, 100; Docs. ADD/4229].

Frances Salmon, grant for 40 years, on 1st July 1823 [A.1817–1832, p. 120].

James Garrod, grant for 40 years, on 2nd July 1832 (fine £80) [A.1817–1832, p. 605]; further grant for 40 years, on 18th September 1848 (fine £80) [R.2, p. 216]; further grant for 40 years, on 17th November 1863[11] (fine £77) [R.4, p. 40].

Notes

1. Or Honyngton, i.e. Horrington.
2. See below n.4.
3. The name also occurs as 'Dinghill' (SRS, 51, p. 9, no. 18), and 'Dunkhill' (L.1681–1701, f. 169).
4. E.1543/4 is stated to be the 30th year of the 60 year term for which Carsleygh's lease had been granted, i.e in 1513 or 1514. It seems that Carsleygh had expressed his intention to repair the house, or to build another on the site to replace Hornyngton's, which had been burnt down. Consequently he was given a concession in rent; for the first twenty years of the term it was set at 6*d.*, and for the next twenty years, at 12*d.* For the third twenty years, it was to be 20*s.*
5. In this year Robert Clement *inhabitat.*
6. The premises are described as 'one tenement with curtilage and garden on the west side of Pyllstrete . . . called Dinghill' (SRS, 51, p. 9, no. 18).
7. Bricke was then in occupation; the rent reverted to the customary 5*s.*.
8. The surveyor proposed an improvement of the rent from 5*s.* to 4*l.*
9. Premises 'once called the Dunghill'.
10. At this time William Parfitt was in occupation.
11. For a plan of the premises, see Docs. ADD/4273 (16).

43

Property No. 62
12/14, Union Street

In the 17th century this property consisted of a dwelling house and a small garden yielding a rent of 6s. 8d. Later, it is not known when, the house was divided into two dwellings. The record of tenancies only begins in the middle of the 16th century:

Thomas Gosse [E1558/9–E1560/1, E1564/5].
Richard Minor [E1584/5, E1586/7–E1589/90].
Widow Myner [E1590/1–E1594/5, E1600/1].
Richard Collins, grant for three lives, on 19th September 1614 [S1649, p. 19].
Daniel Collins, son of John Collins,[1] named as tenant in June/July 1649 [S1649, p. 19[2], E1633/4: paid rent *pro domo in qua ipse inhabitat*].
John Richmond, miner, grant for 40 years, on 3rd October 1660[3] [DD/CC 111997; E1660/1]; grant on surr. for 40 years, on 5th January 1663 [DD/CC 111998].
John Richmond, baker, son of John Richmond (above), grant on surr. for 40 years, on 1st March 1699 (fine 40s.) [E 1698–1699 (DD/CC 110005), p. 90; DD/CC 111995; E1672/3–E1684/5]; regrant on surr. for 40 years, on 1st March 1699 [L1681–1701, p. 228; A.1683–1704, f. 291].
Thomas Richmond [E1685/6–E1688/9[4]].
Abraham Richmond, named as late tenant in 1766 [EB 1762–1771 (DD/CC 110008), p. 217; E1737/8–1744/5].
Widow Richmond [E1689/90].
John Pawley[5] [E1763/4–E1765/6].
Matthew Tucker, gardener, grant for 40 years, on 2nd January 1767 (fine 4l. 4s.) [EB 1762–1771 (DD/CC 110008), p. 217; L.1761–1777, p. 178; DD/CC 111987; E1766/7–E1782/3].
John Moore, sadler, grant on surr. for 40 years, on 2nd December 1783 [DD/CC 111989; DD/CC 111990; L.1777–1789, f. 252; A.1777–1792, p. 165; E1783/4–E1786/7; Docs. ADD/4144].
John Hickes[5] [E1787/8–E1795/6].

George Lovell[5] [E1796/7].
Mr. White[5] [E1819/20; E1822/3].
William Charles, sadler, grant for 40 years, on 29th June 1844 (fine £27) [R.2, p. 37; DD/CC 114080/1, p. 167]; regrant for 40 years, on 5th March 1861 (fine £16) [R.3, p. 378; DD/CC 114080/2, p. 134[6]; cf. Docs. ADD/4221 – proposal for a further regrant for 40 years].

Notes

1. Possibly the brother of Richard Collins.
2. The surveyor proposed an increase in rent from 6s. 8d. to 30s.
3. At this time the premises were in the possession of John Richmond.
4. Thomas Richmond appears in the escheator's accounts for 1690/1–1692/3; and John Richmond, in 1693/4, 1699/1700, and 1725/6–1736/7
5. No grants can be traced in respect of these persons who doubtless were subtenants, though shown as paying the rent.
6. At this time the two dwellings into which the house had been divided were in the respective occupation of Sylvester Dudden and Joseph Sutcliffe.

44

Properties No. 62A and 62B
A House and Garden in Union Street

Property no. 62A was a dwelling house situated on the west side of Union street, or Grope lane as it was formerly called, and property no. 62B a garden lying behind this house. Both properties comprised a single tenement until early in the 19th century, when separate leases were made of each. At the time of the commutation of the estates of the dean and chapter (1866), the two properties passed into the hands of the Ecclesiastical Commissioners; eventually, on the site occupied by the house (property no. 62A), the present Wells public library was built.

In the 14th century the dwelling house belonged to John Roper, steward of the borough of Wells,[1] who by his will devised the rent of 13s. 4d. issuing from this tenement to the dean and chapter on condition that his obit was kept in the cathedral annually on the feast of St Edmund, king (20th November). Alternatively, he instructed his executors to sell the property and to hand over the proceeds to the dean and chapter for the same purpose.[2] A grant of the rent was made on 14th July 1485 by Roper's wife Petronilla and his executors to various feoffees acting on behalf of the dean and chapter.[3] At the time Roper's will was executed, the property was in the tenure of Roger le Webbe and his wife Margery, to whom it had been granted for their lives by Roper. From this time the tenants under the dean and chapter were:

William Jenyngs and Joan his wife, who held the tenancy for their lives at a rent of 6*s.* 8*d.* [E1391/2, E1397/8, E1399/1400, E1400/1, E1408/9, E1417/8[4] E1423/4, E1424/5].
John Forde, grant for life at a rent of 6*s.* 8*d.* [E1433/4].[5]
John Hayne named as inhabitant[6] [E1472/3].
John Goldwegge, grant for three lives[7] [E1490/1,[8] E1503/4, E1505/6, E1508/9, E1509/10, E1511/2,[9] E1513/4].
John Gregory, named as tenant paying a rent of 10*s.* [1515/6, E1518/9, E1520/1, E1524/5].
John Pynner, jun., named as tenant paying 10*s.* rent [E1529/30].
William Boyle and Alice (formerly Cullens) his wife, grant at a rent of 8*s.* because a higher rent could not be obtained [E1543/4].
Alice Boyle (formerly Collens, widow [E1558/9, E1559/60, E1560/1].
Thomas Boyle [E1564/5, E1584/5, E1586/7, E1587/8–E1594/5, E1600/1 ('Boyle')].
William Boyle [E1633/4, E1660/1, E1668/9, E1670/1].
Richard Boyle, claimed in June/July 1649 to hold by copy dated 2nd April 1633, with reversion to John Boyle sen. and John Boyle jun. [S1649, p. 20[11]]
Edward Bowell (Boyle ?) [E1671/2–E1679/80, E1681/2–E1684/5].
Joseph Norton (Nurton) [E1680/1, E1685/6–E1689/90, E1699/1700–E1629/30].
Priscilla Norton, widow [cf. DD/CC 111999].
John Norton, hosier, son of Priscilla Norton, grant on surr. for three lives at a rent of 10*s.*, on 3rd December 1723 [DD/CC 111999; Cal. ii, p. 511; L.1701–1739, p. 260].
John Goldfinch,[12] grant on surr. for three lives, on 5th April 1731 (fine 8*l.*) [DD/CC 112000; L.1701–1739, p. 515; EB1762–1771 (DD/CC 110008), p. 61].
George Goldfinch, grant on surr. for three lives, on 29th October 1763 [L.1761–1777, f. 63; DD/CC 111981; A.1761–1777, p. 81].
William Rood, subtenant under George Goldfinch; grant on surr. for three lives, on 30th June 1780 (fine 10*l.*) [L.1777–1789, ff. 89, 90;

EB 1771–1780 (DD/CC 110009), p. 303; DD/CC 111981a, 111982; A.1777–1792, p. 71, Docs. ADD/4136].

John and Elizabeth Hoare, in possession of a garden,[13] ro which another garden[14] adjoined, both gardens lying behind and lately part of the property in Union street, and comprising property no. 62B; surr. on 29th November 1817 [DD/CC 111923].

John Hoare, vinegar merchant, grant of property no. 62B on surr. (see above) for three lives, on 2nd December 1817, at a rent of 3s. 4d. [DD/CC 111984].

Richard Rawlings, veterinary surgeon, grant on surr. [DD/CC 111985], of property no. 62A for three lives at a rent of 9s., sealed on 3rd June 1829 (fine 105l.) [A.1817–1832, p. 423; DD/CC 114080/1, p. 42].

Notes

1. Ch. 295 (Cal. ii, p. 612).
2. Cal. i, pp. 279–280.
3. Cal. i, p. 280.
4. Rent 6s. 8d., whereas it used to be 13s. 4d.: there is no explanation of the reduction; probably, as in other years no more could be obtained.
5. In E1454/5, a rent of only 3s. 4d. could be obtained, and 4d. was paid for repairs to the paving adjoining (*contra*) the house; in E1458/9 12d. was paid to Thomas Parcyvale as an amerciament for enlarging this paving.
6. Probably a subtenant.
7. Cf. E1543/4.
8. No higher rent than 3s. 4d. could be obtained in this year (also in E1494/5). In E1494/5 10s. 11½d. was paid for repairs.
9. In this year the rent was raised to 10s.
10. This should apparently be 10s.
11. The surveyor stated that the property was worth an annual rent of 2l. 10s.
12. One of the lives named in the lease of 3rd December 1723 to John Norton.
13. Measuring 66 feet in length from east to west, and 19½ feet in width from north to south.
14. Measuring 20 feet in length from north to south, and 6 feet in width from east to west.

45

Property No. 63
23, Chamberlain Street

On the site of this house, situated on the south side of Chamberlain street, stood originally three cottages. The middle cottage, yielding a rent of 6s. 8d., had a well and a garden; towards the end of the 17th century[1] it was united under one roof with the eastern cottage by Archibald Harper, who held leases of both premises. Early in the 18th century all three cottages were made into one tenement by Thomas Millard.

In 1866, with the commutation of the estates of the dean and chapter the property came into the possession of the Ecclesiastical Commissioners.

The tenants of the middle cottage were:

Agnes Edwards (or Gosset), widow, held a life tenancy[2] [C1587/8; E1558/9[3] – E1560/1, E1564/5; C1587/8[4]].
Edmund Sawier [E 1558/9–E1560/1].
John Yonge [E1564/5].
Elinor Sawyer [C1602/3].
William Sawyer sen. and William Sawyer jun. tenants for their lives [Docs.III/152].
Thomas Parker, sen. [C1625/6, cf. SB 1615–1617, n.p.[5]]
Margaret Parker, wife of Thomas Parker, held for her life, together with her son Thomas Parker [cf. SB 1640–1644, n.p.; C1626/7, C1627/8].
Widow Parker [C1634/5, C1636/7], claimed in June/July 1649 an interest by virtue of a grant from the dean and chapter, but produced no evidence to substantiate her claim [S1649, p. 25[6]].
Robert Rowley, sought and was granted a reversion for three lives on 4th January 1640 (fine 10s.) [SB 1640–1644, slip attached to p. 44].
Archibald Harper, clothier, grant for 40 years, on 5th July 1682 [L.1681–1701, f. 21; S1703, p. 183]; regrant on surr. for 40 years, on 29th October 1706 [L.1701–1739, ff. 39, 40; A.1705–1725, f. 25d].

During Mr Harper's tenancy this house was structurally united with the cottage on the east, which was also in his tenure. The tenants of the eastern cottage which yielded a rent of 6s. 8d. were, before the amalgamation:

Widow Everett (Evered) [E1586/7–E1592/3].
Elenor Webb (or Wills), widow [E1593/4, E1594/5, E1600/1].
Bartholomew Cox [cf. E1633/4, E1660/1].
Ann Pope (rent 6s. 8d.) [E1660/1, E1668/9, E1670/1].
Thomas Parker [cf. L.1681–1701, f. 21].
Margaret Parker, widow [A.1705–1725, f. 258].
Archibald Harper (rent 10s. 8d.) [E1671/2, E1672/3, E1698/9–E1704/5].

After the amalgamation, the following are found in possession of the eastern portion of the united building:

Robert Rowley, assignee of widow Parker [S1649, p. 23; Docs. III/152].
Mr Bernard[7] [E1818/9–E1821/2].
Mr Sweeting[7] [E1822/3].

After Mr. Harper, the tenancy of the united middle and eastern cottages passed to:

Thomas Millard, hosier, grant on surr. for 40 years, on 16th December 1728 [L.1701–1739, p. 411; DD/CC 111776; A.1743–1760, p. 99]; further grant on surr. for 40 years, on 14th December 1748 [DD/CC 111784; L.1740–1760, f. 282].

During Mr Millard's tenancy the western cottage was also structurally united with the middle cottage. The earlier tenants of the western cottage were:

William Sherman [Docs. III/152].
Margery and Mary Godwyn [Docs. III/152].
Margery Stone ('now or lately dwelt' therein) [A.1622–1635, f. 34].
Frances Fane, widow [DD/CC 111776, 111784; L.1761–1777, f. 60].

Tenants, after Thomas Millard, of the house formed by structurally uniting the three cottages:

Thomas Millard, apothecary, grant on surr. for 40 years, on 29th October 1763 (fine 12*l.* [L.1761–1777, pp. 60–1, A.1761–1777, p. 80; EB 1762–1771 (DD/CC 110008, p. 68)]; regrant on surr. for 40 years, on 5th December 1781 [A.1777–1792, p. 122; cf. DCR XVII, p. 28; L.1777–1789, f. 172; Docs. ADD/4140]; regrant on surr. for 40 years, on 1st October 1796 (fine 24*l.*) [EB 1780–1798 (DD/CC 110010), p. 262; L.1790–1807, f. 261; A.1792–1817, p. 81; Docs. ADD/4195].

Jonathan Colmer [cf. DD/CC 114080[1], p. 41 cf. DCR XXX1, pp. 56, 62].

Anne Eyre, widow[8] of the Revd Dr Thomas Eyre[9] in whom the property was vested, [cf. EB 1798–1815 (DD/CC 110011 n.p.]; grant for 40 years (lease sealed on 1st October 1813 (fine £60) [A.1792–1817, p. 512; EB 1798–1815 (DD/CC 110011), n.p.]

Revd Thomas Wickham, of Yatton, and Joseph Lovell Lovell, grant for 40 years sealed on 3rd June 1829 (fine £120) [DD/CC 114080[1], p. 41; A.1817–1832, p. 430].

Edmund Sheppard Symes, doctor of medicine, of Bourdon house, Davis street, Berkeley square, Middlesex, grant for 40 years on 31st August 1861[10] (fine £160) [R.3, p. 415].

Notes

1. Cf. S1703, p. 183; L.1701–1739. f. 39; DD/CC 111777.
2. Docs. III/152.
3. The escheator noted that he had not been allowed 2*s*. 11*d*. the cost of repairs to the house – material required: 50 laths and 100 blue tiles.
4. This property belonged to the escheatry lands, and it is not clear why the communar received certain rents.
5. Request for a reversion for three lives.
6. The surveyor considered that the rent should be raised from 6*s*. 8*d*. to 1*l*.
7. Probably a subtenant in occupation of the eastern portion of the house.
8. And sole executrix of the will of Dr Eyre.
9. Canon residentiary and Treasurer of the cathedral, and surviving executor of the will of Thomas Millard, deceased.
10. At this time John Kelway was in occupation.

46

Property No. 64
A Cottage in Beggar Street

This property consisted originally of a cottage with a parcel of ground adjacent, situated on the western corner of the junction of Priest row with Beggar street (the southern part of Chamberlain street). Houses for the elderly have been now built on the site. There is no record how this property came into the possession of the dean and chapter, but it appears in the communar's accounts for the year 1548/9, yielding a rent of 3s. 4d. It may have been a gift from the bishop, for out of the revenue accruing from the property the early accounts show several payments of an annual chief rent of 6d. to the bishop's bailiff; they also show various sums due to the chapel of St. Mary in the cathedral, suggesting that the cottage may have been donated to provide financial support for that chapel and its services. In 1773[1] it is revealed that the cottage had recently been converted into a stable, and in 1862[2] the premises are described as 'a stable with a loft over and a small gig house at the east end thereof with a passage from the stable to Priest row'.

In 1860 the chapter decided to sell the premises by private contract or by public auction, as the chapter clerk should think most advisable[3]. Eventually an offer was accepted in 1862 from Thomas Serel, an accountant and local antiquarian, who proposed to take a lease of the property for three lives on payment of a fine of £35. Mr Serel undertook to build a house or houses on the site within two years, the new building to have a rounded corner turning from Priest row into Beggar street, instead of the sharp corner on the existing old building. This property eventually passed into the hands of the Ecclesiastical Commissioners.

Tenants:

Peter Begger, *nuper inhabitavit* [C1548/9].
Katherine Saverye [C1587/8].
Anthony Willcox [C1587/8[4]].
William Sawyer [C1602/3].
Richard Bourne [C1625/6–C1627/8].

John Bourne [C1634/5, C1636/7].

William Clarke, assignee by copy dated 24th September 1614, claimed in June/July to hold the property for three lives [S1649, p. 20⁵].

Widow Broadway, named as tenant in 1703 [S1703, p. 175].

Archibald Alexander, mason, grant for three lives sealed on 15th February 1720 [A.1705–1725, f. 150].

William Miller, mercer, grant on surr. for three lives, at a rent of 6s., on 1st October 1773⁶ [A.1761–1777, p. 302; L.1761–1777, f. 396; EB 1771–1780 (DD/CC 110009), p. 82; DD/CC 111845; Docs. ADD/4106].

James Cannings, innholder, grant on surr. for three lives, on 2nd July 1781 (fine 6l.) [DD/CC 111847, 111846; A1777–1792, p. 114; L.1777–1789, ff. 148, 150; Docs. ADD/4138].

William Pearce, surgeon, grant for three lives on 2nd December 1800 (fine 10l. 16s.) [DD/CC 111848; A.1792–1817, p. 183; L.1790–1807, ff. 363, 369; Docs. ADD/4201].

Elizabeth Pearce, daughter of William Pearce succeeded to the tenancy.

On the death of Miss Pearce it was resolved to sell the premises by private contract or failing this by public auction, as the chapter clerk should deem advisable [M.1860–1872, p. 31]. One Foster had proposed a lease for three lives and a fine of £50 had been set [M.1860–1872, p. 53]. This proposal was not taken up.

Thomas Serel, accountant, grant for three lives at a rent of 6s., on 6th September 1862 (fine £35)⁷ [DD/CC 111849; 114080/2, p. 143; R3, p. 472; M.1860–1872, pp. 105, 120].

Notes

1. EB1771–1780 (DD/CC 110009), p. 82; DD/CC 111845; A.1761–1777, p. 342.
2. DD/CC 111849; R.3, p. 472.
3. M.1860–1872, p. 472.
4. Rent 2s. 8d.
5. The surveyor considered that the current rent of 6s. could be improved to 14s.
6. The premises are described as a little house with a small garden, lately converted into a stable.
7. The premises are described as a stable with loft over, and a small gig house at the east end thereof, with a passage from the stable to Priest row, bounded by Beggar street on the north and by Priest row on the east.

47

Property No. 65
Tenements in Beggar Street

This property consisted of a dwelling house situated on the south side of Beggar street (now the western end of Chamberlain street), and a garden belonging thereto on the north side of Beggar street. On the east side of the dwelling was a house called the Boot, part of the estate of Peter Davis; on the west side was the chapel of Bubwith's almshouses, the dwelling house being separated from the chapel by a ditch or common sewer. Before 1767 the dwelling house had been converted into two separate tenements. The survey made for the Ecclesiastical Commissioners in 1875 shows that a further conversion had taken place, dividing the house into three cottages, each with a living room, a pantry, and a bedroom.[1] To these properties belonged jointly the garden situated on the north side of Beggar street.

The first recorded owner of this property was Sir George Cobb, bart,[2] from whom it passed into the possession of John Moss, who retained the garden, enclosing it with an orchard, also his property. Later, both tenements were acquired by a surgeon, Benjamin Pulsford, who exchanged[3] them, together with another of his properties, a paddock in Pillmoor[4], for 5, New street,[5] a house belonging to the manor of Canon Grange. Thus the property in Beggar street came into the ownership of the dean and chapter. Two tenancies under that body are recorded, before the cottages passed into the hands of the Ecclesiastical Commissioners at the time of the commutation of the capitular estates:

Trustees named in the will of Benjamin Pulsford (Zachary Bayley and Revd John Prowse), reversion for one life proposed in August 1786; grant for three lives, on 1st July 1799 (fine 16*l*. 15*s*. 6*d*.) [DCR XXIV, p. 57; Docs. ADD/4153, 4190].
John Mason, grant for three lives, on 12th January 1850 [Ch. C., file 51807 pt 1].
Benjamin Pulsford, surgeon, grant for three lives on 4th May 1767 [Docs. ADD/4153].

Notes

1. Ch. C., file 51807 pt 1, copyhold no. 3; file 51807, pt 2, p. 124a.
2. See J. & J.B. Burke, *Extinct and Dormant Baronetcies of England* (London, 1844), s.v. Cobb of Adderbury, p. 121 (a).
3. EB 1798–1815 (DD/CC 110011), p. 57; L.1761–1777, f. 176; DD/CC 111787; DCR XI, p. 35.
4. See Article 86, p. 204.
5. See Article 68, p. 169.

48

Property No. 66
61, High Street

This property, described as a tenement with garden and backside adjoining, was situated on the west side of the corner premises now occupied by Messrs. W.H. Smith and Son. On the north it fronted on to High street, and extended southward to front on to Broad street; it was bounded on the west and east by tenements belonging to the corporation of Wells.[1] On 1st April 1844[2] the chapter declined an offer to purchase this property, having resolved not to alienate any of the possessions of the dean and chapter. However, on 29th September 1845[3] the exchange was authorized of a small portion of the property, a piece of land about 41 feet, for a similar piece of land, part of one of the adjoining premises, inspection having shown that this exchange would not prejudice the property of the dean and chapter.[4]

Eventually property no. 66 was ceded to the Ecclesiastical Commissioners under the arrangements for the commutation of the capitular estates.

The following tenants can be traced:

Humphrey Erle [E1584/5, E1586/7 (Erley), E1587/8–E1594/5, E1600/1–E1633/4] – recording receipts of 13*s.* 4*d.* rent (*pro domo in qua ipse inhabitat*).

Richard James, yeoman, grant for 40 years (of the premises then in his occupation), on 1st July 1574 [L1671–1624, f. 12d; ch. 797 (Cal. ii, p. 708 – abbr.)].

Thomas Wenslie, weaver, grant for 40 years, on 2nd January 1604

[L.1571–1624, f. 190d]; further grant for 40 years, on 1st October 1634 [L.1624–1681, p. 233; DD/CC 112161; E1589/90–E1594/5, E1600/1, E1633/4, E1660/1, E1668/9, E1670/1 recording rent received *pro domo in qua ipse inhabitat]*; named as tenant in June/July 1649 [S1649, p. 12⁵].

Henry Wensly [E1672/3–E1677/8].

Thomas Lane [E1677/8 (Henry Wensley *nunc* Lane), E1678/9, E1699/1700–E1709/10].

William Baylie, of New Inn, Middlesex, grant on surr, for 40 years, on 7th April 1707 [DD/CC 112059; L.1701–1739, f. 43d; A.1705–1725, f. 28d].

Tristan Evans[6] [E1710/1–E1733/4].

Thomas Lovell[6] [E1734/5–E1736/7].

Mr Fox[6] [E1737/8–E1744/5].

Charles Taylor, glazier, grant for 40 years, on 5th December 1749 (fine 2*l*. 2*s*.) [EB 1745–1755 (DD/CC 110006), p. 125; DD/CC 112068; A.1743–1760, p. 121; L.1740–1760, f. 315; E1749/50–E1756/7].

Mrs. Charles Taylor [E1757/8]

Morris Dear[6] [E1762/3].

Robert Pidgeley, baker, grant on surr. for 40 years, on 2nd July 1764 [L.1761–1777, f. 92; A.1761–1777, p. 102; DD/CC 112023, 112024]; regrant on surr, for 40 years, on 1st July 1780 (fine 2*l*. 2*s*.) [EB 1771–1780 (DD/CC 110009), p. 300; L.1777–1789, f. 104; A.1777–1792, p. 74; E1763/4–E1786/7; Docs. ADD/4134].

John Broad, serjeant in the Somerset regiment of Militia, assignee of Robert Pidgeley, on 5th April 1786 [cf. DD/CC 112025; E1787/8–1789/90].

Mrs Broad [E1803/4–E1806/7].

Ellerton Sunter, dealer in horses, assignee of John Broad, on 25th March 1787 [DD/CC 112025]; grant on surr. for 40 years, on 1st October 1794 (fine 5*l*. 5*s*.) [DD/CC 112026; A.1792–1817, p. 42; EB 1780–1798 (DD/CC 110010), p. 159; E1803/4–E1818/9[7]; DD/CC 112092; L.1790–1807, pp. 160, 168; Docs. ADD/4176].

Frances Sunter, daughter of Ellerton Sunter, grant on surr. for 40 years, on 1st October 1813 [DD/CC 112027, 112028; A.1792–1817, p. 512].

Richard Dix, saddler, grant for 40 years at a rent of 14*s*., on 2nd January 1832[8] (fine £40) [DD/CC 112029; DD/CC 114080/1, p. 70; A1817–1832, p. 589].

John Dix [E1818/9–E1822/3].

Thomas Gilling [DD/CC 112030].

William Charles, ironmonger, assignee and subsequently lessee on 9th September 1845 of Thomas Gilling [DD/CC 112030]; grant on surr. for 40 years, on 12th February 1850 (fine £38) [DD/CC 114080/2, p. 31; DD/CC 112031; R.2, p. 269;⁹ Docs. ADD/4255].

Notes

1. For plans of the property, see DD/CC 112029 (1832), and Ch. C. file 51807 pt 2, p. 44a (1875).
2. M.1837–1849, p. 223.
3. Ibid, p. 268.
4. A plan showing the portions of land to be exchanged, was produced in chapter, but was not copied into the minute book, and cannot be traced.
5. The surveyor proposed an increase in rent from 13s. 4d. to 3l.
6. These persons may have been subtenants or assignees.
7. The receipts of rent for these years are specified: 'Mrs Broad since (or now) Sunter's'.
8. The premises are described as a messuage or dwelling house now or lately used as two tenements, with stable and yard adjacent thereto.
9. During this tenancy the chapter gave consent to an exchange of a small piece of land, part of the property, for a comparable piece belonging to an adjacent property, see above, p. 133.

49

Property No. 67
A House at Jacob's Well

Jacob's well was a public pump which stood formerly on the south side of High street, near its junction with Water lane (now Broad street).¹ Eventually this pump was removed into Mill lane,² and has since been abolished. In the 16th century there appears to have been a cross at this place.³ This property was one of Walter Compton's burgages, and an account of it up to 1366, and of its acquisition by the dean and chapter will be found in Appendix III, which deals with these burgages.⁴ The building has disappeared; it seems to have stood on the western corner of the junction of Mill lane with High street, on the site of 55, High street (now a dress shop called 'Mary's'), but evidence as to its location is conflicting.

In a lease of 1362⁵ the property is described as 'a shop with a solar attached in the High street by Jacobeswell, between the messuage of William Bythewood, and that of Cristina relict of John Comehawe'; it seems that the use of the premises was changed after that date, for there are no further references to a shop. In 1542[6] the description is: 'a tenement with a garden adjoining, on the south side of High street and upon the corner opposite Jacobswell, between a tenement of the cathedral church . . . on the east, and a tenement of the commonalty of Wells on the west.' In 1696,[7] the property is 'at a place called Jacob's well in the west part of Mill lane, and the south side of a street (High street) there, and in the east part of a tenement heretofore of Jeoffrey Upton. . . .'

The leases of 1362 and 1542 describe premises situated between two other properties, one of which (that on the east) also belonged to the dean and chapter (1542). The situation described in these leases appears to correspond to that depicted on the map of Canon Grange c. 1825, which shows property no. 67 as having buildings on either side. No premises adjacent on the east, however, are shown as belonging to the manor, while property no. 67 is shown some 80 feet west of (and not opposite) Jacob's well; furthermore, descriptions later than the 16th century place the property at the corner of Mill lane and High street.[8] A plan of 1821[9], also, shows freehold premises on this corner in the tenure of 'John Berryman', with property of the city council on the west. Property no. 67 was held from 1784 to 1832 by Ann Chester Berryman,[10] of whom John Berryman may have been a relation and subtenant; if so this would identify property no. 67 positively with 55, High street. Not enough, however, is known of the early topography of this part of Wells, and of the disposition and ownership of properties there, to explain and reconcile the statements contained in the various descriptions.

After Alice Croceres, who was holding this property under Walter Compton for life in 1366,[11] there is no record of tenants until the beginning of the 17th century:

Morgan Newhooke [C1602/3].
David Price [1625/6–C1627/8].
Isabel Jennings [S1649, p. 20].
David Barrett, grant for three lives at a rent of 6s. 8d. on 2nd April 1633 [S1649, p. 20[12]; C1634/5; C1636/7].
Thomas and Arthur Mattock (representatives of William and Mary Sands, of Carrick O'Foyle, Ireland) [SRO, DD/FS box 27.
Charles Baron, apothecary, grant by T. and A. Mattock, on 17th October 1696 (fine 109l. [SRO, DD/FS, box 27.

Elizabeth Barrett [S1703, p. 183].
David Harris [S1703, p. 183].
Mary Wills, widow [DCR III, p. 12].
Thomas Wills, woolcomber, tenant by virtue of a copy dated 24th February 1720, surr. [DCR III, p. 12].
James King, innholder, grant for three lives on 25th February 1741 (fine 2*l.*) [DCR III, p. 12; DCR XII, p. 81; Docs. ADD/4097]
James Newman, tenant by reversion for three lives (fine 6*l.* 6*s.*) [DCR XII, p. 81; EB 1762–1771 (DD/CC 110008), p. 377; Docs. ADD/4097].
Ann Chester Berryman, tenant 1784–1832 [DD/CC 114080/1]
John Berryman, ? 1821 (Wells city records, 381, 26) proposed for reversion (fine 8*l.*) on 7th December 1784, [Docs. ADD/4148].

Notes

1. See William Simes's map of 1735; also *The Estates of the Wells City Council* (June 1821), Wells city records, ref. 381, plan 26, which depicts 'Jacob's pumps' in the position shown by Simes.
2. SRO, DD/SAS/SE 123.
3. E1543/4 refers to the *crux apud Jacobb's well.*
4. See below, p. 223.
5. Cal. i, p. 369.
6. *SRS* 46, p. 107.
7. SRO, DD/FS, box 27.
8. The map of Canon Grange seems to have been inaccurately drawn at this point.
9. *The Estates of the Wells City Council* (Wells city records, 381), plan 26.
10. See General Terrier, DD/CC 114080[1] under property no. 67.
11. Cal. i, 270.
12. The surveyor recommended an improvement of the rent to 3*l.* 6*s.* 8*d.*

50

Properties Nos. 67A and 67B
7, 8, and 9, Mill Street

These properties are variously described in leases and surveys, thus: a house in *le Mulle lane*[1]; a toft or vacant place between two dwelling houses in a *venella* called *le Mullane* (1381[2]); a messuage and fishpond (*pissinum*) in Mullane (1396[3]); a tenement with garden 60 feet long and 40 feet broad (1575[4]); two slaughter houses and a little yard adjacent (1649[5]); slaughter houses (*c.* 1665[6]); a stable set in Millpond lane (1765[7]); a stable and two small yards (*c.*1825[8]); and, a two-stall stable and gig-house (1875[9]). It appears that the two properties stood on the site now occupied by 7, 8, and 9, Mill street. In 1837 the chapter received a proposal to purchase the fee of 'the spot numbered 37' from a Mr. Berryman (probably William Charles Berryman). The chapter raised no objection 'provided they are borne harmless as to the expenses'[10], but it seems that the sale was not proceeded with, for the property no. 67A (the 'spot numbered 37') came into the hands of the Ecclesiastical Commissioners at the time of the commutation of the capitular estates in 1866[11].

Tenants under the dean and chapter:

John Martel paid 3*s.* rent because the house was wholly in ruins [E1372/3, E1380/1].
Thomas Jay, burgess, grant of a toft or vacant place in *le Mullelane*, for three lives, on 18th November 1381 [Ch. 414 (Cal. ii, p. 636; E1381/2; E1391/2], the lessee covenanted that within two years he would rebuild, and thereafter maintain the house, in consideration whereof the rent was adjusted – 20*d.* for the first 14 years, and 6*s.* 8*d.* thereafter [Cal. i, p. 291].
John Wareyn, canon, tenant in 1396 [Ch. 488 (Cal. ii, p. 650)].
Simon Sodbury and Mary his wife, tenants of Wareyn in reversion at a rent of 1*d.* (property: one messuage with fishpond in Mullelane) [Ch. 488 (Cal. ii, p. 650)].
Robert Sloo, canon, John Arthur jun. of Bishopworth, and Thomas Turney of Tadewyk, grant (with other properties) of a messuage and fishpond in Mullelane, on 6th April 1396 [Ch. 488 (Cal. ii, p. 650)].
Thomas Stoke and his wife, grant for their lives at a rent of 10*s.* [E1423/4[12]].
John Lichfeld and Alice his wife, grant for their lives at a rent of 5*s.* 4*d.* whereas it used to be 13*s.* 4*d.* [1433/4, E1438/9, E1439/40, E1454/5, E1455/6, E1458/9, E1461/2, E1468/70].
John Harefield[13] and his wife Alice, grant for their lives at a rent of 5*s.* 4*d.* [E1445/6].
William Linge, tenant of a stable *super la Mylle Poole* [E1558/9]; *iuxta la Mille Poole* [E1559/60, E1560/1].
William Godwine, *alias* Linge, grant for 30 years, on 6th January 1548 [E1564/5.]

Mary Godwin and William her son, grant for 40 years of a tenement with garden in Mill lane, at that time in her tenure, on 1st October 1575 at a rent of 4s. 6d. (fine 4l. [L.1571–1624, f. 31].

Ralph Sinock, victualler, grant for 40 years, on 3rd April 1605 (fine 40s.) [L.1571–1624, f. 202]; regrant for 40 years sealed on 2nd January 1637 (fine 3l. [A.1635–1645, f. 24; SB 1638–1640, p. 8].

Ralph Sinox pretended an interest in June/July 1694 'but it is in no way evident by what tenure he holds' – 'he has demised to an undertenant' (not named) [S1649, p. 25[14]].

David Harris, cordwinder, grant for 40 years, on 5th October 1671 [DD/CC 112088; SRS 72, p. 32].

George Brock, currier, grant on surr. for 40 years, on 29th July 1697 [DD/CC 112089; A.1687–1704, f. 272; L.1681–1701, f. 203; S1703, p. 176].

George Brook[15], currier, grandson of the above, grant on surr. for 40 years, on 17th April 1727 [DD/CC 112090; A1725/1744, f. 27; L.1701–1739, p. 368]; further grant on surr. for 40 years, on 3rd December 1765 [L.1761–1777, f. 127; DD/CC 112091].

John Brock, currier, son of George Brock, grant (of a stable in Millpond lane) for 40 years, on 10th December 1765, at a rent of 4s. 6d. (fine 16l. 16s.) [A1761–1777, p. 136; EB 1762–1771 (DD/CC 110008), p. 146; DD/CC 112091]; further grant on surr. for 40 years, on 1st April 1800 (fine £22) [L1790–1807, f. 353; EB 1798–1815 (DD/CC 110011), p. 88; A.1792–1817, p. 170; Docs. ADD/4192].

William Charles, saddler, grant for 40 years sealed on 5th December 1816 [A. 1792–1817, p. 560; Docs. ADD/4231] further grant on 5th April 1832 (fine £16) [R.2, p. 366; A.1832–1840, p. 39].

Notes

1. E1372/3.
2. Ch. 414 (Cal. ii, p. 636, abbr.).
3. Ch. 488 (Cal. ii, p. 650).
4. L.1571–1624, f. 31.
5. S1649, p. 25.
6. DD/CC 111736 25/33.
7. A.1761–1767, p. 136.
8. DD/CC 111748.
9. Ch. C. file 51807, pt. 1, leasehold 8 – this seems to relate to property no. 67A only, cf. the plan in Ch.C. file 51807 pt. 2, p. 40a.
10. M.1837–1949, p. 3.

11. It is not certain whether property no. 67B was taken by the Ecclesiastical Commissioners, see above n. 9.
12. For this year only 3s. 4d. was received, whereas (noted the escheator) it used to be 13s. 4d.
13. This name seems to be an error for 'Lichfeld'.
14. The surveyor recommended an increase in the rent, from 3s. 6d. to 1l.
15. *Sic*, in error for Brock.

51

Property No. 68
13, High Street

Early in the 14th century the property which stood on this site was in the possession of William de Chelworth, who had an interest also in other premises in High Street.[1] In 1350[2] the property was described as 'two selds (shops) with solars above them'. By the middle of the 16th century it appears to have extended southward from High street to the 'watercourse called the Millestreme', and to have included a barton and a garden, and also two rear houses (*posteriores domus*) which stood on the north bank of the stream. The whole tenement at this time was virtually destroyed, being very ruinous and almost fallen down (*quasi diruta, valde ruinos et pene collapsos*). Some of the defects and deformities were such as to need extensive repair work, which was thought likely to prove very costly. However restoration was carried out by John Hillacre[3] under a repairing lease.[4] In the 19th century the property was used as a brush factory, being described as a dwelling house with factory, shop, sheds, and other outbuildings, with a timber yard where the garden had been. When the Ecclesiastical Commissioners assumed ownership[5] under the arrangements for the commutation of the capitular estates, the premises were still in use as a brush factory. At present, with other premises on the east, the property has been absorbed into a supermarket.

After the death of William de Chelworth we find the following tenants:

Juliana de Chelworth, widow of William de Chelworth, who married secondly Robert Boret.
Robert Boret, in right of his wife Juliana.

Adam de Tettebourne and his wife Alice, grant for the life of Juliana Boret, on 22nd March 1350 [Cal. i, pp. 368–369].

Thomas Sherston, tenant in 1363[6] [Cal. i, p. 368 (R.III, f. 113d)].

John Hillacre, grant for 80 years, the lessee at his own charges to sufficiently repair and if necessary rebuild the property by Michaelmas 1550 – rent for 71 years, 13s. 4d. and for 9 years, 57s. 4d.; grant made on 16th March 1546 [L.1546–1565, f. 2; C1547/8, C1549/50[7], C1550/1[7], C1553/4[7], C1557/8[8], C1559/60[8], C1560/1[9], C1568/9[10]].

Mary Hillacre, widow [C1587/8].

Robert Hillacre [C1602/3].

Sir Thomas Hughes [C1625/6].

William Bushel, grant for 40 years, rent 53s. 4d. on 10th January 1624 [DD/CC 112049; L.1624–1681, p. 1; C1626/7, C1627/8].

Edward Browning[11] [C1635/6, C1636/7].

John Cox, linen draper, named as tenant (apparently an assignee) in June/July 1649 [S1649, p. 7[12]].

Charles Baron, grant[13] on surr. for 40 years, on 14th October 1681 [L.1681–1701, f. 4; DD/CC 112087; S1703, p. 174]; further grant for 40 years, on 6th April 1708 [DD/CC 112060; L.1701–1739, f. 44d; A.1705–1725, f. 36]; further grant[14] for 40 years, on 26th September 1741 [L.1740–1760, f. 61; A.1725–1744, f. 219d; DD/CC 112067].

Daniel Gell, grant sealed on 1st October 1751 [A.1740–1760, f. 152].

Sarah Gell, widow, grant on surr. for 40 years, on 3rd January 1757 (fine 12l.) [EB 1756–1762 (DD/CC 110007), p. 52; L.1740–1760, f. 499; A.1743–1760, p. 244].

Elizabeth Brunt, widow, grant on surr. for 40 years, on 1st July 1772 (fine 12l.) [EB 1771–1780 (DD/CC 110009), p. 21; L.1761–1777, f. 345; A.1761–1777, p. 281; Docs. ADD/4100].

Edward Goldborough, mercer, grant on surr. for 40 years, on 6th December 1787 [L.1777–1789, f. 461; A.1777–1792, p. 258]; regrant[15] on surr. for 40 years (fine 40l.) [L.1790–1807, f. 458; A.1792–1817, p. 252; EB 1798–1815 (DD/CC 110011), p. 193; Docs. ADD/4155, 4209].

Henry Sampson Michell, of Bruton, grant for 40 years, sealed on 30th September 1818 [A.1817–1832, p. 25; cf. Docs. ADD/4244].

Joseph Parsons, brush manufacturer, grant for 40 years, on 14th January 1847 [R.2, p. 156; A.1817–1832, p. 611].

Joseph Parsons, son of the above, purchased the tenancy on 7th February 1852[16] [DD/CC 114080/2, p. 71].

Notes

1. See below, Appendix III, 'Compton's Burgages'.
2. Cal. i, pp. 368–369.
3. C1553/4, *per eum quasi reedificatur*.
4. L.1546–1565, f. 2 (1546).
5. See Ch. C. file 51807, pt 1, leasehold tenancy 29, plan (1875), file 51807, pt 2, p. 82a.
6. Sherston is mentioned as tenant in other documents of 1363: Cal. i, p. 370 (R.III, f. 116d), pp. 370–371 (R.III, f. 117).
7. Premises then in the occupation of Robert Hooper, assignee.
8. Premises then in the occupation of Morgan Gitto (? subtenant).
9. Premises then in the occupation of John Haggat (? subtenant)
10. Premises then in the occupation of Cicelie Haggat (devisee ?).
11. Apparently an assignee or subtenant.
12. The surveyor recommended an increase in rent from 53s. 4d. to 8l.
13. Previous tenants whose names are recited in the lease: Tristram Towse, John Davis. There is no trace of grants to these persons, who may have been subtenants.
14. According to the lease, Samuel Walter, goldsmith, held a subtenancy under Charles Baron.
15. Probably made on 3rd January 1803 (see Docs. ADD/4244).
16. There is no record of a grant.

52

Property No. 69
11, High street

This property was originally one of Walter Compton's burgages, devised by him to the dean and chapter.[1] It was charged with an annual payment of 8s. to the vicars choral for the observance of the obit of John Hubard, anciently founded in the cathedral church.[2] One tenant under Compton, Adam de Chelworth, used the wine cellar of the house as a tavern. In about 1444–1445 the premises were rebuilt, and defaults in payment of rent during the tenancy of Thomas Tanner (?1392–?1422) suggest that the building had become dilapidated and uninhabitable; in C1445/6 a sum of 21l. 6s. 6d. was expended *circa nová edificatione* of the premises. According to C1455/6 these were at that time converted into two tenements. In 1454[3] the property was described as a tenement newly built, lying between the street and the water on the south, that is, the mill stream running from St. Andrew's spring.[4] In C1568/9 the property is designated 'the Catherine Wheel'; this is the first reference, in a document or entry relating primarily to these premises, to the name by which, in later years, they were generally known. The designation, however, was not new, for a lease of 1546[5] refers to the tenement commonly called of late the Katheryne Whele. Possibly the tavern in the wine cellar had traded under this sign, and the name had survived in popular usage. At the beginning of the 18th century the premises were divided, and leases of the Catherine Wheel regularly reserved to the dean and chapter, two lower rooms and two chambers above them, with a passage thereto. This reserved portion was eventually united with property no. 70 (9, High streeet).

The premises passed into the hands of the Ecclesiastical Commissioners at the time of the commutation of the capitular estates. In the survey made for the Commissioners in 1875 they are described as a tenement consisting of a confectioner's shop, dining parlour, sitting room, pantry, and kitchen; two sitting rooms and four bedrooms on the first floor, and two bedrooms over;[6] a scullery and bakehouse, with a storeroom over on the site of a malthouse, the remaining part of the malthouse being used for lumber and storage; a tiled wagon shed and a piggery.[7] The whole property then extended southward 290 feet from the street. It has lately been converted into a supermarket.

Tenants under Walter Compton:

Adam de Chelworth.
Henry Bouedich, burgess, and his wife Juliana,[8] grant[9] for their lives at a rent of 6 marks, on 28th February 1362[10] [Cal. i, p. 370 (R.III, f. 116); p. 270 (R.I, 254d and 279d)].

Tenants under the dean and chapter:

Thomas Tanner and his wife Isabel, grant for their lives[11] [C1392/3, C1400/1, C1417/8].
William Langford and his wife Christine, grant for their lives [C1428/9].
John Adams and William Voel [C1446/7].
John Adams and his wife Alice, grant for 40 years, on 3rd March 1454 [DD/CC 112047, C1446/7].
William Canyngton and John Adams [C1448/9][12].
Alice, wife of William Canyngton, and John Adams [1449/50][12]
John Adams and John Touker [C1455/6, C1461/2][12].
Richard Burnell and Alice Adams [C1470/1][12].

Richard Burnell and William Stikelpathe [C1473/4][12].
Richard Burnell and William Edmonde [C1478/9][12]
Richard Burnell and Robert Broke [C1490/1].[12].
Richard Harte and John Walshute [C1504/5].[12].
John Walshate, grant extended from 80 to 99 years[13] [Cal. ii, p. 175; C1568/9].
Thomas Brewster and John Walshute [C1513/4[14]].
Robert Houper and William Walshute [1534/5; C1537/8][14].
William Welshott [C1547/8,[15] C1559/60,[16] C1560/1[16] C1561/2[16], C1568/9[16]].
Thomas Tugwell, innholder, grant for 40 years at a rent of 53s. 4d., on 2nd January 1587 [L.1571–1624, f. 93; A1571–1599, f. 37; C1602/3 (lessee's name shown as Tuggle)].
William Welshote, mercer and Isabel his wife, grant for 40 years, on 29th September 1608 [Cal. ii, p. 213].
Christopher Kempe, grant for 40 years, on 5th January 1614 (fine 80l. payable in 8 audits) [Cal. ii, p. 367; A.1608–1622, f. 94d].
Henry Southworth, grant for 40 years [A.1608–1622, ff. 126d, 133d; DD/CC 112048; C1625/6].
Dr. Duck[17] and William Bull [C1626/7, C1627/8].
John Gibbons, grant on surr. for 40 years, on 1st April 1640 [SB 1637–1640, p. 59; A.1635–1645, p. 70; C1634/5, C1636/7].
Mrs. Gibbons, named as tenant in June/July 1649 [S1649, p. 12[18]].
Thomas Nixon, surgeon, grant for 40 years at a rent of 53s. 4d., on 5th January 1667 [DD/CC 112033; L.1624–1687, p. 608; *SRS* 72, p. 11].
Charles Baron, grant for 40 years sealed on 14th October 1681 [SRS 72, p. 90]. On 22nd January 1702 a survey of the premises was made by Dr Creyghton, precentor, and Mr. Marshall Bridges, chancellor, overseers of the houses at that time.[19] The survey showed that extensive repairs were necessary; these were to be executed upon three months notice [Docs. ADD/4072].
Mrs. Prowse, named as tenant in 1703 [S1703, p. 189].
Joseph Taylor, grocer, grant for 40 years on 2nd October 1704 [L.1701–1739, f. 24; A.1783–1784 f. 341]; grant (excepting two lower rooms and two rooms over, lying on the east of the premises granted, with the passage thereto) on surr. for 40 years at a rent of 46s. 8d., on 3rd July 1722[20] [L.1701–1739, p. 214; A.1705–1725, f. 175; DD/CC 112061].
Susanna Taylor, widow, relict of Joseph Taylor (above), grant (excepting the two lower rooms &c) on surr. for 40 years on 2nd January 1740 [DD/CC 112065; DD/CC 112066; L.1740–1760, f. 9; A.1735–1744, f. 208d.].

Stephen Taylor, maltster, grant on surr. for 40 years, on 2nd January 1759 (fine 15*l.*) [EB 1756–1762 (DD/CC 110007), p. 133; DCR VIII, p. 15; L.1740–1760, f. 573].

Maurice Davies, maltster, and Benjamin Plummer of Shepton Mallet, innholder, grant (excepting the two lower rooms &c.) on surr. for 40 years, on 5th December 1779 (fine 20*l.*) [EB 1771–1780 (DD/CC 110009), p. 275; L.1777–1789, f. 80; A.1777–1792, p. 52; cf. Docs. ADD/4129].

Maurice Davies, maltster, grant (excepting, as before, the two lower rooms &c.) on surr. for 40 years, on 1st April 1796 (fine 26*l.* 2*s.*) [A.1792–1817, p. 66; L.1790–1807, f. 228; A.1792–1817, p. 528; cf. Docs. ADD/4183a, 4183b].

Robert Davies, grant (including property no. 70) for 40 years, sealed on 14th July 1827 (fine £120) [A.1817–1832, p. 308; DD/CC 114080/1, p.12].

William Chester Berryman, wine and spirit merchant, grant for 40 years, on 2nd January 1861 (fine £315) [R.3, p. 356].

Notes

1. See Appendix III, p. 223.
2. A cancelled entry in *Liber Albus I*, dated 29th September 1289 (Cal. i, p. 151, R.I, f. 115) states that a seld or shop in High street, formerly held by Augustine the cobbler, was granted to Walter de la Roche by the chapter at a yearly rent of 4*s.* payable towards the obit of Walter Huberd, but there is nothing to identify this seld with a building on the site of property no. 69; nor is the cancellation of the entry explained.
3. DD/CC 112047.
4. Cf. Cal. ii, p. 213.
5. L.1546–1565, f. 2.
6. These were the rooms reserved to the dean and chapter, see above.
7. Ch. C. file 51807 pt 1, leasehold property 41; plan, file 51807 pt 2.
8. Or Joan, see Cal. i, p. 370 (RIII, f. 116).
9. Including the moiety of a wine cellar used by Adam de Chelworth as a tavern, for which the rent was one rose.
10. It was stipulated in this grant that when Walter Compton or his wife Margery should die, the surviving partner, if he or she did not desire to move to another house, might have a room for life in the tenement leased to Bouedich and his wife, with free ingress and egress.
11. Thomas and Isabel Tanner had died by C1421/2, see marginal note on the account roll.
12. Rent received for two tenements newly constructed.
13. Date of grant not known.
14. Rent received for two tenements newly constructed.

15. Rent received for a tenement newly built in the time of William Longforde.
16. Property then in the tenure of John Body (?a subtenant).
17. The bishop's vicar general; see *CHW*, Article 5, p. 56.
18. The surveyor proposed an improvement in the rent from 53*s*. 4*d*. to 16*l*.
19. The overseers of the houses were elected to supervise the canonical houses belonging to the dean and chapter (see *CHW*, p. xi), and this is a rare instance of their being deputed to survey another type of property.
20. Reserving the lessor's right to bring in and use ladders or any other necessary instruments for repairing the two lower rooms &c.

53

Property No. 70
9, High Street

In various 14th century descriptions[1] of the 'Catherine Wheel'[2] reference is made to a tenement on the east to which belonged certain selds (shops) held by Thomas de Draycote, a burgess of Wells.[3] The map of Canon Grange (*c*.1825) shows a building (property no. 70) on the east of the 'Catherine Wheel', situated at the rear of another building not belonging to the manor, fronting on to High street. From most leases of the 'Catherine Wheel' during the 18th century were excluded two lower rooms with two bedchambers over them (*duo conclavia cum eorum cubiculis*[4]) situated on the east side of a passage; and these premises formed property no. 70. They were eventually thrown into, used and occupied as part of the banking house of Vincent Stuckey of Langport, to whom the reversion had been sold for £140 11*s*. under the provisions of the Land Tax Redemption Acts. They have since been converted into flats for private occupation.

The first tenant of whom we have record was John le Bouyer (Boghiare),[5] who held the tenement on the east of the 'Cathering Wheel' early in the 14th century. The separation of what became property no 70 from the 'Catherine Wheel' is recorded in a lease of 1704, and in that year also a grant of the separated premises was made to

William Haines,[6] barber, grant for 40 years, on 2nd October 1704 [DD/CC 112058; A.1683–1705, f. 341; L.1701–1739, f. 23].
After the death of William Haines *c*.1710, various complicated transactions ensued, involving his widow, Priscilla, and his son Robert, and

his daughters Priscilla and Jane, and also Peter Davis, to whom the premises were made over as security for a mortgage of 100*l*.[7] Eventually the tenancy came into the hands of John Haines, of Coxley; he was followed by:

Simon Collins, grant by John Haines, on 26th March 1742 and 25th July 1746.

John Collins, barber and peruke maker, grant for 40 years, on 1st July 1765 (fine 15*l*.) [EB 1762–1771 (DD/CC 110008), p. 124; A.1761–1777, p. 127; L.1761–1777, f. 121].

John Burland, of Essex street, Strand, Middlesex, assignee of John Collins under a mortgage for 125*l*., on 8th November 1765 [SRO, DD/FS, box 3, bdl. 1].

James Penny, goldsmith, assignee of John Berkeley Burland, executor and legatee of John Burland, having discharged the debt due to the last-named under the mortgage, on 1st January 1780 [SRO, DD/FS, box 3, bdl.1].

John Collins, peruke maker, grant for 40 years, on 2nd January 1797 (fine 15*l*.) [A.1792–1817, p. 87; L.1790–1807, f. 268; EB 1780–1798 (DD/CC 110010), p. 303].

Anne Collins, only child and heiress of John Collins.

John Buncombe Hoare, tallow chandler, grant for 1 year, on 24th March 1808 [SRO, DD/FS, box 3, bdl. 1].

William Charles, shopkeeper, assignee of Anne Collins, on 25th March 1808; grant for 40 years sealed on 2nd January 1817 (fine 12*l*.) [A.1792–1817, p. 562, cf. A.1817–1832, p. 308; Docs. ADD/4240].

Robert Davies, grant (with property no. 69) for 40 years sealed on 3rd December 1829 [A.1817–1832, p. 492].

William Charles Berryman, purchaser of tenancy from Robert Davies.

Vincent Stuckey, of Langport, banker, lessee for 40 years from 3rd December 1829 [A.1817–1832, p. 492]; purchaser of property on 1st April 1830 for £140. 11*s*. [A.1817–1832, p. 514].

Notes

1. Cal. i, pp. 369 (1361), 371 (1361 and 1363).
2. See above, article 52, pp. 142–3.
3. Cal. i, p. 371 (1361 and 1363).
4. A1683–1704, f. 341.
5. Cal. i, p. 369.

6. Before William Haines, two tenants are named: William Hettisplace and Ralph Conyers; it is not clear whether these persons were tenants in chief, or only subtenants (see SRO, DD/FS, box 3, bdl. 1).
7. See SRO, DD/FS. box 3, bdl. 1; DD/CC 112062; DCR VIII, p. 13.

54

Property No. 71
Gildenhurst

Gildenhurst was a meadow situated in the eastern part of Coxley field, and is described in F1457/8 as two closes thrown into one, and in a lease of 1567[1] as near Wynapledore.[2] In recent time it formed the western portion of a large and irregularly shaped field, numbered 2496 on the tithe commutation map, and bounded on the east by the Keward brook. The large field was bisected by the Wells branch of the Somerset and Dorset Railway; Gildenhurst, containing 3 acres, 3 roods, 9 perches lay on the west of the railway line.[3] This land passed into the hands of the Ecclesiastical Commissioners at the time of the commutation of the capitular estates. Its tenants under the dean and chapter were:

William le Veyl, his wife Dionisia, and their son Thomas, grant (including other properties) for their lives, on 11th July 1316 [Cal.i, p. 157].
John Tregodek paid rent 6s. 8d. [F1457/8, F1480/1].
John Beynton [F1500/1, F1505/6].
John Jonys [F1549/50[4]].
John Nashe [F1564/5[4]].
Thomas Leigh [F1587/8–F1589/90].
Widow Leigh [F1590/1–F1594/5].
Katherine Coward, grant (with other properties) for three lives, on 1st October 1567 [L.1571–1624, f. 32].
Widow Edwards [F1619/20, F1620/1].
Thomas Coward, grant for three lives, on 30th September 1606 [A.1591–1607, f. 196]; further grant for three lives, on 1st July 1611 [DD/CC 112579; A.1608–1622, f. 41d; S1649, p. 15[5]].
Gideon Brooke, husbandman, grant for three lives, on 9th April 1661 [DD/CC 112588; Ch. 829 (Cal. ii, p. 714)].

John Allam, of Coxley, husbandman, grant on surr. for three lives, on 2nd January 1655 (L.1681–1701, f. 45; A.1683–1704, f. 53d].

William Higgens, innholder, grant for three lives sealed on 4th January 1714 [L.1701–1729, f. 74d; A.1705–1725, f. 88d].

Nicholas Marsh, innholder, grant on surr, for three lives, on 3rd September 1719 [L.1701–1739, p. 148; A.1705–1725, f. 143d].

James Cannings, innholder, and Anne his wife, grant on surr. for three lives, on 22nd April 1740 [L.1740–1760, f. 1; A1725–1744, f. 208d].

Sarah Cannings, spinster, grant on surr. for three lives, on 1st October 1778 (fine 9*l.*) [EB 1771–1780 (DD/CC 110009), p. 267; L.1777–1789, f. 42; A.1777–1792, p. 21; Docs. ADD/4127].

James Cannings, innholder, grant on surr. for three lives (fine 84*l.*) on 6th June 1803 [A.1792–1817, p. 266; L.1790–1807, f. 487; Docs. ADD/4212].

Thomas Fuller, grant on surr. for three lives, on 3rd December 1805 (fine 21*l.*) [L.1790–1807, f. 555; A.1792–1817, p. 334; Docs ADD/4232].

John Rexworthy [cf. DD/CC 110051].

William Inman Welsh, grant for three lives, on 21st April 1846 (fine £36) [R.2, p. 47 DD/CC 114080[2], Docs. ADD/4251], regrant for three lives, on 16th September 1857 (fine £16) [R.3, p. 127].

Notes

1. L.1571–1624, f. 32.
2. ? 'Appletree meadow'; this must have been a field in the locality, but its situation is not known.
3. For plans, see R.3, p. 127, and Ch. C file 51807 pt 2, lease 39.
4. '*Richard Pawlet nuper tenuit*'
5. The surveyor recommended an improvement in the rent from 6*s*. 8*d*. to 46*s*. 8*d*.

55

Property No. 72
Castlemead

Castlemead was a meadow, 2½ acres in area, situated in the Wells east field, bounded on the west by the Beryl stream and on the south by the

Chilcote stream. On the 1930 edition of the 1:2500 Ordnance Survey map of Somerset (Wells section)[1] it is numbered 2580. On the same map, near Castlemead, there is a field numbered 2585, part of which was called Limkiln (Limekill) close. Castlemead is sometimes described as a close near, or opposite the limekiln, for it was only some 50 yards from Limekiln close.

Castlemead is a corruption of Carswell's (Caswell's) mead, an early tenant or subtenant having borne this name. Another designation, Cole's close survived into the late 19th century[2] from C1587/8, when the land was held by one Richard Cole, and from C1634/5 and C1636/7, when it was in the tenure of John Coles. Castlemead passed into the possession of the Ecclesiastical Commissioners in 1866, and in the survey made for them in 1875, it is described as having upon it a small tiled shed.[3]

This field appears to have been originally part of the estate of Peter Orum,[4] and was once held by Walter Magot, from whom Richard de Bamfeld, canon of Wells, acquired it.[5] De Bamfeld (*temp.* Edward I) donated it, with other lands to the dean and chapter, partly to make provision for certain pious and charitable objects.[6]

The tenants of Castlemead[7] under the dean and chapter appear to have been:

Richard Orum.
Agnes Orum, widow and probably devisee of Richard Orum.
Robert Pade and Alice his wife, grant for their lives by Agnes Orum on 13th February 1431 [Ch. 596 (Cal. ii, p. 670)].
John Giffard, ?tenant under Agnes Orum.
Robert Pade, grant by John Giffard for three lives of land in Carswellmede, on 20th February 1446 [Ch. 623 (Cal. ii, p. 674)].
Peter Orum, probably son and devisee of Agnes Orum.
William Wyott, grant by Peter Orum for three lives of ½ acre of land in Casswelmede, on 25th December 1464 [Ch. 671 (Ch. ii, p. 684)].
Thomas Cornysshe, bishop of Tinos and precentor, grant of ½ acre of meadow lying in Casswelmede, for 60 years, on 20th September 1510 [Cal. ii, p. 223].
Roger, Thomas, Richard and Mary Edgworth, grant (i) of the reversion of ½ acre close of meadow in Castelmede or Casswelmede between a great stone on the east and a hedge or fence (*sepes*) on the west; and (ii) of 1 acre of meadow enclosed by itself in the west part of Castelmede; both grants made on 19th May 1541 (fine 26s. 8d.) [WCL, Book of Court Rolls, *temp.* Henry VIII, f. 49d].

Ludovicus Shepperd [S1570, f. 7d].
John Smith, grant for 40 years, on 4th July 1585 [S1570, f. 7d].
Richard Cole [C1587/8].
Mary, wife of Dr. William Powell, archdeacon of Bath, grant on 1st April 1596 (fine 40s.) [DD/CC 114066, p. 300].
John Cole [C1602/3].
Samuel Biss, tenant of 2 acres of pasture 'called Collclose' [SB 1615–1617, n.p.]
Gilbert Attwood sen., yeoman, grant of land 'abutting on . . . Limekill', on 1st October 1619 [L.1571–1624, f. 231d]; grant renewed on surr. for three lives, on 2nd January 1628 [DD/CC 111947; L.1624–1681, p. 53].
Jonah Loxton, paid rent *pro clauso prope Lymekill* [C1625/6].
Francis Loxtone [C1626/7, C1627/8].
John Coles [C1634/5, C1636/7; EB 1640–1642 (DD/CC 110004), p. 32; SB 1640–1644, n.p.: 'holds Casselesmeade for lives'].
Dorothea Alderley, daughter of Arthur Alderley, tenant in reversion for three lives, c.1640 (fine 3l. 6s. 8d.) [DCR II, p. 50]; June/July 1649 [S1649, p. 21^s;] 1703 [S1703, p. 173].
Arthur Alderley, vicar choral, tenant in reversion for three lives of 'a meadow called Cassell's meade', on 10th September 1642 (fine 5 marks) [EB 1640–1642 (DD/CC 110004), p. 32].
Thomas White, grant of various parcels of land[9] in Lymekill close for three lives sealed on 26th October 1667 [*SRS* 72, p. 7].
Mathew Cutler held a reversion for life by copy of court roll; he sold his interest to the following [Docs. ADD/4068]:
Avy Broderip, paid rent in 1723 for 'a close near the limekiln' [SRO, DD/WM 43].
Francis Broderip claimed tenancy for life in 1764 by copy dated 1721 [EB1762–1771 (DD/CC 110008), p. 127].
John Broderip, brother of the above, tenant in reversion for three lives, 1st July 1765 (fine 10l.) [DCR X, p. 49; EB1762–1771 (DD/CC 110008), p. 127]; licensed on 2nd January 1770 to demise to any person for any term [DCR XIV, p. 9; DD/CC 111789; Docs. ADD/4094].
Sarah Jenkins, spinster, grant for 99 years [DD/CC 111790].
William Rood, assignee of Sarah Jenkins under mortgage [DD/CC 111790].
Clement Tudway and Revd Dr Thomas Eyre, trustees under the marriage settlement of Thomas Abraham Salmon and Frances his wife, grant in reversion for three lives, on 1st August 1810 [DCR XXVI, p. 52; Docs. ADD/4222].

Notes

1. Section XLI 5.
2. Ch. C.file 51807 pt 1, 'in hand'2.
3. The map of Canon Grange c. 1825, shows a small building in the centre of the field.
4. Chs. 705, 706 (Cal. ii, p. 691).
5. See Article 60 (land in High Mead), 81 (land at Dulcote), and 85 (land at Wookey Hole).
6. Cal. i, p. 107; Ch. 145 (Cal. ii, p. 578).
7. In some cases, it will be observed, grants were made of apparently only portions of the field.
8. The surveyor noted 'we find John Coles in present possession, but by what he holds the property is unknown to us, because he has produced no copy or other evidence to manifest his estate'. An improvement in the rent from 6s. 8d. to 2l. was recommended.
9. Including Castlemead, see Article 56, p. 153.

56

Properties Nos. 73 and 74
Hackman's Well and Broad Close

These two fields lay on the south side of Bath road, between the road and the Chilcote stream. On the 1:2500 Ordnance Survey map of Somerset, Wells section,[1] they are numbered 2579 (Blackman's Well), and 2575 (Broad Close). They do not occur in the records of the dean and chapter under these names but from a 19th century document[2] it appears that they were formerly 'in several divisions', and in the occupation of Clement Tudway, to whom on 2nd December 1800[3] a grant was made of various lands including 4½ acres of arable land in the Wells east field, comprising five fields designated as follows: 'Harper's acre' (1 acre), 'Under the Hedge' (½ acre), 'At the Bush' (1 acre), and 2 acres at the corner of the east fields. The three first named fields are specified regularly in grants of land in this district, and it would appear that they were the 'several divisions' which properties Nos. 73 and 74 together comprised. This is the more probable because the three fields so named, usually with the 2 acres at the corner of the east field, were always leased as a single tenement, and never individually. It seems that 'Harper's acre', 'Under the Hedge' and 'At the Bush' were combined into one field at the beginning of the 19th century during the tenancy of

Clement Tudway, which was then divided into two portions, 'Blackman's Well', and 'Broad Close'. It is not known why the western portion was called 'Blackman's Well'.

In some documents the ½ acre field 'Under the Hedge' is described as 'shuttin[4] up towards Buriall', or 'reaching towards Buriall', or 'near Buriall'. The land in question is not, strictly, near Beryl[5], but it lies pointing,[6] as it were, in the direction of Beryl, and this is what the descriptions seem to mean. It is not known in what corner of the Wells east field the two acres lay, nor what the names 'Under the Hedge', and 'At the Bush' signified, but they probably referred to prominent natural features; 'Harper's acre' doubtless derives from an early owner or lessee.

Eventually these lands came into the possession of the Ecclesiastical Commissioners, whose survey made in 1875[7] confirms the identification of 'Broad Close' and Blackman's Well' with the 4½ acres. A housing estate has now been built on these fields, and 'Broad Close' is commemorated by a road of that name.

The following tenants of the 4 acres are recorded:

Edward Barker, of the city of London, grant (including 25 The Liberty[8]) for 40 years, on 1st October 1594 [L.1571–1624, f. 144].
Gilbert Attwood, grant (including Castlemead[9]) for three lives, on 1st October 1619 [L.1571–1624, f. 231d; DD/CC 112581]; regrant on surr. for three lives on 2nd January 1628 [DD/CC 111947; L.1624–1681, f. 53; S1649, p. 15].
Thomas White, grant (including Castlemead) on surr. for three lives, on 26th October 1667 [L.1624–1681, p. 592].
George Bampfield, grant on surr. (including 25, The Liberty) for three lives, on 12th October 1672 [L.1624–1681, p. 664].
Margaret Bampfeild, widow, grant on surr (including 25, The Liberty) for three lives on 2nd August 1688 [L.1681–1701, p. 87].
John Davis, grant (including 25, The Liberty) on surr. by Margaret Bampfeild, for three lives, on 1st April 1691 [L.1681–1701, f. 127].
Robert Creyghton, precentor, named as tenant in 1703 [S1703, p. 180].
Charles Baron sen., grant (including other lands), for three lives, on 13th November 1714 [L.1701–1739, f. 83].
Peter Davis, grant (including other lands), for three lives, on 9th July 1724 [L.1701–1739, f. 268].
Revd Henry Layng, of Paulspury, grant (including 25, The Liberty), on surr. for three lives, on 27th August 1730 [L.1701–1739, p. 480]; change of lives made on 2nd October 1732 [L.1701–1739, p. 541].

153

George Andrews and George Carey, in possession in 1752[10] [EB 1745–1755 (DD/CC 110006), p. 257].

Catherine Westley and George Andrews, grant[11] for two lives or the remainder of a term of 99 years determinable thereon [DD/CC 111977].

George Carey, yeoman, grant on surr. for three lives, on 2nd July 1753 [L.1740–1760, f. 423; DD/CC 111978; A.1743–1760, p. 172; DD/CC 111977].

Joseph Bacon, grant (including other lands) on surr. for three lives, on 2nd July 1761 [DD/CC 111931].

Richard Gould, grant (including other lands), on 21st January 1762 [cf. L.1790–1807, f. 354].

Clement Tudway, in lawful possession, and surr. on 2nd September 1800 [L.1790–1807, f. 354]; grant (including other lands), for three lives, on 2nd December 1800 [L.1790–1807, f. 370; A.1792–1817, p. 183; DD/CC 110051; Docs. ADD/4196].

Premises legally vested in Edward Foster and Revd Thomas Whalley, who proposed in 1815 a new lease for three lives, a fine of £330 being set [Docs. ADD/4235].

Notes

1. Section XLI 5.
2. Cf. DD/CC 110051.
3. L.1790–1807, f. 370.
4. In one document 'suting' (shooting).
5. Beryl is a locality on the west side of Knapp hill; various spellings are found: Burial, Berriall, Buriell, Buryall, Burriall, Beryall, etc. In earlier time, Beryl may have denoted a locality different from that to which the name now applies. W. Phelps (*History and Antiquities of Somersetshire,* ii (London 1839) p. 24) suggests that Beryl may be a corruption of Burgh-hill.
6. See Ch. C file 51807 pt 2, p. 97a, and the map of Canon Grange c.1825, also the Tudway estate map, SRO, DD/TD, lands 23 and 24.
7. Ch. C. file 51807 pt 1, leasehold 36.
8. See *CHW*, Article 9, p. 95.
9. See above, Article 55, p. 00.
10. No grant can be traced; Andrews and Carey were probably subtenants. They surrendered with a view to a new lease, possibly that next recorded.
11. It may have been for this grant that Andrews and Carey surrendered the last recorded lease (see DD/CC 111978), and for which a fine of 20*l.* was paid.

57

Property No. 75
Land in the South Part of Wells Park

It has proved impossible to locate this land. The communar records receipts of a rent of 16s. *pro clausis propa (sic) lez parka*, or *pro clausa prope le parka;* while in 1827 the land is described simply as 'that piece or close of meadow land containing half an acre situate . . . in the south part of Wells Park . . .' It did not pass into the hands of the Ecclesiastical Commissioners, having been sold in 1827, consequently no description nor plan of it appears in the survey made in 1875. The only existing plan occurs on the map of Canon Grange *c.* 1825; this shows a field situated on the north side of a bend in the Chilcote stream, between the stream and Southover, but not reaching as far as that street. Houses and other buildings stand on the site now, and it would appear that Silver street traverses it before making a junction with Southover.

The following tenants held this meadow:

George Lambert of Dulcote [C1587/8].
William Sawyer [C1602/3, C1625/6].
Thomas Hicks [C1634/5].
Widow Hicks [C1636/7].
Dorothy Clement (late widow Hicks), tenant in 1703 [S1703, p. 178].
John Brock, grant for his life, on 29th October 1722 [EB 1771–1780 (DD/CC 110009), p. 62]; tenancy in reversion for three lives granted, on 1st December 1772 [DCR XIII, p. 50 (fine 3*l.* 10*s.*)].
Edmund Broderip, grant for three lives, on 5th December 1826 [DCR XXXII, p. 104]; purchased from the dean and chapter [DD/CC 111797, A1817–1832, p. 292].

58

Property No.76
A Paddock at Portway

This meadow, containing in area three roods, was situated on the north side of the road (now A371) from Wells to Cheddar. The communar received the rent for this field, and in C1553/4 noted that the land pertained to the chapel of St Mary, the income from it presumably being applied to the maintenance of the fabric and the services of the Lady chapel in the cathedral. The rent was originally 1s. 8d. and was increased to 5s. in C1553/4. In 1866 this property passed into the possession of the Ecclesiastical Commissioners. The following tenants are recorded:

Thomas Zayer [C1587/8].
William Sawyer [C1602/3, C1635/6[1]].
Mrs Beaumond [C1634/5, C1636/7].
John Beaumont, in June/July 1649, claimed an interest, but produced no supporting evidence [S1649, p. 22[2]].
Maurice Beaumont, grant of a copy for three lives, on 1st July 1700 (fine 2l. 3s.) [EB 1698–1699 (DD/CC 110005), p. 120].
Henry Beaumont, tenant in 1703 [S1703, p. 175].
Joseph Beaumont, grant by copy for three lives, on 1st July 1765 (fine 5l. 5s.) [EB 1672–1771 (DD/CC 110008), p. 143; Docs. ADD/4096].
John Beaumont and William Hunt, grant by copy dated 1st July 1765, surr. on 4th December 1787 [DCR XVIII, p. 26].
James Haynes, grant by copy for three lives, on 5th December 1787 (fine 15s.) [DCR XVIII, p. 31; EB 1780–1798 (DD/CC 110010, p. 302; Docs. ADD/4157].
William Pulsford, admitted tenant in reversion on 6th December 1796 [DCR XXIII, p. 65].
John Dawbin, grant for three lives, on 28th February 1832 [DD/CC 114080/1].

Notes
1. Receipts of rent were recorded for C1526/7 and C1527/8, but no names of tenants.
2. The surveyor proposed an improvement in rent from 5s. to 8s. 4d.

59

Property No. 77
Paulsgrove

Paulsgrove was a field of about seven acres in area, situated on the south side of Breach lane, and some 60 yards from the junction[1] of the lane with the road from Wells to Glastonbury (now A39)[2]. At the beginning of the 18th century this field was owned by Peter Davis, who had assigned it to John Paine jun. on 9th September 1732[3]. It came into the hands of the dean and chapter as the result of an exchange between Davis and Paine. Paine held under the dean and chapter 2 acres of meadow or pasture 'against Walcombe field', and several other parcels of land; all these lands he ceded to Davis in return for Paulsgrove, paying as consideration a sum of 86l. 13s. 4d. The dean and chapter thus assumed ownership of Paulsgrove,[4] which Paine continued to hold as subtenant, while Davis, by a lease made on 9th July 1724, became tenant under the dean and chapter of the lands formerly in Paine's tenure. Eventually Paulsgrove was sold in 1827 to Edmund Broderip. After the exchange between Davis and Paine we find the following tenants of Paulsgrove under the dean and chapter:

John Paine, tenant for three lives at a rent of 26s. 8d. [cf. DD/CC 112594].
Francis Paine, apothecary, son of John Paine, grant on surr. for three lives, on 1st April 1742 [L.1740–1760, ff. 86, 87; A.1725–1744, f. 230; DD/CC 112411].
Viscount Palmerston and Revd John Paine, both or one of them in lawful possession, surr. on view of a new lease [DD/CC 112412].
Revd John Paine, prebendary of Barton St David, canon residentiary, and subdean, grant on surr. [DD/CC 112412] for three lives, on 1st April 1766 (fine 8l. 8s.) [DD/CC 112413; EB 1762–1771 (DD/CC 110008), p. 181].
Robert Tudway and Elizabeth Frances Paine, spinster, grant on surr.

for three lives on 12th December 1774 (fine 14*l.*) [L.1761–1777, f. 463; A.1761–1777, f. 463; A.1761–1777, p. 341; EB 1771–1780 (DD/CC 110009), p. 116; Docs. ADD/4108].

James Brookes, grazier. grant on surr. for three lives, on 1st July 1792 (fine 80*l.* [DD/CC 112415; EB 1780–1798 (DD/CC 110010), p. 205; A.1792–1817, p. 51; L.1790–1807, f. 196; Docs. ADD/4180].

Benjamin Brookes, grazier, grant on surr. for three lives,(fine 26*l.*) on 1st October 1803 [A.1792–1817, p. 274; L.1790–1807, f. 492; DD/CC 112416; Docs. ADD/4212].

Edmund Broderip, grant for three lives, on 2nd April 1820 [A.1817–1832, p. 78; DD/CC 112411]; purchased from the dean and chapter on 10th March 1827 for £212 12*s.* 11*d.* [DD/CC 112418; DD/CC 111795; A.1817–1832, p. 277].

Notes

1. This junction is nearly opposite Sugar Loaf farm, and about 1½ miles from Wells; Breach lane is not labelled.
2. For plan see SRO. DD/SRB (c668).
3. L.1740–1760, f. 86.
4. DD/CC 112410.

60

Property No. 78
Land in High Mead, West Horrington

This property, containing 1½ acres, situated on the north side of the road from Wells to Chilcompton (now B3139),[1] consisted of a small piece of arable ground[2] fronting on the road, and, behind this, a meadow or pasture, part of a larger field – both portions forming one field.[3]

Originally the land belonged to Walter Magot, who gave it to Richard de Bamfeld, canon of Wells, who in turn donated it, with other properties, to the dean and chapter, for the observance of his obit.[4] This was one of the properties taken in hand by the Ecclesiastical Commissioners at the commutation of the capitular estates.[5]

The following are known to have been tenants under the dean and chapter:

William, Joan and Thomasine Tarrye claimed in 1570 to hold this and other lands by a copy dated 20th November 1547 [S1570, f. 7].

William Baylye, grant ? of a reversion (with other lands) for three lives, in 1616 [SB 1615–1617, n.p.].

Thomas Attwood, tenant (with other lands) in June/July 1649 [S1649, p. 22].

William Salmon [cf. DD/CC 112531].

George Lax, tenant in 1763 [EB 1771–1780 (DD/CC 110008), p. 77].

Thomas Lax, of East Horrington, yeoman, grant on surr. for three lives at a rent of 6*d.*, on 2nd January 1764 (fine 3*l.* 3*s.*) [EB 1771–1780 (DD/CC 110008), p.77; L.1761–1777, f. 87; DD/CC 112531; A.1761–1777, p. 87].

George Lax, grant for three lives, on 1st April 1817 [A.1792–1817, p. 563; DD/CC 112532; DD/CC 112533 Docs. ADD/4241]; regrant for three lives, on 28th February 1832 [SRO, DD/LX box 6 bdl. 50]; regrant for three lives sealed on 29th August 1836 [A.1832–1840, p. 225].

Notes

1. See the plans in SRO, DD/LX box 1, bdl. 2; and Ch. C. file 51807 pt 2, p. 78a.
2. On the tithe map, no. 886.
3. On the tithe map, part of no. 885.
4. Cal. i, p. 107; Ch. 145 (*temp.* Edward I), Cal. ii, p. 578.
5. See Ch. C. file 51807 pt 1, lease 27.

61

Property No. 79
Land on Mendip

This land, in area 9 acres 2 roods 32 perches, lay on the south side of the road from Hill Grove (on the main road from Wells to Bristol, now A39) to Priddy, near Priddy road farm.[1] It came into the possession of the dean and chapter in 1800, as the result of an exchange involving land at Dulcote called Kingshay end, under the provisions of the Wells Enclosure Act of 33 George III.[2] Included in this exchange was land on Haymoor.[3] The tenant of the Mendip land at the time of the enclosure award was Charles William Taylor, whose tenure continued under the dean and chapter. Eventually this land passed into the possession of the Ecclesiastical Commissioners in 1866.

After Charles William Taylor the tenants were:

Alexander Popham, master in Chancery, devisee in trust, grant (with other lands) on surr. for three lives, on 1st October 1800 [L.1790–1807, f. 358; DD/CC 112573].

Henry Rycroft, of Curzon street, Mayfair, and Thomas Lewis, of Nassau street, Soho, grant (with other lands) on surr. for three lives at a rent of 4s. 4d., on 15th May 1813 [DD/CC 112573a].

Philip William Skynner Miles, of Kingweston, Glos., and Charles Newdegate Newdegate, of Arbury Priory, Warwks., grant (with other lands) on surr. for three lives, on 16th September 1857 (fine £140) [R.3, p. 125; DD/CC 114080[2], p. 82; DD/CC 112574 (fine £142); DD/CC 112575] (fine £80).

Notes

1. For plans, see DD/CC 1779; Enclosure award (1793), SRO, Q Re 81; Ch. C. file 51807 pt 2, p. 90b, cf. also Docs. ADD/4194c.
2. DD/CC 112614.
3. See below, Article 62.

62

Property No. 80
Land on Haymoor (I)

This pasture, containing 3 acres, 1 rood, and 10 perches, lay below Ben Knowle hill, on the east side of Haymoor drove. It belonged originally to the rectory of St Cuthbert, and under the Wells Enclosure Act of 33 George III was allotted to Sir Charles William Taylor, with land on Mendip,[1] in respect of land at Dulcote called Kingshay end.[2] The farm of the rectory passed into the hands of Sir C.W. Taylor and Alexander Popham, master in chancery, as trustees and executors of the will of Peter Taylor, and they surrendered their interest to the dean and chapter on 1st October 1800.[3] This land on Haymoor eventually passed into the possession of the Ecclesiastical Commissioners at the time of the commutation of the estates of the dean and chapter. The tenants under that body after the surrender of 1800 were:

Alexander Popham, master in chancery, grant (with other lands) for three lives, on 1st October 1800 (fine £450) [L.1790–1807, f. 358; DD/CC 112573].

Francis Popham, heir of the above, devisee [DD/CC 112616].

Henry Rycroft, of Curzon street, Mayfair, and Thomas Lewis, of Nassau street, Soho, grant (with other lands) on surr. for three lives, on 15th May 1813 [DD/CC 112573a].

Philip William Skynner Miles, of Kingweston, Glos., and Charles Newdegate Newdegate, of Arbury Priory, Warwks., grant (with other lands) for three lives, on 16th September 1857 (fine £140) [R.3, p. 125; DD/CC 112574]; further grant (with other lands) on surr. [DD/CC 112575] for three lives, on 24th September 1859 (fine £80) [DD/CC 114080/2, pp. 82, 105].

Notes

1. See above, Article 61.
2. DD/CC 112614.
3. DD/CC 112614.

63

Property No. 81
Land on Haymoor (II)

The dean and chapter acquired this strip of meadow, containing 2 roods and 20 perches, situated near Battlebury on Haymoor, by exchange[1] under the provisions of the Wells Enclosure Act of 33 George III, for ½ acre of arable land on the north side of Tucker street.[2] At the time of the enclosure award (1793) both properties were in the tenure of Robert Michell, who surrendered the meadow on Haymoor, which had been awarded and allotted to William Melliar. It was taken in hand by the Ecclesiastical Commissioners in 1866. After the exchange, the tenants under the dean and chapter were:

Sir Charles William Taylor, grant for three lives by copy at a rent of 3s. 4d. on 1st October 1794 (fine 5l.) [EB 1780–1798 (DD/CC 110010), p. 166; DCR XXI, p. 41; DD/CC 111791].

Henry Rycroft, of Curzon Street, Mayfair, and Thomas Lewis, of Nassau street, Soho, grant (with other lands) on surr. for three lives, on 15th May 1813 [DCR XXVII, p. 75; DD/CC 112573a].

Philip William Skynner Miles, of Kingweston, Glos., and Charles Newdegate Newdegate, of Arbury Priory, Warwks., grant (with other lands) for three lives, on 16th September 1857 (fine £140) [R.3, p. 125; DD/CC 114080/2, p. 82; DD/CC 112574]; further grant for three lives, on 24th September 1859 (fine £80) (DD/CC 114080/2, p. 105.

Notes

1. DD/CC 111791; DD/CC 1781[6] (plans of properties exchanged); Enclosure award, SRO, Q Re 81; A.1792–1813, p. 43; L.1790–1807, f. 172.
2. See below, Article 67.

64

Property No. 84
Meadow on Knowle Moor (I)

This meadow, in area 14 acres, 1 rood, lay on the south side of the road from Bleadney to Easton, about ½ mile west of Knowle bridge. It became the property of the dean and chapter on 28th September 1795,[1] in exchange, under the Wells Enclosure Act of 33 George III, for land at Wookey Hole.[2] At the time of the commutation of the capitular estates, this meadow became the property of the Church Commissioners. The following were tenants under the dean and chapter:

John Band, of Wookey Hole, grant for three lives, on 1st July 1796 at a rent of 10s. [A.1792–1817, p. 68; DD/CC 112569].

Revd Herman Drew, of Combrawleigh, Devon, grant on surr. for three lives, on 1st July 1805 [DD/CC 112570; L.1790–1807, f. 539; A.1792–1817, p. 320; DD/CC 112571].

Notes

1. DD/CC 112568; A.1792–1817, p. 52; DD/CC 1781[6]; Enclosure award, SRO, Q Re 81, p. 68.
2. See below, Article 85.

65

Property No. 85
Land on Knowle Moor (II)

This land, containing 3 acres, 2 roods, 10 perches, is situated on Knowle moor, bounded on the south east by Knowle Moor drove, and on the south west by Stock's drove. It came into the possession of the dean and chapter in c 1866.

It was always granted by the dean and chapter with a pasture on Haymoor, and details of the tenancies[2] will be found in the article[3] on that land.

Notes

1. DD/CC 112614; Docs. ADD/4194a, 4194b.
2. See EB 1798–1815 (DD/CC 110011, p. 95 (1800); L. 1790–1807, f. 358 (1800); DD/CC 112573 (1800); A. 1792–1817, p. 180 (1800); DD/CC 112616 (1813); A. 1792–1817, p. 503 (1813); R.3, p. 125 (1857); DD/CC 112574 (1857); DD/CC 112575 (1859).
3. See above, Article 62.

66

Property No. 86
Land in Burcot Mead

This meadow or pasture, containing 2½ acres, was described in 1840 as 'situated at Coxley near the turnpike road leading from Glastonbury to Wells (in common with other lands)'.[1] It lay between the road (now A39) and a stream, probably the Keward brook, its eastern boundary being some 66 yards from the road. Neither the plans[2] of the ground, nor the descriptions in leases, allow identification of the field, however; nor do we know how it came into the possession of the dean and chapter. Eventually it passed into the hands of the Ecclesiastical Commissioners. The record of its tenants begins in 1649.

Thomas Attwood, tenant (with land in High Mead) in June/July 1649 [S1649, p. 22].[3]

William Salmon [EB 1762–1777 (DD/CC 110008), p. 64].

John Whereat, of Coxley, yeoman, grant for three lives at a rent of 4s. 5d., on 2nd February 1764 (fine 52l.) [EB 1762–1777 (DD/CC 110008), p. 64; L.1761–1777, f. 85; A.1761–1777, p. 95; DD/CC 112534].

Samuel Whereat, of Coxley, yeoman, grant on surr. (John Whereat having died), for three lives, on 12th December 1775 (fine 4l. 10s.) [EB 1771–1780 (DD/CC 110009), p. 179; A.1761–1777, p. 362; L.1761–1777, f. 505; DD/CC 112535; Docs. ADD/4112].

Susannah Teek, of Polsham, widow, in whom the tenancy was legally vested after the death of Samuel Whereat [EB 1780–1798 (DD/CC 110010), p. 21]

Robert Teek, of Coxley, yeoman, son of Susannah Teek, grant on surr. [DD/CC 112536] for three lives at a rent of 4s. 5d., on 1st October 1790 (fine 18l.) [EB 1780–1798 (DD/CC 110010), p. 21; L.1790–1807, p. 22; A.1777–1792, p. 297; DD/CC 112537; Docs. ADD/4165].

Matthew Teek, grant on surr. for three lives, on 2nd April 1804 (fine 8l. 8s.) [DD/CC 112538; A.1792–1817, p. 283; Docs. ADD/4213].

James Teek, of Polsham, yeoman, grant on 23rd February 1839 [DD/CC 112539]; regrant on surr. [DD/CC 112540] for three lives, on 22nd June 1841 [R.1, p. 329; DD/CC 112541]; grant on surr. [DD/CC

112542], for three lives, on 25th July 1854[4] (fine £17) [DD/CC 112543; R.2, p. 472].

Notes

1. DD/CC 112544.
2. See margin of lease dated 22nd June 1841, R.1, p. 329; also Ch. C. file 51807, pt 2, p. 76a.
3. The surveyor recommended an improvement in the rent for the whole tenement of 4s. to 2l. 9s. 4d.
4. For a plan of the premises, see Docs. ADD/4273(38).

67

Property No. 92
Land in Tucker Street

The earliest description of this land is: a close of pasture estimated to contain ½ acre, on the north side of Tucker street.[1] A plan drawn in connexion with an enclosure award and exchange in 1793[2] shows a field situated at the west end of Tucker street, but it cannot be more exactly identified. Under the provisions of the Wells Enclosure Act it was exchanged for land on Haymoor[3] in 1794. The record of lessees begins in the 14th century in the accounts of the communar, which show those who paid the annual rent of 3s. 4d.

Thomas Zayer [C1587/8].
William Sawyer [C1602/3].
Richard Bourne [C1625/6–C1627/8].
Alexander Towse [C1634/5–C1636/7].
Henry Baron, tenant in June/July 1649 [S1649, p. 22[4]].
Arthur Baron, tenant in 1703 [S1703, p. 174].
Francis Duncombe [cf. DCR III, p. 5].
John Moss and his son, John, tenancy in reversion for three lives, on 26th October 1741 [DCR III, p. 5].
Jacob Nicholls, claimed tenancy by copy dated 26th October 1741 for three lives [EB 1745–1755 (DD/CC 110006), p. 302].[5]

Robert Michell, grant for two lives, on 3rd December 1754 [cf. EB 1780–1798 (DD/CC 110010), p. 166]; grant on surr., on 1st October 1794 [DCR XXI, p. 40[6]; A.1792–1813, p. 43; DD/CC 111701; L.1790–1807, f. 172; Docs. ADD/4178].

Notes

1. S1649, p. 22.
2. DD/CC 1781[6].
3. See Article 63 above.
4. The surveyor recommended an improvement of the rent (3*s.* 4*d.*) to 8*s.* 8*d.*
5. Nicholls sought a reversion for three lives, for which a fine of 10*s.* 6*d.* was set, but there is no evidence of a grant.
6. Between Jacob Nicholls and Robert Michell, Joseph Nicholls is stated to have been the tenant; but no grant to him can be traced; there may be confusion in the records between Jacob and Joseph Nicholls.

Part II Various Unnumbered Properties, Parts of the Manor of Canon Grange

68

5, New street

This property was situated between property no. 57 (3, New street)[1] on the south and the house called 'The Rose and Crown', formerly 'The White Lion' (7, New street, now the Trustee Savings Bank), on the north. In a post-Restoration rental[2] it is described as 'in Chamberlain street, at the end of New street'. It does not appear on the *c*. 1825 map of Canon Grange, having been exchanged for property no. 65.[3] In the 18th century it was apparently used as a blacksmith's shop. The record of tenants begins at the end of the 16th century in the accounts of the communar.

Christopher Haine, paid rent 6*s*. 8*d*. [C1587/8, C1602/3].
Margery Hedd, *alias* Haine, *nuper fide Lightfoot* [C1625/6–1627/8].
George Hoell [C1634/5, C1636/7].
John Harris, in possession by one copy, and after him Sibil Lightfoot and Grace Cooke by another copy, *c*. 1627 [SB 1636–1641, p. 16].
John Cook, tenant in reversion for three lives in *c*. 1627 (fine 20*s*.) [SB 1636–1641, p. 16].
Widow Howell, in June/July 1649, pretended an interest by virtue of a grant by the dean and chapter [S1649, p. 24[4]].
Michael Howell, named as tenant in 1703 [S1703, p. 184].
Bartholomew Sperring, claimed tenancy by virtue of a grant dated 2nd November 1747 [EB 1762–1771 (DD/CC 110008), p. 218].
Benjamin Pulsford, surgeon, grant on surr. for three lives, on 9th December 1766 (fine 3*l*. 3*s*.) [EB 1762–1771, p. 218; DCR XI, p. 14], grant to the dean and chapter in connexion with an exchange for property no. 65, on 2nd May 1767 [DD/CC 111788; A.1761–1777, p. 185; DCR XI, p. 34; L.1761–1777, f. 176; EB 1762–1771 (DD/CC 110008), p. 242].

Notes

1. See above, Article 38.
2. DD/CC 111736, 25/33.
3. See above, Article 47.
4. The surveyor recommended an improvement of the rent of 6s. 8d. to 2l.

69

Cristesham's Inn or The George Inn (now 7, High Street)

The college of St Anne and St Catherine on the Mountroy[1] was not the first provision made by bishop Ralph Erghum for the accommodation of chantry priests (chaplains or annuellers) who ministered at altars in the cathedral. Soon after his coming to Wells in 1388 he obtained from Nicholas Cristesham, a burgess who had been elected thirteen times to represent the city in Parliament,[2] a tenement in the High street near the high cross, and with it, four acres of land.[3] This tenement stood on the site now occupied by the National Westminster bank.[4] Bishop Erghum, however, was apparently not satisfied with Cristesham's inn as a *hospitium* for the annuellers – it may have proved too small, or in too public a place, for he made provision in his will for the erection of a new college on the Mountroy, and thither, when it had been completed, the chaplains removed. Cristesham's inn was then vested in the dean and chapter, with the intention that the revenue derived therefrom should be applied to the support of the chantry priests in their new college.

Subsequently Cristesham's inn served as a public lodging house, and was named The George. When the chantries were dissolved under Edward VI, the inn was acquired[5] by John Ayleworth (then receiver general for Somerset), and William Lacy, the purchasers of the Mountroy college.[6] In his history of the cathedral, Nathaniel Chyle states that the house 'continues still (c. 1680) an inn and the same sign of the George.'[7] It appears that the Corporation of Wells eventually obtained an interest in the inn, for among the properties of the Corporation in 1821 it is included with the note: 'A fee farm of eight shillings is payable out of the George inn premises to the Corporation.' The tenant at that time was Thomas Lax, and a pencilled note records that the property was sold to him.[8] Tenants were also under obligation to pay to the dean and chapter an annual pension of 2*l*. 6*s*. 8*d*., which was entered in the manorial accounts as 'for Mountroy from the George inn'. For 1785, 1787, 1790, and the period 1791–1802, this sum was paid by James Cannings, while according to rentals of 1828, 1830, and 1831, the same pension, plus 8*s*. for the land tax was received from John (not Thomas) Lax, who is designated 'owner'. According to Dr. T.S. Holmes,[9] the George inn 'in 1854 was sold by the Ecclesiastical Commissioners to Stuckey's Banking Company'. Nothing is known about the title of the Commissioners to this property; Dr Holmes's statement may simply imply that they authorized the discontinuance of the payment to the dean and chapter of the annual pension, which does not appear in the accounts after the date of the sale.

Notes

1. See Appendix I.
2. R.V. Sellers, 'The Chantry College in the Mountroy at Wells', WNH&A Soc., *Report* 1959–1960, p. 11, n. 39.
3. Ibid, and see Cal. i, p. 442.
4. T.S. Holmes, *Wells and Glastonbury* (London, 1908), p. 63.
5. *Cal. Pat. Rolls*, 1547–8 pp. 406–407, *SRS* 77, pp. 14–15.
6. See Appendix II, p. 220.
7. Reynolds, p. xxxiv.
8. *Wells Corporation Lands and Tenements, 1821* (WML), plan no. 20
9. Op. cit., p. 64.

70

A Copyhold tenement in Chamberlain Street

The location of this property is not known; it does not appear on the map of Canon Grange, and in the documents relating thereto it is simply described as a cottage with garden adjacent. It is not known how or when the dean and chapter acquired it, nor in what circumstances it passed from their possession. The following tenants can be traced:

William Smith, tenant in right of his wife Hester for three lives, by copy dated 23rd October 1637 [S1649, p. 18]; tenant in June/July 1649 [S1649, p. 18[1]].

Robert and Susanna Balch, tenants for their lives by copy granted by Esther Smith [SB 1640–1642 (DD/CC 110004), p. 14; cf. SB 1640–1642, n.p.].

Adrian Bower, tenant in reversion for three lives, c. 1639 [DCR II, p. 49 (fine 12s. 6d.); SB 1637–1640, p. 58].

Thomas Willis, tenant for three lives in right of his wife Elinor [DCR II, p. 47].

Bartholomew Cox, tenant in reversion, on 27th October 1641 [DCR II, p. 47].

Notes

1. The surveyor recommended an improvement of the rent of 8s. to 3l.

71

Brown's Gate

Brown's gate,[1] through which Cathedral Green was entered from Sadler street,[2] is one of the several gates or towers built by bishop Bekynton.[3] It was often let with properties nos. 53 and 54, which were adjacent to it on the south side.

In pursuance of plans to improve the city, it had been proposed to remove Brown's gate in 1841, but the chapter objected.[4] On 18th September 1848[5] it was reported that the gate was in a state of dilapidation, and the chapter clerk was instructed to require the tenant to effect the necessary repairs without delay. On 1st July 1864[6] the chapter was told that Mr Ramsay, the occupant of the house adjoining the gate on the south, had complained that 'the gate in its present state was a nuisance to his home'. The chapter's surveyor was asked to report on the condition of the gate and its connexion with Ramsay's house, and on the uses to which it had been put by Ramsay. This report was considered on 10th November 1864,[7] and order was given that such repairs only as were absolutely necessary should be effected, and that

Mr Ramsay should be reminded that his occupation of the gate was on sufferance,[8] and that its use as a larder or as a drying room must be discontinued. On 2nd April 1867[9] repairs costing £40 – £50 were authorised by the chapter, and on 30th July 1867[10] the chapter's surveyor was asked to submit a plan for the restoration of the west side of the gate.

Forty years later the chapter again had Brown's gate under consideration. On 1st November 1906[11] it was reported that the only means of access to the room in the tower was from the adjoining house on the south. To forestall any future claim upon the gate by the occupant of this house, the chapter clerk was directed to press for a door rent and to make the best possible arrangement for reserving the gate to the dean and chapter. On 31st December the chapter was informed that the occupant of the house had paid the door rent, but refused to admit the dean and chapter's right of way through the house to the room in the tower; the door had been bolted and barred to prevent trespass from the house. It was decided to ask Mrs Parfitt, who occupied the house, to rent the tower room at 5s. yearly, and the chapter's surveyor was asked to report on the cost of making a stair on the north side of the arch to provide access to the room.[12] He reported that this would be difficult and expensive,[13] and the matter was finally concluded by an agreement to let the room at an annual rent of 1s., conceding to the dean and chapter the right to enter and view the room.[14] In 1908 the room was converted at a cost of £38 into a comfortable living room,[15] by Mrs Parfitt's successor, Miss Ranken to whom it was decided to grant it at a rent of £2.[16]

In connexion with the commutation of the estates of the dean and chapter, one of the buildings exempted from the properties to be transferred to the Ecclesiastical Commissioners was 'a tower commonly called or known as "Brown's gate or Baron's gate"'.[17]

Tenants:

Gyles Wallis, pewterer, grant (including property no.54, and a house in New Street) for 40 years at a rent of 6s. 8d., on 1st July 1580 [L.1561–1624, f. 55; Cal. ii, p. 302].

George Upton, grant for 40 years at a rent of 2s., on 1st July 1585 [L.1571–1624, f. 74]; further grant 'of the gat howse called Brownes gat to make up the years that now he hath in the same to xl tie years'; charge *pro foedis sigilli*, 53s. 4d., sealed on 1st October 1597 [A.1571–1599, f. 112]; further grant for 40 years, on 1st October 1601 (Docs. V/3).

William Clutterbuck, tenant for 3 years to come on 3rd January 1639: 'he has a price (10*l*.) given him by the chapter, but has refused it; upon which refusal David Flood, vicar choral, desires to take it at the same price or such a fine as shall be . . . thought fit' [SB 1637–1640, p. 60].

James Clutterbooke, grant for 40 years, on 9th January 1660 [DD/CC 112485; cf. SB 1637–1640, p. 39].

Jane Edmonds [cf. DD/CC 112496]

Robert Warmall, grant (including properties nos. 53 and 54) on surr. for 40 years, on 6th December 1692 [DD/CC 112496; L.1681–1701, f. 146].

Mary Warmall, tenant in 1703 [S1703, p. 193]; grant (including properties 53 and 54) for 40 years, on 4th January 1713 [L.1701–1739, f. 73; DD/CC 112502].

Frances Brown, spinster, grant (including properties nos. 53 and 54) on surr. for 40 years, on 1st July 1752 (fine 20*l*.) [L.1740–1760, f. 383; EB 1745–1755 (DD/CC 110006), p. 211].

Ann and Elizabeth Brown, spinster, executors of the will of Frances Brown [cf. DD/CC 112508].

Thomas Maynard, tiler and plasterer, purchased tenancy on 14th March 1754 [DD/CC 112508].

Joseph Lovell, grant (including properties 53 and 54) on surr. for 40 years, on 1st April 1765 (fine 10*l*.) [EB 1762–1771 (DD/CC 110008), p. 137; L.1761–1777, f. 115; Docs. ADD/4146].

George Lax and George Lovell, surr. in July 1800, with a view to a new grant to John Conway, grant for 40 years (fine £27) in July 1800 [Docs. ADD/4195].

C.K. Parrott tenant (including properties 53 and 54) in 1924 [M.1919–1938, p. 105].

Notes

1. During the years the gate has had various names. Brown's gate is the earliest; Baron's gate occurs on the map of Canon Grange *c*. 1825, and is possibly a corruption of the earlier name. The 'dean's eye' is found in 1866 (J.H. Parker, *The Architectural Antiquities of the City of Wells* (Oxford and London), 1866, p. 40), and was doubtless a complimentary imitation of the 'bishop's eye' in the Market Place.
2. The road through the gate was closed in the 7th decade of the present century.
3. See Pevsner, p. 316.
4. M.1837–1849, p. 116.
5. Ibid, p. 346.

6. M.1860–1872, p. 190.
7. Ibid, p. 200.
8. Presumably because he was only a subtenant.
9. Ibid, p. 272.
10. Ibid, p. 280.
11. M.1904–1918, p. 55.
12. Ibid, p. 58.
13. Ibid, p. 67.
14. Ibid, p. 65.
15. Ibid, pp. 123, 126.
16. Ibid, p. 128.
17. *London Gazette*, 27th July 1866 (Schedule B).

72

A Messuage in Elm

The village of Elm or Great Elm lies about two miles north-west of Frome. The messuage owned by the dean and chapter there was a cottage; its location is not known, nor is there any evidence how it came into the possession of the dean and chapter. The only sources of information concerning the property and its tenants are the fabric accounts, in which are recorded receipts of the rent of 12*d*. For the 18th and 19th centuries the cottage is not mentioned in the records, and at the end of the 17th century there appears to have been difficulty in obtaining the rent, which caused complications in the accounts, so that the chapter decreed on 1st October 1694[1] that 'the arrears . . . upon the messuage in Elme shall . . . be left out of the charge of the fabric account from henceforth until farther order'. This property does not appear in the survey and valuation of 1875 made for the Ecclisastical Commissioners after the commutation of the capitular estates, and it probably ceased to belong to the dean and chapter in the 18th century. The few tenants known to us are recorded in the fabric accounts as paying the rent:

Richard Bythewode, of Buckland Dinham, tenant and occupant [F1390/1].
Formerly held by John Bythewode [F1457/8].
John Payne, formerly held by Nicholas Bythewode [1480/1].
Thomas Payne [F1492/3–F1505/6].

175

John Grenelake [F1549/50].
Edmund Bower [F1589/90; F1619/20; F1663/4–F1688/9].
Adrian Bower [F1625/6, F1626/7].

Notes

1. A.1683–1704, f. 242.

73

A House in New Street

This house was sold *c.* 1806; consequently it does not appear on the map of Canon Grange. From descriptions in leases and other documents it appears that it was situated on the east side of New street, and, according to a grant of 1552,[1] that on its south side stood a cottage belonging to the estate of the city of Wells. The city owned two houses on the east side of New Street – the present no. 12,[2] and that now called 'Patch House'.[3] In 1821 the latter was in the tenure of a Mrs Torriano who, according to the estate plan[4] of the premises, also held property on the north. At this time she held under the dean and chapter the house with which we are here concerned. From this it may be inferred that this house lay on the north side of 'Patch House'.

'Patch House', or the building that stood on the site is designated in 1592[5] the 'inn called "The Saracen's Head",' but it was not long used for this purpose, being described in 1599[6] as a dwelling house 'late being an inn called "Sarison's Head".' A document of 1782[7] confuses the house with which we are concerned, with that on the south, referring to the former as 'the "Saracen's Head" now called Mountroy,' although it is not so named in any earlier lease. The latter designation appears to have originated in a mistaken assumption that the college of St Anne and St Catherine for chantry priests on the Mountroy,[8] on the site of which 'The Cedars' now stands, was situated on or near the site of the property that is the subject of this article.[9] It may be to this property that Phelps refers: 'At the upper end of (New) street stood a large building in the Elizabethan style with gable windows, called

Mountroy, heretofore . . . built . . . for the residence of . . . chantry priests . . . the edifice was taken down in 1830'.[10]

Late in the 13th century this property, described as a messuage, garden and dovecote, was in the possession of a canon of Wells, William de Pulton. By his will, before the statute of mortmain (1279), he bequeathed to the dean and chapter for his obit the rent of 13s. 4d. issuing from the property. After Pulton's death, the premises passed into the hands of a burgess of Wells, Walter de Middleton. The escheator had no difficulty in collecting the rent until 1340, in which year, for no reason stated, Middleton ceased payment. The property had then come into the ownership of another burgess, John le Markaunt, who paid the arrears of rent on Middleton's behalf, and acknowledged the entitlement of the dean and chapter to the payment of 13s. 4d. on each 1st January, binding himself, his heirs and assignees (being owners of the property) to fulfil their obligation in this matter; he allowed that the dean and chapter might distrain for any arrears, and in return Middleton and Markaunt were acquitted of liability for the arrears of rent already incurred. The emphasis in several documents relating to this matter on the fact that Pulton's bequest antedated the statute of mortmain, suggests that Middleton may have doubted the legality of the bequest, and may have withheld payment accordingly.[11]

At some time during the 13th century the property came into the hands of Richard Horsford; from him it passed to vicar choral, John Bovyndon, and from Bovyndon to a canon of Wells, Richard Harewell, by whom, on 1st August 1402,[12] it was granted to the dean and chapter. The following tenants under the dean and chapter can be traced:[13]

John Stone, mason, and his wife Juliana, grant on 25th March 1370(?) [Ch. 369 (Cal. ii, p. 627)].
Nicholas Rodeway *inhabitavit* [E1423/4; E1424/5].
Richard Horsford and Walter London [E1439/40–1490/1].
Richard Bowe, Alice his wife, and Thomas their son, grant for their lives at a rent of 8s. 4d. [E1494/5; E1503/4; E1511/2].
Alice and Thomas Bowe (Richard Bowe deceased) [E1513/4; E1515/6; E1518/9; E1520/1].
Thomas Bowe (Alice Bowe deceased), grant for life [E1524/5; E1529/30].
Richard Rosemounde *alias* Martyn [E1543/4].
Thomas Hagget, yeoman, grant for three lives at a rent of 13s. 4d., on 2nd October 1552[4] [L.1546–1565, f. 59[15]].
Nicholas Byngam, of Warminster, Wilts., yeoman, grant for 40 years, on
24th June 1592 [L.1571–1624, f. 132d].

Alice Lowman, of Sowlie, Devon, widow, grant for 40 years, on 24th June 1599 [1571–1624, f. 166].

William Clutterbooke sen., grant for 40 years, on 3rd January 1614 [S1649, p. 7[16]; DD/CC 112148].

Joseph Moreton [cf. DD/CC 112151].

Richard Hickes, grant on surr. for 40 years, on 6th May 1679 [DD/CC 112151].

John Day, grant on surr. for 40 years, on 5th February 1701[17] [DD/CC 112158; L.1701–1739, f. 5d; S1703, p. 182].

Matthew Irish, hosier, grant for 40 years, on 27th February 1706 [DD/CC 112158; L.1701–1739, f. 42d; A.1705–1725, f. 27d]; regrant on surr. for 40 years, on 9th July 1724 [L.1701–1739, p. 264; A.1705–1725, f. 205d; DD/CC 112162].

Martha Baron, widow, grant for 40 years, on 10th October 1743 [A.1743–1760, p. 41].

John Lafausille, grant on surr. [DD/CC 112122] for 40 years, on 10th December 1759 (fine 7*l*.) [DD/CC 112120; L.1740–1760, f. 590; A.1743–1760, p. 308; EB 1756–1762)DD/CC 110007), p. 168].

Ann Lafausille,[18] widow, grant on surr. for 40 years, on 3rd December 1776 (fine 7*l*. 7*s*.) [A.1761–1777, p. 375; EB 1771–1780 (DD/CC 110009), p. 200; L.1761–1777, p. 526; Docs. ADD/4118].

Ann Lafausille, widow, and her daughter Helen Lafausille, grant on surr. for 40 years (fine 36*l*.) on 30th September 1782[19] [A.1777–1792, p. 139; L.1777–1789 ff. 207, 209; DD/CC 112121; DD/CC 112123, Docs. ADD/4141].

Hon. David Anstruther, grant on surr. for 40 years, on 6th December 1792 (fine 5*l*. 10*s*. [L.1790–1807, f. 110; A.1777–1792, p. 360; DD/CC 112124; EB 1780–1798 (DD/CC 110011), p. 124; Docs. ADD/4200].

Charles Torriano,[20] grant on surr. for 40 years, on 15th October 1804 [DD/CC 110053; DD/CC 110054].

David Maunsell, grant by C. Torriano for 40 years, on 15th October 1804 [A.1792–1817, pp. 295, 337]; purchaser under the provisions of the Land Tax Redemption Acts [A.1792–1817, p. 295; L.1790–1807, f. 556; DD/CC 110011; Docs. ADD/4217].

Notes

1. L.1546–1565, f. 59.
2. See *Estates of Wells City Council* (Wells city records, ref. 381), plan 6.

3. See ibid, plan 5. This house was formerly known as 'Mountroy' – not to be confused with the house opposite in New street, 'Mountroy', used until recently as the judge's lodging.
4. Ibid, plan 5.
5. L.1571–1624, f. 132d.
6. Ibid, f. 166.
7. SRO, DD/TD, box 41, CB3.
8. See Appendix I.
9. This mistaken assumption, recorded on the 1:500 and 1:2,500 ordnance survey maps of Wells, has led to the naming of Mountery (sic) road.
10. W. Phelps, *The History and Antiquities of Somersetshire* (London 1836), ii, p. 15.
11. For this matter, see Cal. i, p. 241 (R.I, f. 202d); p. 242 (R.I, f. 203); pp. 463, 464 (R.III, ff. 324d, 325)
12. Ch. 507 (Cal. ii, p. 653); Cal. i, p. 469.
13. From E1408/9–E1438/9, the property is described by the escheator as *domus Richardi Horsford*, although Horsford's interest had long ceased.
14. Thomas Hagget was already dwelling in the house.
15. The premises are described as a tenement, with barton and garden.
16. Subtenant in June/July 1649, Edward Webb; the surveyor recommended an increase in the rent from 13s. 4d. to 3l.
17. At this date the premises were in the possession of a subtenant, Thomas Muttlebury.
18. Daughter of Martha Baron (see above).
19. The premises were then in the possession of a subtenant, Richard Chapple Whalley (DD/CC 112123).
20. Mr. Torriano had married Hester, daughter of Ann Lafausille (DD/TD box 41/3).

74
A Tenement on the North Side of Chamberlain Street

The description of this property in the leases made of it afford no clue to its location, and it is not shown on the map of Canon Grange. It was sold in 1826,[1] and is described in the deed of conveyance as a dwelling house with a small court adjacent, heretofore a garden. It yielded a rent of 10s. to the communar. It was held by the following tenants:

John Smyth, clerk, grant for three lives, on 2nd January 1552 [L.1546–1565, f. 62].
John Dane, notary [C1587/8].
Austeyn Bullman, pewterer, grant for three lives, on 1st October 1588

[L.1571–1624, f. 109d]; further grant for three lives, on 24th June 1599 [L.1571–1624, f. 165d; C1602/3].

Daniel Tuthill, mercer, grant for three lives, on 1st April 1614 [Ch. 820 (Cal. ii, p. 712); C1625/6].

Richard Allford, of Lyme, merchant (late Daniel Tuttell) [C1626/7; C1627/8].

Daniel Tuthill [C1634/5; C1636/7]; pretended an interest in June/July 1649, but produced no confirmatory evidence [S1649, p. 25²].

Thomas Starr, 'plumer'³, grant on surr. for 40 years, on 6th April 1689 [L.1681–1701, f. 99; A.1683–1704, f. 142; S1703, p. 191].

Thomas Millard, named as tenant in 1703 [S1703, p. 187⁴].

Mary Evans, widow, grant on surr. for 40 years, on 4th April 1717 [L.1701–1739, p. 118; A.1705–1725, f. 122d].

Hon. George Hamilton, grant on surr. for 40 years, on 12th January 1720 [A.1705–1725, f. 160d; L.1701–1739, p. 118] – The house being 'very ruinous and in decay' and the lessee 'being desireous to take the same down, and convert the premises into some other improvement . . .' covenanted 'that such alterations shall be without prejudice to the . . . dean and chapter, and that he will at the expiration of fourteen years of the . . . terme . . . renew the present lease, and pay one years purchase for the fine at such renewing, and so from time to time afterwards at the expiration of every fourteen years renew in like manner . . .'; further grant on surr. on 14th December 1736 [DD/CC 111780; A.1725–1744, f. 165d]; further grant on surr. for 40 years, on 1st October 1750 (fine 4*l.*) [EB 1745–1755 (DD/CC 110006), p. 147; DD/CC 111786; A.1743–1760, p. 135; L.1740–1760, f. 337⁵]; further grant on surr. for 40 years, on 2nd January 1762 (fine 4*l.*) [DD/CC 111850; DCR VIII, p. 34; L.1761–1777, p. 16; A.1761–1777, p. 36].

Zachary Baily, grant on surr. for 40 years, on 1st October 1776⁶ [L.1761–1777, f. 520; A.1761–1777, p. 373; DD/CC 111851; EB 1771–1780 (DD/CC 110009), p. 186].

Robert Tudway, grant on surr. for 40 years, on 3rd January 1791 (fine 4*l.*) [EB 1780–1798 (DD/CC 110010), p. 37; DD/CC 111852; L.1790–1807, ff. 34, 38; DD/CC 112131; Docs. ADD/4115, 4160, 4171].

William Melliar, purchaser for £42 under the acts relating to the redemption and sale of land tax, on 2nd May 1826 [A.1817–1832, p. 233; DD/CC 111796; cf. DCR XXXI, pp. 56, 62].

Notes

1. DD/CC 111796.
2. The surveyor recommended an improvement in the rent from 10s. to 1l. 13s. 4d.
3. Starr was paid 56l. 7s. 8d. for roofing the chapter house with lead (c.1690), (Cal. ii, p. 471); See also Cal. ii, p. 475: paid 36l. 15s. for leading the quire.
4. In this survey the property is described as 'in Chamberlain street on the north side, late Archibald Harper, once Ann Pope's', yielding a rent of 10s. 8d.; no grants to these persons can be found.
5. It is here noted that the lessee's undertaking to convert and improve the property had been fulfilled.
6. The lessee undertook to continue the covenant in the 1720 lease to the Hon. George Hamilton, now deceased.

75

Penniless Porch

This gate-tower, built by bishop Bekynton, was probably so called because it was a customary place for beggars to solicit alms of those who were going to the cathedral, not because alms were usually distributed there, as is sometimes said. It was one of the properties reserved to the dean and chapter at the time of the commutation of the capitular estates. From 5th October 1688[1] the gate and two chambers over it were regularly included in grants of 25, Market Place, and became part and parcel of property no. 26.[2] On 16th June 1848[3] this arrangement ceased, for on that date the two chambers were granted for 40 years in consideration of a fine of £11 to Edward Parfitt the tenant of the adjoining property no. 24[4] on the south. This lease stipulated that the lessee must repair the gate, but must not make any alteration thereto without the leave and consent of the dean and chapter.[5]

Notes

1. DD/CC 112338; L1624–1681, p. 615.
2. See above, Article 19.
3. DD/CC 112250; R.2, p. 207, Docs. ADD/4252.
4. See above, Article 17.
5. R.2, p. 205.

76

The Choristers' or Organist's House

This house, described in *Historia Major* as a 'fair dwelling'.[1] was newly built[2] for the choristers by bishop Ralph of Shrewsbury in c.1354. In April of that year the abbot of Glastonbury granted to the dean and chapter for building this house 40 loads of stone from the abbey's quarries at Doulting.[3] On 6th May 1459[4] bishop Bekynton issued a commission to M. Hugh Sugar and M. John Stokes enjoining them at his own expense to carry out the profanation and appointment of 'a portion of the churchyard . . . adjoining the wall of the house or dwelling of the choristers . . . to be walled in and enclosed for the enlargement of the said house and . . . for the use of the choristers".

J.H. Parker describes[5] the house as he saw it, in the middle of the 19th century: "It is one of the smaller houses of the fifteenth century, the plan of which was that of the letter T, the hall forming the top stroke and the rest of the house the stem, but the house has been almost entirely spoiled during the last [18th] century, vile additions having been made to it, encroaching on the small space originally left between the house and the [west] cloister, and destroying the outlines of the house. . . . The interior also is spoiled by modern partitions, now becoming more old-looking and more rotten than the original roof of the hall which remains . . . The singing school[6] and Organist's house are part of one design, and never ought to have been separated . . . [The doorways] which connected the house with the singing school have been blocked up, the porch under the school is concealed by a modern wall, and the two doorways opening into it are also blocked up."

The choristers probably ceased to live in the house in the time of queen Elizabeth I, when the school was united with the grammar school. The organist and master of the choristers certainly had the house as his official residence from early in the 17th century. In 1649 the surveyor for the Parliament found that it was in the occupation of "the widow Oker"; John Oker or Okeover was appointed organist in 1620, but it is not clear whether the widow Oker was the wife or the mother of the organist. The description in the survey is: "all that messuage or tenement commonly called the choristers' house, with a court and backe yard thereunto adioyneing, adioyneing in the east unto the cloysters. . . , in the south east unto the late bishopp's stables, in the north to the cathedrall churchyard and in the south west unto a house [16 Market place[7]] in the occupation of Alexander Jett gent. . .".[8]

During the tenure of the house by John Brown (organist 1663–1674) bishop Creyghton had apparently drawn the chapter's attention to the condition of the roof, for on 1st April 1671[9] the overseers of the houses were requested "to inspect the dilapidations of the choristers' house and inquire carefully who was competent to repair it, so that the roof might be put in order immediately, and the bishop might be fully satisfied." In C1695/6 the dean and chapter also accepted responsibility for the maintenance of the building, paying 7*l*. 13*s*. to the master of the choristers, Thomas Webb, towards its repair.[10] William Perkins, organist 1820–1859, seems to have had no doubt of the liability of the dean and chapter, for he submitted bills totalling £14. 17*s*. in respect of damage by fire. On 2nd January 1837[11] payment of these was authorized as soon as he had effected a fire insurance in a sum of £300 with the Sun office. Uncertainty still persisted as to liability for maintenance of the house. On 3rd January 1848[12] the chapter had before it a bill for repairs to the roof; the steward was asked to investigate, and to report whether in the past the chapter had usually paid such bills. There is no record of the steward's report.

Perkins's death on 11th November 1860 brought to a head the question of liability for the upkeep of the choristers' house. A surveyor was asked to assess how much the late organist's representatives would have had to pay in respect of dilapidations, had he been collated to the house. In other words the assessment was to be made in the same manner as for a canonical house; furthermore, it was resolved that Perkins's successor, Charles Williams Lavington, should be required to enter into an agreement to execute in future all such repairs as he would be liable to execute had he been collated to the house. Thus the intention was to treat the choristers' house as a canonical house, and the organist as a canon residentiary as far as repairs were concerned. Meanwhile John Henry Parker, the antiquary, sought a repairing lease, which was refused.[14] It appears that Perkins had granted a subtenancy to a Mr Teek, who was in occupation from 1851 to 1861.

On 2nd December 1862, the chapter ordered that the house be repaired at its own charges. It was evidently uninhabitable, and the chapter decided that Lavington should be put in possession of a suitable residence, and paid £15 annually, presumably as compensation for the rent he might have received by letting the choristers' house, as Perkins had done.[15] Eventually, Lavington was permitted to occupy the canonical house now 3, The Liberty.[16]

The chapter now ordered that all the buildings of the choristers' house, except the 'old hall' be pulled down under proper superintendence, and that measures be taken to prevent the 'old hall' falling into decay."[17] Consideration was also given to the possibility of erecting a new house with the same accommodation as the old, using the old materials in the new building, but this was not proceeded with.[18]

After further debate,[19] however, it was resolved to pull down the ruins of the 'old hall', and to put the gable end in a safe state for preservation.[20]

In a copy of J.H. Parker's *Architectural Antiquities of . . . Wells*, in Wells Museum library, there is a note on page 22 written by the Wells antiquarian, Thomas Serel: "The organist's house was destroyed, partly in 1869, and partly in 1870. The first work of destruction in 1869 was the selling of the lower part or stem of the T, and pulling it down. Many hundred loads of stone went to build a house in St Thomas street by Isaac Brown the cathedral mason, who had purchased the walls. The remaining part of the house being the hall on top of the T, fell down or rather the roof fell in on April 12 1870 between 5 and 6 in the afternoon. This fall was caused by the removal of the other part in 1869. Shame! Shame!"

Usually the organist and master of the choristers took possession of the house on appointment.[21] There are, however a few instances of specific grants or assignments:

John Broderip [1741–1771], assignment on 30th September 1741, for as long as he should hold office. [Cal ii, p. 538].
Robert Parry (1773–1781), assignment on 1st July 1773 [A.1761–1777, p. 229].
Dodd Perkins, grant on 1st July 1781 [A.1777–1792, p. 114].
William Perkins, assignment on 1st July 1820 [A.1817–1832, p. 62].

Notes

1. *Habitacionem pulchram pro choristis ecclesiae Wellensis*, SRS 39, p. 68.
2. *Mansum pro choristis do novo construxit*, Hist. Min, SRS 39, p. 55.
3. B.M. Arundel MS 2 14v; see L.S. Colchester and J.H. Harvey, 'Wells Cathedral', in *Archaeological Journal*, 131, p. 208, n. 57.
4. *Reg. Bekynton*, SRS 48, p. 318.
5. *The Architectural Antiquities of Wells* (Oxford and London, 1866), pp. 22ff., illustration, plate XXI, plan, plate XXII.

6. Over the west cloister.
7. See Article 17.
8. S1649, p. 1; the surveyor considered that the property was worth a rent of 20s.
9. SRS 72, p. 29.
10. Cal. ii, p. 476.
11. M.1831–1837, p. 167.
12. M.1837–1849, p. 332.
13. M.1860–1872, p. 55; on 4th March 1862 a letter from Lavington was read in chapter, the contents of which are not disclosed, ibid., p. 102.
14. Ibid, p. 119.
15. Ibid, p. 127; Teek had paid a rent of £15 a year.
16. See *CHW*, p. 26.
17. M.1860–1872, p. 213, 9th February 1865.
18. Ibid, p. 264.
19. Ibid, pp. 303, 304, 309, 314, 332, 341, 349, 354, 361; M.1873–1976, p. 25.
20. WCL, Fabric Order Book, 1821–1918, p. 59.
21. A biographical list of organists is given in *The Organs and Organists of Wells Cathedral* (Friends of Wells Cathedral, 1974), pp. 15–24.

77

A House in Sadler Street

This house appears to have stood on the site of 4, Sadler street, but all we know of it comes from the descriptions in charters and leases relating to the adjoining premises on the south,[1] in which reference is made to it. In a charter dated 7th April 1418,[2] it is described as 'a burgage of the *annuellarii* newly built and lately acquired by the dean and chapter from William Northlode for the use of the said *annuellarii*.'[3] By this time the chantry priests were in residence at their college on the Mountroy, so this house could not have been intended as supplementary accommodation to that afforded by the nearby Cristesham's inn;[4] like that *hospitium* after the departure of the *annuellarii*, it was evidently a property administered by the dean and chapter for the support and benefit of these priests.

This property is not shown on the map of Canon Grange, and there is no record of its having been disposed of. The following tenants can be traced:

Richard Dorfylde, tenant in April 1561 [L.1571–1624, f. 9].
Grace Thomas, widow, tenant in October 1633 [L.1624–1681, p. 197; cf. S1649, p. 8].

Rachel Thomas, tenant in January 1660 [DD/CC 112482].
Jacob Thomas [cf. DD/CC 112359; L.1701–1739, f. 17].
— Thomas, widow, tenant in April 1704 [DD/CC 112359; L.1701–1739, f. 17].
George Rush, saddler, tenant, in May 1721 [L.1701–1739, f. 196]; in March 1735 [DD/CC 112063].
John Bartlett, brazier, tenant in December 1750 [DD/CC 112507; L.1740–1760, f. 343; DD/CC 112069]; not in possession in February 1792 [DD/CC 112073].
Mr Fievez shown as occupant in January 1828 [SRO, DD/FS, box 27 (c/648); A.1817–1832, p. 334a]; continued in occupation until *c*.1850 –he may have been a subtenant.

Notes

1. Property no. 51, see above, Article 32.
2. Ch. 552 (Cal. ii, p. 662, abbr.).
3. Cf. Ch. 513 (Cal. ii, p. 654).
4. See above, Article 69.

78
A House on the North East of the Undercroft

W. Byrne's engraving (1802) based on a monochrome water-colour painting by T. Hearne, 'The East End of Wells Cathedral'[1] shows a small house with a south facing gable end lying between 'The Rib' and the undercroft of the chapter house. No reference to this house is to be found before the early years of the 17th century, at which time it appears to have been rebuilt, and possibly enlarged. In 1615[2] it is described as 'a certain old house', in F1619/20 as *domus nuper aedificata*, and in more, though somewhat confusing, detail in 1634:[3] 'a tenement or house or part of a building whereupon there is now a new house built, and . . . a plot of ground adjoining, lying . . . upon the church camery of the west[4] side next unto the canonicall howse[5] wherein sometime Dr. Rogers did dwell, and now Dr. Gerard Wood, archdeacon of Wells, inhabiteth, which said plot of ground extendeth and runneth in length north and south from the said old howse or new buildinge now or lately new built wholely unto the south doore next unto a chappell on the north side of the quier . . . inclusive, and in breadth east and west as now lieth and heretofore hath soe layen, within the distuance of two foote of the wall of the said Dr. Woode's canonicall howse unto the treasure howse[6] wall viz: unto the corner of the treasure howse next unto the said new erected howse and extending no farther than the corner of the east end of the casting howse and unto the wall adjoyning to the treasure howse on the south . . .' It would appear that this house lay on the south side of St Andrew street, more or less opposite the entrance to Vicars' Close, and that its curtilage consisted roughly of all the land between 'The Rib' and the undercroft, extending southward as far as the wall of the chapel of Corpus Christi. The 'south door on the north side of the quier', mentioned in this and succeeding deeds, must refer to the doorway, now blocked, formerly leading from the undercroft on the south. In 1897 the architect reported: 'On the South side [outside the undercroft] were found fragments of foundations (apparently mediaeval) & a concrete floor about level with that of the undercroft — remains of the small building whose roofline shows upon the Chapter house, & which was entered through the doorway now closed with modern walling put together with black mortar.'[7]

It is interesting to note that the casting house for lead for the roofs of the cathedral and for pipes and guttering adjoined the undercroft. Reference is made to it in an abortive grant to Augustine Benford, a vicar choral, on 3rd October 1634[8], in consideration of a fine of 12d., of 'a little howse or roome' 6 feet wide and 8 feet long 'adjoyning to the howse wheare the lead is usually cast'. Dr. Wood, dwelling in 'The Rib', opposed this grant, and he protested against the giving to Benford of permission to make a window in the room or shed, although the lease had not been sealed, declaring that such permission was contrary to the good of the fabric and 'scandalous to the church'. He was supported by the treasurer, Dr Robert Creyghton, who asserted that 'it is nott fitt the window should be made until the lease be sealed', while the chancellor, Dr. Young, consented to the window 'in case it be not against the good of the church, otherwise not.'[9] This contention smouldered on for six months, then on 1st April 1635 the chapter 'upon mature deliberation (after hearing many inconveniences showen by Dr Wood)' revoked the grant made to Benford in 1634, 'holding the same graunte to be unlawful'.[10] Unfortunately no record was made of the particulars of Dr Wood's objections, so we do not know what were the 'inconveniences' against which he protested.

It is not clear what eventually happened to this house. The leases record a continuous tenancy until near the end of the 18th century, and it was evidently standing when Hearne's painting was made.[11] But it seems that it was demolished after that, for a deed of collation to 'The Rib' of 8th November 1816[12] states that on the west side thereof (i.e., on the former curtilage of the 'old house newly built') lay an orchard and a garden. By June 1842[13] this orchard and garden had become 'part of the lawn or pleasure ground' attached to 'The Rib', for which the tenant of that house was charged by the dean and chapter a rent of £1. 2s. 8d. He also paid £1. 7s. 4d. annually for two store rooms, described as 'adjoining the entrance to the cathedral yard'[14]. If this entrance was that from St Andrew street, it would seem that the two store rooms may have been all that remained of the old house.

On 1st January 1903 it was brought to the notice of the chapter that the rent of £1. 2s. 8d. for the lawn or pleasure ground was being paid by the tenant of 'The Rib' to the Ecclesiastical Commissioners, who laid claim to the land on the west of the way from St Andrew street to the Camery and the Masons' Yard. On 11th February 1903[15] the chapter resolved to resist the Commissioners' claim, and to assign the pathway to 'The Rib'. Accordingly, on the west side of the entrance from the street to the pathway was set a post of Doulting stone, triangular in section, lettered on its west face 'D & C' and on its east face 'RIB'.[16] On 8th May 1903[17] an agreement was concluded between the dean and chapter and the tenant of 'The Rib'. (Henry Leighton Goudge), by which, in consideration of the dean and chapter making no claim upon him (i.e., for rent) in respect of the piece of grass 'which is called the Camera' lying between his garden and the chapter house (i.e., the undercroft), he acknowledged that the piece of grass in question was the property of the dean and chapter, although it was not fenced off from his ground, and further, he agreed to allow the chapter to use the gravel path separating his land from that of the dean and chapter, and to keep this path in repair as necessary.

Tenants of the old house newly built:

John Brint, sacrist [cf. A1608–1622, f. 106d; F1619/20–F1626/7].

John Attwell, notary public, grant at a rent of 6s. 8d., on 1st July 1615 [A.1608–1622, f. 106d; F1619/20–F1626/7]; the lessee to have 'so much ground allotted to him as shalbe allowed by the master of the fabric'.

Augustine Benford, vicar choral, grant on surr. for 40 years, on 20th March 1634 [Cal. ii, p. 406; L.1624–1681, p. 213]; regrant on 20th October 1635 [SRO, DD/SAS c/795; CH 33, p. 251].

Humphrey Marsh, sexton, grant for 40 years, on 20th March 1633 (Docs. V/17); in possession June/July 1649 [S1649, p. 13[18]; BB 1, p. 20a;[19] F1663/4–F1664/5]; regrant on surr. for 40 years, on 12th January 1661 (Docs. V/17).

Widow Marsh [F1667/8–F1669/70].
Jane Edmunds, daughter of Humphrey Marsh, [cf. L1681–1701, f. 148].
John Edmunds [F1676/7–F1677/8].
Widow (Jane) Edmunds, [F.1678/9–F1683/4; F1688/9].
Robert Warmall, grant for 40 years, on 6th November 1692 [BB 18, p. 1; A.1683–1704, f. 217; L.1681–1701, f. 148; Cal. ii, p. 472; Docs. V/32]; regrant on 1st August 1694 [SRO, DD/SAS, C/795, CH 33, p. 170]; the lessee undertook 'not to let or sell his estate or any part thereof, except to those who shall first put in sufficient security to the dean and chapter to keep the dean and chapter freely exonerated and discharged from all charge of such men, women, and children as may be onerous or troublesome to them and to the Liberty', also, not to 'keep in the house or ground any noisome cattle or swine or any horde or geese to the annoyance or disturbance of the church, nor build or make any privy or such noisome house' near to the cathedral or to the canonical house ['The Rib'].
Mary Warmall, widow, named as tenant in 1703 [S1703, p. 193]; grant on surr. for 40 years, on 4th January 1713 [L.1701–1739, f. 71d; Docs. V/38, 39].
Richard Cupper, apothecary, grant for 40 years sealed on 4th January 1714 [A.1705–1725, f. 88d].
Lawrence and Elizabeth Orchard, of East Coker, grant on surr. for 40 years at a rent of 6s. 8d. on 2nd October 1732 [L.1701–1739, p. 546; A.1735–1744, f. 101d; Docs. V/47, 48].
Thomas Hughes, grant on surr. for 40 years, on 26th April 1757 (fine 5l.) [EB 1756–1762 (DD/CC 110007), p. 57; L.1740–1760. f. 510 (dated 27th April); Docs. V/57; A.1743–1760, p. 248].
Thomas Moore, named as tenant before Alexander Watts [Reg. Willes (SRO, D/D/B 28,) f. 82].
Alexander Watts, shopkeeper, grantee of Thomas Hughes for 40 years, on 3rd June 1757 (fine 100l.)[Docs. V/58].
John Hicks, baker, grantee of Alexander Watts, under a mortgage for 50l., on 13th May 1764 [Docs. V/89 cf. ADD/4174[20]].

Tenant of the orchard and garden:

Dodd Perkins, organist, named as tenant in 1816 [Reg. Beadon (SRO, D/D/B 33), p. 122].

Notes

1. Hearne's original water-colour, now in the possession of the dean and chapter is reproduced in L.S. Colchester (ed) *Wells Cathedral: a history*, (Open Books, 1982). Plate 79.
2. A.1608–1622, f. 106d.
3. Cal. ii, p. 406.
4. *sic* for east; west was copied into descriptions for a long time, but is clearly an error.
5. See *CHW*, Article 15, p. 137.
6. The undercroft was formerly the treasury of the cathedral.
7. WCL Fabric Record Book, p. 32.
8. A.1622–1635, f. 163d.
9. Ibid, f. 164d.
10. Ibid, f. 173.
11. c.1780.
12. *Reg. Beadon*, SRO, D/D/B 33, p. 122.
13. M.1837–1842, p. 172.
14. Ibid, p. 172.
15. M.1893–1804, pp. 391, 394.
16. A stone of Draycott conglomerate, flat, not triangular, is still in position, appropriately lettered.
17. R.5, p. 187.
18. The surveyor recommended an improvement in the rent of 6s. 8d. to 5l.
19. It is stated that Marsh 'hath (at a deare rate) purchased the remaynder of an estate granted to Aug. Benford.'
20. The premises are here described as 'a house and garden called the North Camera.'

79

St Andrew's Acre, North Wootton

It is not known where this acre of meadow land in 'Woottonesmede' was situated, nor how it came into the possession of the dean and chapter, on whose behalf the master of the fabric received for it an annual rent of 2s. this was increased to 2s. 6d. in F1457/8, of which amount 2s. was remitted in F.1480/1, because the land had been ruined on account of drought (*quod periit per nudacionem aquarum*) in that year. Nothing more is heard of this land until its sale, on 10th March 1827[1] with Paulsgrove[2] for £212. 12s. 11d. to the then tenant, Edmund Broderip.

St Andrew's Acre was held by the following:

John Philpys of Wootton, and his son Robert, tenants for their lives [F1457/8; F1480/1 ?; F1492/3 ?].
Thomas Brows [F1500/1; F1505/6].
Stephen Bakehowse, *nuper tenuit* [F1549/50].
Thomasina Fitzjames, now the wife of William Stourton [F1549/50].
William Sturton [F1564/5; F1587/8–F1589/90].
Widow Sturton [1590/1–1594/5].
Mr. Morgan, of Worminster [F1619/20; F1620/1].
Widow Morgan, of Worminster [F1622/3; F1626/7].
M. Baskervile [F1663/4; F1664/5].
M'ri Morgan modo in tenura [F1667/8; F1668/9; F1670/1; F1672/3].
John Morgan [F1673/4–F1675/6; F1676/7–F1683/4].
Allen Lawe, bailiff of the Liberty, tenant from 29th September 1685, during the pleasure of the dean and chapter, rent 2*s*. 6*d*. [A.1683–1704, f. 95d (13th December 1686)].
Elizabeth Moore [cf. DD/CC 111795; DCR XXVIII, p. 29].
Joseph Bacon, tenant for two lives, by copy dated 25th February 1741 [EB 1771–1780 (DD/CC 110009), p. 137].
Charles Bacon, tenant in reversion, on 13th December 1774 (fine 15*l*.) [EB 1771–1780 (DD/CC 110009), p. 137; DCR XV, p. 54)].
Edmund Broderip, grant for three lives, on 3rd January 1814 (fine £18) [EB 1798–1815 (DD/CC 110011, n.p.; DCR XXVIII, p. 29)]; purchased the property on 10th March 1827 [DD/CC 112418; A1817–1832, p. 277].

Notes

1. DD/CC 112418; A.1817–1832, p. 277.
2. See above, Article 59, p. 157.

80

Longstring, Clay Furlong, and a Close near Balletrow

These three fields lay in Milton field, north of Monday's meadow. Longstring,[1] contained 2 acres and is described in 1526[2] as 'lying in a close called Hancock's close', and in 1661[3] as having Clay Furlong (1 acre) on the west. Longstring and Clay Furlong were usually let as a single tenement at a rent of 6s. 8d. and appear to have been united and enclosed from the open field, being described in 1661[3] as 'now lying altogether in one close'. The field thus formed is shown as no.88 on the 1930 1:2,500 ordnance survey map of Somerset.[4] On the same map the adjacent field no. 89 appears to be that generally designated 'a close near Balletrow'. The location of Balletrow[5] and the meaning of the name cannot be ascertained. In F1457/8 this close is described as 'an acre of formerly arable land between Boltrew and Mylton, now enclosed with a quickset hedge and ditched by M. John Reynolds'.[6]

The close near Balletrow, Clay Furlong and Longstring, having previously been thrown together in one piece, were exchanged on 28th September 1795[7] under the provisions of the Wells Enclosure Act of 33 George III for 6 acres of meadow or pasture on Queen's Sedgemoor.[8]

Tenants of Longstring with Clay Furlong:

Richard Pomerey [F.1500–1; F.1505–6] (Longstring).
Henry Proctor *alias* Butler [Ch. 744 (Cal. ii, p. 699)] (Longstring only).
Thomas Cornish, bishop of Tinos and Precentor, grant by Henry Proctor (Longstring only) for 80 years (Ch. 744 (Cal. ii, p. 699)].
Walter Stryde, burgess, assignee of Thomas Cornish (Longstring only) [Ch. 744 (Cal. ii, p. 699)].
William Butler [F.1549–50] (Longstring).
Robert Kirton [F.1564–5] (Longstring).
Peter Archer [F.1589–90] (Longstring).
Elizabeth Slatford, daughter of John Slatford of Oxford [cf. DD/CC 112589].
Thomas Heath, grant (Clay Furlong only) for three lives, on 8th July 1661 [DD/CC 112589; cf. Ch. 827 (Cal. ii, p. 713)].
Richard Thomas, grant on surr. for three lives sealed on 4th July 1685 [A.1683–1704, f. 7; S1703, p. 192[9]].
Matthew Baron, grant on surr. for three lives on 4th October 1711 [DD/CC 112553^A; L.1701–1739, f. 66d; A.1705–1725, f. 66].
John Moss, grant for three lives on 1st December 1761 [DD/CC 112556; L.1761–1777, p. 37; Docs. ADD/4092].
Matthew Phipps *alias* Tucker, gardener, grant on surr. for three lives, on 15th October 1762 (fine 3*l*.) [DD/CC 112557; EB 1762–1771 (DD/CC 110008), p. 10; L.1761–1777, f. 19; A.1761–1777, p. 52].
Matthew Tucker sen., gardener, grant for three lives, on 9th December 1780 (fine 6*l*. 15*s*. [DD/CC 112560; A.1777–1792, p. 99; L.1777–1789, f. 128; Docs. ADD/4132].

Edmund Brodrip proposed a surr. of the tenancy, legally vested in him, with a view to a new grant [Docs. ADD/4181b].

Charles Tudway, purchased the tenancy for 200*l.*, on 3rd January 1781 [SRO, DD/SAS (c/151), 3/4].

Robert Michell, purchased the tenancy from Charles Tudway for 280*l.* [SRO, DD/SAS (c/151), 3/4].

Tenants of the close near Balletrow:

John Reynold [F1457/8; F1480/1; F1492/3].

Thomas Cornysshe bishop of Tinos and precentor, grant for 60 years, on 20th September 1510 [Cal. ii, p. 223].

Roger Edgworth, grant for three lives, on 1st March 1552 [L.1546–1565, f. 63d].

William Butler [F1549/50].

Robert Kirton [F1564/5].

Peter Archer [F1584/5–F1587/8; F1589/90].

Thomas Zayer [C1587/8; C1602/3].

Thomas Sowthworth, grant for three lives, on 1st October 1612 [Docs. V/5; A1608–1622, f. 53].

Widow Archer [F1619/29; F1620/1; F1622/3; F1626/7].

William Brady, grant for three lives, on 2nd January 1623 (fine 6*l.* 13*s.* 4*d.*) [A.1622–1635, f. 15d; C1634/5; C1636/7;].

M. Sowthworth and John Wookie [C1625/6].

John Wookie [C1626/7; C1627/8].

Richard Stacy, grant for three lives, on 2nd April 1623 [S1649, p. 14]; in possession June/July 1649 [S1649, p. 14[10]]; further grant for three lives at a rent of 5*s.*, on 9th January 1660 [DD/CC 112586; L.1624–1681, p. 367]

M. Lane [F1663/4; F1664/5].

Martha Hole, widow, grant on surr. for three lives, on 8th December 1674 [L.1624–1681, p. 692].

Thomas Cooper, mercer, grant on surr. for three lives, on 30th October 1688 [DD/CC 112592; DD/CC 112593; A.1683–1704, f. 132d; L. 1681–1701, f. 92 S1703, p. 178].

Richard Hobbs[11] [cf. A.1705–1725, f. 66].

Matthew Baron, sen., grant for three lives sealed on 4th October 1711 [A1705–1725, f. 66].

Thomas Cowper, mercer, grant on surr. for three lives, on 3rd September 1719 [DD/CC 112554; A.1705–1725, f. 143d; L.1701–1739, f. 143].

James Melliar, property legally vested in [DD/CC 112558].

Matthew Phipps *alias* Tucker, sen., gardener, grant on surr. for three lives, on 2nd December 1772 (fine 7*l*.) [DD/CC 112559; A.1761–1777, p. 286; EB 1771–1780 (DD/CC 110009), p. 23; L.1761–1777, ff. 360, 364, Docs. ADD/4099c]

Charles Tudway, grant by Matthew Tucker on 11th November 1779 on purchase of tenancy for 189*l*. [SRO, DD/SAS (C/151), 2/3].

Matthew Tucker, grant for three lives, on 2nd December 1792 [cf. EB 1780–1798 (DD/CC 110010), p. 222].

Edmund Broderip, grant in consequence of enclosure, on 28th September 1795 [L.1790–1807, f. 198; Docs. ADD/4181].

Notes

1. South of Ash lane and east of Kennion road there were several fields called Longstring, doubtless division of a large field bearing that name. These fields are not to be confused with the Longstring with which we are here concerned.
2. Ch. 744 (Cal. ii, p. 699).
3. DD/CC 112589.
4. Sheet XLI 5.
5. Many different versions of this name are found: Boltrew (1458), Balitrow (1510), Ballytroe (1552), Balletro (1578), Bellatroe (1612), Ballitroe (1623), Ballytrowse (1700), Bella Trea (1795), and Battle Tree (1795).
6. John Reynold(s) was successively prebendary of Combe IV, and Ilton; and subdean.
7. SRO, DD/SAS (c/151) 2/4; L.1790–1807, f. 198; A.1792–1817, p. 83; EB 1780–1798 (DD/CC 110010), p. 232.
8. See below Article 87; see also Enclosure Award, SRO, Q Re 81, p. 69.
9. According to this survey, p. 174, the tenant of both Longstring and Clay Furlong was Matthew Baron, who may have been a subtenant or assignee – see the next entry.
10. The surveyor recommended an increase of rent from 5*s*. to 1*l*.
11. Probably a subtenant.

81

Lands at Dulcote

In return for his long service, bishop Robert (1136–1166) gave to Ralph Martre half a hide and half a virgate of land at Dulcote – amounting roughly to 65 acres. Subsequently, *c*.1150, the bishop assigned[1] this land to the cathedral towards an increase in the lights, on condition that Martre should continue to hold the land under the dean and chapter, paying annually as rent three wax candles, one of 3 pounds, and two of 2 pounds. At this time also the dean and chapter accordingly made a grant [2] of the land to Martre and his heirs, subject to the same payment.

This holding was augmented c.1300 by certain lands given to the cathedral for various pious purposes by Richard de Bamfeld, who had obtained them from Walter Magot.[3] This gift comprised 6½ acres of mowing grass in the meadows of Dulcote, 2 acres of arable land in Wells, and 16½ acres of arable land in one field, and 15½ acres of arable land in another field. It is not clear from the terms of this gift whether the two last mentioned lots of arable land were in Dulcote, or in Wells.

From the middle of the 16th century the lands of the dean and chapter at Dulcote were generally let as a single holding consisting of 14 acres of arable in Dulcote west field, 14 (or 13[4]) acres of arable in Dulcote east field, and 2½ acres of mowing grass in Dulcote mead, at an inclusive rent of 10s. The 2½ acres would appear to correspond to the 6½ acres in Dulcote meadows of Bamfeld's donation – save for the discrepancy in acreage, probably due to inaccurate measurement or estimation at the time the gift was made. It is tempting, therefore, to identify the arable land in the Dulcote west and east fields with the 16½ acres and 15½ acres in separate fields of Bamfeld's donation, allowing again for inaccuracy in measurement or estimation. This would mean that Bamfeld's lands were preserved, and granted, as a single holding.

The lands assigned to the dean and chapter by bishop Robert and held by Ralph Martre were not distinguished by individual names or acreages, consequently their history cannot be traced. Apart from Bamfeld's lands, however, the dean and chapter had other possessions in Dulcote, but it is not known how or when these were acquired:

One acre of arable land in the east field, described as *iuxta rivum ibidem pro*[5] *viam viz. semitam erga partē orientalē* was granted for 40 years on 4th July 1566[6] to John Smith; this land, in 1649, was in the tenure of George Saunders.[7]

Certain fields called Red hill, Torr hill, Torr field, and Scarlet Witheys,[8] are named with other fields in a grant made by the dean and chapter on 21st January 1762[9] to Richard Gould. Among these other fields was another in Dulcote, Kings hay end (1 acre), in respect of which, in 1793, land on Haymoor and Mendip was awarded to Charles William Taylor under the Wells Enclosure Act of 33 George III.[10] Kings hay end was granted to Taylor on 1st October 1800[11] in exchange for an acre of meadow land in East Wells field.

195

The following grants were made of Bamfeld's lands in Dulcote east and west fields (14 acres and 13/14 acres respective) and in Dulcote mead (2 acres):

John Deverells, grant for three lives at a rent of 10s., on 13th August 1545 (fine 33s. 4d.) [SB 1545, f. 33a].
John Nele and Frideswede Hardeman,[12] claimed a copyhold tenancy [S1570 f. 7[13]]
John Nele, paid rent 10s. for lands at Dulcote [C1662/3].
Alice Foster *alias* Gallington, paid rent 10s. for lands at Dulcote [C1625/6–C1627/8]; grant, on 2nd October 1634 [DD/CC 114068].
Joan Collywood, held for four lives by copy dated 9th May 1618 at a rent of 10s. [S1649, p. 19[14]; C1634/5; C1636/7].
James Cox, tenant in reversion for three lives for a fine of 10l. [cf. S1649, p. 20; DCR II, p. 48].
Sarah Alderley, tenant in reversion after James Cox for three lives [cf. S1649, p. 20].
Alice Rodney *alias* Cutler, tenant [EB 1698–1699 (DD/CC 110005), p. 28].
Matthew Cutler, tenant in reversion for two lives, on 6th October 1699 (fine 15l.) [EB 1698–1699 (DD/CC 110005), p. 28; S1703, p. 181].
Claver Morris, Doctor of Physic, grant for three lives, on 2nd October 1704 [DD/CC 111929; L.1701–1739, f. 20d]
Richard Gould, grant (with other properties) for three lives, on 21st January 1762 [DD/CC 111930; DD/CC 110028, p. 1; A.1761–1777, p. 38; L.1761–1777, f. 10; Docs. ADD/4102].

Notes

1. Cal. i, p. 53, ch. clxxvii.
2. Ibid, ch. clxxvi.
3. Ch. 145 (Cal. ii, p. 578).
4. Some grants specify 13 acres and others 14, probably due to an error in measurement.
5. ? an error for *prope*
6. Cf. S1570, f. 7d.
7. S1649, p. 23. No rent was noted by the surveyor, who made no recommendation as to improvement.
8. These fields are also shown on the Tudway estate map of Dulcote, SRO, DD/TD.
9. DD/CC 111930; L.1761–1777, f. 10. (Docs. ADD/4102a).
10. SRO, Enclosure Award, Q Re 81, p. 53; DD/CC 111932.
11. DD/CC 111932;L.1790–1807, f. 361; A.1792–1817, p. 180.

12. Two of the lives named in the grant to J. Deverells in 1545.
13. Doubtless owing to error, no mention is made in this survey of the 14 acres in the east field.
14. The surveyor recommended an improvement of the rent to 3*l*. 10*s*.

82

Three Corner Close

Before the 19th century, at the beginning of which a realignment of the turnpike road to Bristol was made, New street branched into two roads at its northern end. The western branch ran directly to Milton, becoming the 'old Bristol road'. The eastern branch joined College lane opposite Stoberry lodge, and ran thence to connect with Walcombe lane and with the turnpike road to Bristol. A short road joined College lane to the western branch, thus forming the base of a triangle having its apex at the bifurcation of New street.[1] Within this triangle of roads lay the field called three corner close.

The earliest reference to this field occurs in a city rent roll of 5 Henry VI (1426–1427):[2] *una* [sic] *splottum*[3] *inter* . . . *viam regiam ducentem versus Bristolem ex parte occidente, et viam regiam tendentem versus Bathoniam ex parte oriente.* In a grant of 1465[4] the close is described as being 'at the end of New street between the road from Bristowe on the west and the road from Bathe on the east'. The name first occurs in the survey of 1649:[5] 'one close of pasture commonly called the three cornered close . . . between the way leading towards the orchard called Sare orchard on the west side, and the close of meadow sometime belonging to the late college in Mountroy lane . . . on the east.'[6]

In 1801 the close, described as lately pasture, but then, a garden, was sold to Admiral Holloway under the provisions of the legislation of 38 and 39 George III for the redemption and purchase of land tax. Soon afterwards the close was destroyed by the construction of the realigned turnpike road already mentioned, the western and eastern boundary roads being closed.

It is not known how this field came into the possession of the dean and chapter. In the middle of the 15th century it was in the tenure of William and Margaret Chaundeler,[7] who, on 11th April 1463[8] granted it to Thomas Yong and his wife Alice. The rent of 11*s*. 8*d*. was received on behalf of the dean and chapter by the escheator, which suggestss that the close was donated to the cathedral to provide for an obit, perhaps that of William and Margaret Chaundeler. The tenants under the dean and chapter were:

Richard Rosemunde *alias* Martyn, grant for 60 years, on 26th September 1544 [E1558/9; E1559/60 E1560/1; E1564/5; E1584/5; E1586/7; E1587/8].

William Godwin [E1588/9–E1594/5].

Nicholas Weeks, grant on 2nd January 1598 [A.1571–1599, f. 113d; E1660/1].

George Paulett, of Gotthurst [*sc* Goathurst], sealing of grant decreed on 1st July 1609 [A.1608–1622, f. 23d].

Ezekiel Barkham [cf. DD/CC 112147; L.1624–1681, p. 343; E1633/4; S1649, p. 1^9].

Margaret Barkham, widow [cf. L.1624–1681, p. 343; DD/CC 112147].

Ezekiel Jett,[10] of the city of London, haberdasher, grant for 40 years, on 7th January 1660 [DD/CC 112147; L.1624–1681, p. 343; E1661/2].

Charles Penny, silversmith, trustee for the children of George Mattock, grant on surr. for 40 years, on 2nd October 1749 [DD/CC 112167; EB 1745–1755 (DD/CC 110006, p. 117; cf. E1668/9; E1670/1–E1672/3; E1695/6; E1698/9–E1735/6] regrant for 40 years, on 2nd October 1749 [A.1743–1760, p. 118; L.1740–1760, f. 300].

James Penny, silversmith, grant for 40 years on 2nd January 1760 [L.1740–1760, p. 300; EB1756–1762 (DD/CC 110007), p. 162; A.1743–1760, p. 295; Docs. V/59; L.1740–1760, f. 592; DD/CC 112135]; regrant on surr. for 40 years, on 12th December 1775 (fine 3*l.*) [EB 1771–1780 (DD/CC 110009), p. 180; A.1761–1777, p. 362; L.1761–1777, f. 508; Docs. ADD/4113].

Richard Gould, grant on surr. [Docs. V/67] for 40 years, on 20th February 1792 (fine 4*l*. 19*s.*) [EB 1780–1798 (DD/CC 110010), p. 81; DD/CC 110028, p. 17; DD/CC 112137, L.1790–1807, ff. 73, 79; A.1777–1792, p. 337; E.1790/1–E1798/9]

George Nickless, undertenant, [cf. Docs. V/90].

John Holloway, rear-admiral of the red, purchased on condition of payment of £42. 16*s*. 8*d*. under the acts of 38 and 39 George III, for the redemption and purchase of land tax, on 7th December 1801 [Docs. V/90; E1799–1800–E1801/2].

Notes

1. These roads appear clearly on a map of the bishop's manor (1827), DD/CC 7183.
2. DD/CC 111736 22/33.
3. *Splottum*, a piece of land (Dorset).
4. Winchester college MS 19415.
5. S1649, p. 1.
6. It is interesting to observe that the western boundary road is described as 'the way leading towards Sare orchard', not the road to (or from) Bristol. This is the first reference to Sare orchard in descriptions of the close; on Sare orchard, which at one time must have been an important locality, see *CHW*, pp. 50, 51.
7. William and Margaret Chaundeler were the parents of Thomas Chaundeler, Chancellor of Wells, dean of Hereford, and warden of New college Oxford.
8. Winchester college MS 19415.
9. The surveyor proposed an improvement in rent from 11*s*. 8*d*. to 18*s*. 6*d*.
10. He was the son of Alexander Jett, the Chapter Clerk.

83
A Piece of Waste Ground on the East Side of the New Works Gardens

In 1629 Valentine Powell sought a grant of a piece of waste ground measuring 20 feet by 12 feet 'lying at the head of New Works gardens, abutting westwards unto a garden in the tenure of Mr George Bull,[1] and eastwards to the pallace greene, and southward to the bishop's brewhouse.'[2] A grant made in 1687[3] gives different measurements: 16 feet broad from east to west at the south end, 24 feet broad from east to west at the north end, and 34 feet long from north to south. On this land, with the consent of the chapter one tenant, William Westley erected a stable.[4] It would appear that this piece of land was eventually joined with the garden on the west (property no. 28).

East of the waste ground, as the description of 1629 indicates, lay a plot of land belonging to the bishop; this formed part of a close called the Conygree. The Conygree is not shown on Simes's plan of 1735, but seems to have been part of the eastern portion of the present recreation ground. This plot of land was granted by the bishop for 21 years to Benjamin Andrews[5] on 24th February 1803,[6] and is described in that lease as being 28 perches in area, bounded on the north by a wall dividing it from the back mill stream running from the hatches out of the moat, on the east by the bishop's private road (now the west moat road) from the Palace to Chanter's meadow (part of the Park), on the south by the other part of the Conigree, and on the west by the garden[7] and a stable[8] lately belonging to Peter Layng.[9]

The piece of waste ground appears to be part of the site of the building designated 'Brush Factory' on the 1:500 (1886) ordnance survey map of Wells.

Tenants of the waste ground:

William Westley, grant for 40 years at a rent of 2s. 6d. on 1st October 1687 [DD/CC 112348; L.1681–1701, f. 77; A.1683–1704, f. 109]; the lessee undertook not to abuse or defile the public way leading to the New Works gardens from the Market Place, by any horse or beast he might keep in the stable (which he had been permitted to erect); and not to hinder any tenant of a house in the New Works from bringing ashes or other domestic rubbish on the void space near the stable reserved for that purpose, provided such rubbish was removed annually.[10] Regrant (with other properties) on surr. for 40 years on 5th February 1702 [DD/CC 112356; L.1701–1739, f. 2d; A.1683–1704, f. 310; S1703, p. 194].

Revd John Pope, chancellor of the diocese of Bath and Wells, grant (with other properties), for 40 years, on 1st July 1720 [DD/CC 112399; L.1701–1739, p. 167; A.1705–1725, f. 152].

Margaret Pope, widow, grant on surr. (with other properties) for 40 years, on 11th December 1734 [DD/CC 112409; L.1701–1739, p. 636; A.1725–1744, f. 138]; regrant on surr. for 40 years, on 14th December 1748 (fine 16l.). [L.1740–1760, f. 285; EB 1745–1755 (DD/CC 110006), p. 102].

Andrew Cross of Broomfield, Somerset, grant on surr. (with other properties) for 40 years, on 20th June 1763 (fine 16l.) [EB 1761–1771 (DD/CC 110008), p. 36; DD/CC 112273; L.1761–1777, f. 48].

George Layng, grant (with other properties) on surr. for 40 years, on 2nd January 1777 (fine 20l.) [EB 1771–1780 (DD/CC 110009), p. 209; DD/CC 112274; L.1761–1777, f. 534].

William Jeboult, of Taunton, organist, legal tenant in 1791 [DD/CC 112276].

Peter Layng, grant (with other properties), on surr. for 40 years, on 3rd January 1791 (fine 37l.) [EB 1780–1798 (DD/CC 110010), p. 79; DD/CC 112277; L.1790–1807, f. 35; A.1777–1792, p. 302].

Notes

1. Probably a subtenant of Nicholas Willowby, tenant of property no. 28, to which the garden mentioned pertained.
2. SB 1629–1637, p. 11.
3. DD/CC 112348.
4. See DD/CC 112348. William Westley was the Chapter Clerk.
5. Tenant of the garden adjoining on the west.
6. DD/CC 112239.
7. Property no.28.
8. Built on the waste ground by William Westley, see above, p. 199.
9. The lessee of properties nos. 28 and 30, see Articles 20 and 21 above.
10. From this, it appears that the waste ground served as a rubbish tip for the New Works houses.

84

A Messuage/House in Tucker Street

Richard, son of Richard le Touker, granted c.1290 to the dean and chapter a rent of 5s. to be paid 'out of his messuage in the street of the fullers', for distribution to the poor by the communar for the benefit of the soul of Roger de Cruk, canon and provost, on the day of Roger's anniversary.[1] This messuage is described as situated between the messuage of William the fuller and that lately belonging to Richard Horner, but these particulars do not allow of an exact identification. Payments of rent by the following tenants are recorded in the accounts:

John Gurdell [E1380/1(3s.); E1381/2 (6s. for two years); E1391/2 (3s.); E1397/8 (3s.); E1400/1 (3s.); E1402/3 (10s.)].
Henry Camel [F1390/1 (16d.)].

At the beginning of the 15th century the property appears to have come into the possession of the prior and convent of St John in Wells, who paid a rent of 16d. until the surrender of the priory in 1539. After this date the accounts of the master of the fabric continue to show receipts of 16d. rent until the beginning of the 18th century. Nothing is known of the eventual fate of this property; it is not enumerated among those belonging to Canon Grange at the beginning of the 19th century.

Note

1. Ch. 135 (Cal. ii, p. 575); Cal. i, p. 468.

85

Lands at Wookey Hole

This property consisted of fifteen scattered pieces of land,[1] comprising 14 acres of arable in one field, 13 acres of arable in another field with a great sheepfold, and 2½ acres of mowing grass – in all 29½ acres lying on the north west side of the village of Wookey Hole. Like their land in High Meads, West Horrington,[2] and certain of their lands at Dulcote,[3] the lands of the dean and chapter at Wookey Hole were originally owned by Walter Magot, who gave them to Richard de Bamfeld, canon and probably prebendary of Dinder, who in turn donated them to the cathedral as a part-provision for his obit.[4] The entire holding was exchanged in 1795 for a meadow on Knowle moor,[5] under the provisions of the Wells Enclosure act of 33 George III, and passed eventually into the hands of the Ecclesiastical Commissioners in 1866. The tenants under the dean and chapter were:

John de Ho, vicar choral, grant of the 29½ acres on 30th March 1294 at a yearly rent of 16s. towards the service of St Edmund's altar for four years, after which the lessee shall pay 18s. towards the service of St. Edmund's altar for four years, after which the lessee shall pay 18s. annually so long as he holds the land, and keeps the sheepfield in repair [Cal. i, p. 108].
Roger de Milton [cf. Cal. i, p. 449].
William de Luttleton and Walter de Coumptone, grant for their lives of the 29½ acres at a rent of 16s., on 25th January 1333 [Cal. i, p. 449; Ch. 267 (Cal. ii, p. 607)].
William Bultinge and John his son, claim to hold for three lives by copy dated 11th May 1533 at a rent of 10s. [S1570. f. 7; C1587/8]
Joanna Boulting [C1602/3].
John Boulting, tenant for three lives by copy dated 4th April 1626 [S1649, p. 20[6]; C1625/6; C1626/7; C1627/8] regrant for three lives, on 22nd October 1639 [DD/CC 114089; cf. S1649, p. 20; C1634/5, C1636/7].

Widow Boulting,[7] named as tenant in 1703 [S1703, p. 175].

John Boulting, joiner, grant on surr. for three lives, on 20th July 1722 [L.1701–1739, p. 220; DD/CC 112576].

Thomas Cooper, of Bristol, carrier, grant on surr. for three lives, on 25th August 1737 [DD/CC 112577; L.1701–1739, p. 722; A.1721–1744, f. 176d; Cal. ii, p. 533].

Sarah Cooper, widow, grant on surr. for three lives, on 2nd December 1741 [L.1740–1760, f. 81; DD/CC 112578].

William Taylor, grant[8] on surr. for three lives, on 7th November 1764 (fine 14*l.*) [EB 1762–1771 (DD/CC 110008), p. 81; DD/CC 112564; A.1761–1777, p. 117; L.1761–1777, f. 100].

Charles Wolfram Cornwall, Alexander Popham, and Isaac Schomberge, being lawfully seized of the premises, William Taylor having died, grant on surr. for three lives, on 1st October 1778 (fine 30*l.*) [EB 1771–1780 (DD/CC 110009), p. 252; L.1777–1789, ff. 34, 39; A.1777–1792, p. 21; DD/CC 112565; DD/CC 112566].

John Band, received 15 fields at Wookey Hole in exchange for land on Knowle moor containing 16 acres 1 rood, on 1st July 1796 [Enclosure Award, 1793, SRO, Q Re 81, p. 68; DD/CC 1781/6 no. 282; DD/CC 112568; A.1792–1817, p. 52; L.1790–1807, f. 235]; in legal possession and surr. on 1st September 1795 [DD/CC 112567].

Revd Herman Drewe, proposed a lease for three lives (fine £75), n.d. [Docs. ADD/4224]

Notes

1. For plan of the whole property (1795), see DD/CC 112572.
2. See above, Article 60.
3. See above, Article 81.
4. Ch. 145 (Cal. ii, p. 578)
5. See above, Article 64.
6. The surveyor recommended an improvement of the rent of 10*s.* to 10*l.* 10*s.*
7. cf. Docs. ADD/4073.
8. This grant contains a provision for the payment, on the death of one of the lives named, of his best goods or 3*l.* as heriot at the choice of the dean and chapter.

86

A Paddock on Pillmoor

Pillmoor lies on the west side of the hamlet of Launcherley, but the exact location of this paddock, containing 3 roods 38 perches, cannot be ascertained. One description gives its southern boundary as the Drove, doubtless the road shown on the south of the property on the plan made for the Ecclesiastical Commissioners in 1875.[2] This field came into the possession of the dean and chapter by an exchange made on 2nd May 1767.[3] It had been in the tenure of a surgeon, Benjamin Pulsford, who exchanged it and two tenements in Beggar street (the western prolongation of Chamberlain street) for a house on the site of 5, New street.[4] The owners of the paddock before Pulsford are not known. After the exchange it was regranted to Pulsford for three lives at a rent of 6s. 8d. on 2nd May 1767;[5] the tenants thereafter under the dean and chapter until the paddock was taken in hand by the Ecclesiastical Commissioners were:

William Pulsford, devisee under the will of Benjamin Pulsford [EB 1798–1815 (DD/CC 110010), p. 57].
Trustees (Zachary Bayley and Revd John Prowse) appointed under B. Pulsford's will claimed the tenancy by virtue of a copy dated 5th December 1786 [EB 1798–1815 (DD/CC 110010), p. 57.]; tenants in reversion for three lives, on 1st July 1799 (fine 14*l*.) [EB 1798–1815 (DD/CC 110010), p. 57; DCR XXIV, p. 57].
William Inman Walsh, grant for three lives at a rent of 2s. 2d. on 2nd April 1846; in occupation of a subtenant, Isaac Small, who claimed on 28th September 1842, to hold the freehold, because it had been purchased by his father nearly 30 years ago, or since; Small in any case sought a reversion to himself [DD/CC 111800].

Notes

1. DD/CC 111800.
2. Ch. C. file 51807 pt 2, p. 128a.

3. L.1761–1777, f. 196; EB 1762–1771 (DD/CC 110008, p. 242).
4. See above, Article 68.
5. DCR XI, p. 35; L.1761–1777, p. 176.

87

Land on (Queen's) Sedgemoor.

The fields called Longstring and Clay Furlong, with a close near Balletrow, were exchanged on 28th September 1795[1], under the provisions of the Wells Enclosure act of 33 George III,[2] for 6 acres of meadow or pasture on Queen's Sedgemoor. This land, measuring 462 feet in length and 192 feet in width at its southern end, was bounded[3] on the north by an old rhine against Harter's hill,[3] and on the south by the lane called Short Drove[4] near its junction with Bourton Bridge Drove. In redemption of land tax, this meadow was sold in March 1827 to George Rich for £78.[5] After the exchange the property was held under the dean and chapter by

Edmund Broderip, grant for three lives at a rent of 11s. 8d., on 3rd December 1795 [L.1790–1807, f. 206; A.1792–1817, p. 60; L.1790–1807, f. 198; DD/CC 112562; Docs. ADD/4181c].

Notes

1. See above, Article 80.
2. DD/CC 112561; A.1792–1817, p. 53.
3. L.1790–1807, f. 198.
4. Or Middle Drove (Docs. ADD/4181c).
5. DD/CC 112563, 112563a.

88

Various Parcels of Land

Among the possessions of the dean and chapter were certain parcels of land which were not numbered[1] among the properties of the manor of Canon Grange, and which are mentioned only infrequently or incidentally in the records. In most cases the descriptions are insufficient to allow of precise identification.

A rental compiled in the time of Charles II[2] includes among the properties of the manor 'one acre of meadow in Polesham meade lying north and south, abutting on the south side of a great withy tree there' – a landmark which has doubtless long disappeared. This land may have been part of the estate of Peter Orum, for a rental of 1522/3[3] records a payment of 2s. 8d. by Robert Bekham for an acre of pasture in Polesham mede. Other tenants under the dean and chapter were:

William Tarrye, grant on 20th November 1548 [S1570, f. 7]
Thomas Attwood jun., grant on 1st October 1588 [SB 1615–1617, n.p.; DD/CC 114066]
[William Baylye] sought a reversion for three lives in 1616 [SB 1615–1617, n.p.]
Thomas White, grant on 26th October 1643 [DD/CC 111740].
Mrs. White, named as tenant in Dr Healy's 'New Survey', c.1710 [DD/CC 111736].
Charles Baron, grant on surr. for three lives, on 13th November 1714 [L.1701–1739, f. 83].
Peter Davis, grant (with other properties) on surr. for three lives, on 9th July 1724 [L.1701–1739, p. 268].
It would appear that this land had passed out of the possession of the dean and chapter before 1800.

* * * * *

One of the smaller properties owned by the dean and chapter lay in the Wells east field, a close of two acres of meadow or pasture called Horsepool close, described in 1431[4] as 'one parcel lying near the horspole near the water there'. The horsepool in East Wells is not shown on Simes's plan, nor on the map of Canon Grange, nor on any ordnance survey map;[5] it seems to have been situated on the south side of the Bath road, and may have been fed by the Beryl stream. This conjecture is supported by the common description of Horsepool close as 'land on the south side of East Wells' – East Wells being the ancient name of St Thomas street and of its eastward prolongation, Bath road. In fact, a document of 1755[6] describes the close as 'situated at the upper end of East Wells above the horsepool, having on the north 'the king's highway leading from Wells towards London, commonly called the London way, right over against a place where sometime stood a cross called Fayre cross.' On the other hand, a survey of the bishop's manor made in 1685[7] refers to 'land . . . in Stoborow feilds abuttinge against the Horsepool in East Wells, the land being on the west thereof'. This suggests that the horsepool may have been situated on the north side of the Bath road. In the absence of more precise evidence, however, its situation and that of Horsepool close must remain uncertain; but it appears probable that the latter lay on the south side of Bath road. The following tenants can be traced:

Richard Orum.
Agnes, widow of Richard Orum.
Robert Pade and Alice his wife, grant by Agnes Orum for their lives at a rent of 8s., on 13th February 1431 [Ch. 596 (Cal. ii, p. 670)].
John Gyffard.
Robert Pade, grant for three lives by John Gyffard, on 20th February 1446 [Ch.623 (Cal. ii, p. 674)].
Peter Orum.
William Wyotte, grant by Peter Orum for three lives, on 25th December 1464 [Ch.671 (Cal. ii, p. 684)].
John Levett, smith [C1587/8].
Alice, Agnes, and Joan Levett, daughters of John Levett, grant for their lives at a rent of 5s., on 31st March 1579 [L.1571–1624, f. 48d].
Joan Levett [C1602/3].
Richard Bourne [C1625/6; C1626/7; C1627/8].
Michael Hunt [C1634/5; C1636/7].
John Prickman, of the city of London, merchant, grant for 40 years at a rent of 5s., on 1st April 1630 (fine 5l.) [L.1624–1681, p. 67].
Stephen Joyce.
Joan Joyce, grant on 3rd July 1741 [DD/CC 111979a].

Margaret Richards.

Joan Joyce, grant by Margaret Richards for 99 years, on 9th August 1755 (fine 27*l*.) [DD/CC 111979a].

Clement Tudway, grant[8] on surr. for three lives at a rent of 1*s*., on 2nd December 1800 [L.1790–1807, f. 370; DD/CC 111933]; surr. [DD/CC 111934] for use by the dean and chapter during the life of John Paine Tudway.

Trustees for John Paine Tudway (Revd Edward Foster, and Revd Richard Thomas Whalley) grant on surr. on 7th December 1815 [EB 1798–1815 (DD/CC 110011) n.p.; DD/CC 111934].

* * * * *

We turn now to two acres of pasture 'lying next to the field called Stowebarrowefeld [Stoberry field]', as the field is described in a lease of 1580[9]. In 1649[10] it is described as 'in the south side of Stowburrough field', and in 1661[11] as 'two acres more or less of meadow or pasture situated against Walcombe field on the east side of Trapp gate.' On an estate map of Walcombe dated 1748[12] there is a plot of land (acreage not stated) marked 'Dean and Chapter', lying north of the road running eastward from Walcombe hamlet. There is nothing to identify this land with the two-acre pasture; nor is anything known of Trapp gate.

In 1732 the two-acre pasture was exchanged for Paulsgrove.[13] The tenants of the two-acre pasture under the dean and chapter were:

Dr. [Philip] Bisse, grant on 1st October 1580 [A.1571–1599, f. 15; C1587/8; C1602/3].

Samuel Bisse [cf. C1625/6].

Gerard Woodd, archdeacon of Wells, paid 6*s*. 8*d*. rent [C1625/6; C1626/7; C1627/8; C1634/5; C1636/7; cf. DCR I, p. 6].

Thomas Maycock, grant for three lives at a rent of 6*s*. 8*d*., on 3rd January 1618 [Ch. 821 (Cal. ii, p. 712); A.1608–1622, f. 143; S1649, p. 17[14]].

Margaret Trym, widow, grant for three lives at a rent of 6*s*. 8*d*., on 8th April 1661 [DD/CC 112587].

Thomas White [L.1701–1739, p. 268].

Mrs. White, named as tenant in 1703 [S1703, f. 195].

Charles Baron, sen., grant on surr. for three lives, on 13th November, 1714 [L.1701–1739, f. 83].

John Paine, jun., assignee for three lives under an exchange for Paulsgrove, on 29th September 1732 [DD/CC 112594; DD/CC 112410].

* * * * *

Another small unidentifiable piece of pasture, in area about one rood, lay in Chamberlain street. It was called Reck's close, or Recke close. In a rental of the time of Charles II[15] we find the entry: 'a garden (½ acre) . . . once called Reke close . . . not known who now holds', but in his 'New Survey' Dr. Richard Healy makes no mention of this land, either as pasture or a garden, suggesting that the dean and chapter had disposed of it before *c*.1710. The following tenants are recorded:

Thomas Zayer, paid rent 4*s*. [E1558/9–E1560/1; E1584/5; E1586/7–E1594/5; E1660/1].
Humphrey Palmer [E1633/4].
Bartholomew Cox [E1660/1] claimed to hold in 1649, but produced no confirmatory evidence [S1649, p. 18[16]].
Ann Pope [E1660/1; E1668/9; E1670/1].

Notes

1. Properties numbered 82, 83, 87, 88, 89, 90, and 91 cannot be traced; some of these numbers may have been allocated to lands dealt with in this article.
2. DD/CC 111740.
3. Docs. VI/12.
4. Ch. 596 (Cal. ii, p. 670, abbr.).
5. This horsepool must not be confused with the horsepool depicted on Simes's plan and on the map of Canon Grange, lying between the south cloister and the Palace gate, which has now been drained.
6. DD/CC 111979a.
7. SRO, DD/CB 36 (acc. c/1432).
8. Horsepool close had been purchased by Clement Tudway, and had recently been acquired by the dean and chapter by exchange with Kings hay end at Dulcote, cf. L.1790–1807, f. 361; A.1792–1817, p. 180.
9. A.1571–1599, f. 15.
10. S1649, p. 17.
11. DD/CC 112587.
12. DD/WM 1/419: 'A Survey of Walcombe and Pen . . . part of the manor of Emborow belonging to John Hippesley Cox', taken by William Burnet 1748.
13. DD/CC 112594; see Article 59.

14. The surveyor recommended an improvement in the rent from 6s. 8d. to 2l. 13s. 4d.
15. DD/CC 111740.
16. The surveyor proposed an improvement in the rent of from 4s. to 6s. 8d.

APPENDIX I

The 'New Works of Bishop Bekynton

The houses, 3–25, Market Place, were built by Bekynton at this own expense[1] on ground on the north side of the market place. This ground was 243 feet long and 36 feet wide, and encroached northward upon the cathedral churchyard 24 feet 8 inches. Other houses were built by the bishop upon ground on the west of the churchyard alongside Sadler street; this ground was 89 feet long, and varied in width from 30 feet at the north end to 37 feet at the south end; it also encroached eastward upon the churchyard 23 feet 3 inches at the north end, and 18 feet at the south end.[2] 16, Market Place (property no. 24)[3] is also described[4] as 'a tenement in New Works', indicating that it was believed that Bekynton's scheme included the east side of the market place.

The ground on the north of the market place and that on the west of the churchyard was the property of the see, and the history of the two plots is not easy to trace; in attempting to do so, it will be convenient to deal with them together, although we are here concerned only with that on the north of the market place. The earliest reference to these grounds occurs in a licence in mortmain granted on 26th November 1423[5] to the dean and chapter to acquire for pious purposes from bishop Nicholas Bubwith certain lands and rents to the value of 40 marks. The pious purposes are not specified, but it is likely that they related to the foundation of Bubwith's chantries at the altar of St Saviour on the north side of the nave of the cathedral, particularly as another licence in mortmain, granted on the same day, authorized the dean and chapter to accept from the bishop, and to appropriate, the church of Buckland Abbas,[6] which the Chantry Commissioners, in their survey of 1548, recorded as one of the endowments of these chantries.[7] It would also seem that the lands mentioned in the licence of 1423 included the two plots north of the market place and west of the churchyard, for 28th August 1432[8] a commission was set up to enquire whether the king (Henry VI) would be prejudiced by the authorization of a grant to the dean and chapter of the two plots, in part satisfaction of the lands and rents worth 40 marks, for the acquisition of which letters patent (the licence of 1423) had recently been issued. The commission found in favour of the dean and chapter, and on 21st June 1453,[9] licence was granted to two feoffees, precentor Thomas Boleyn and John Trevenaunt, canon and prebendary of Combe XII, empowering them to alienate in mortmain to the dean and chapter the two plots 'in support of certain charges and works of piety for the safety of the soul of Nicholas late bishop of Bath and Wells, and the souls of his parents and benefactors.'

It is curious that despite the letters patent of 1423, there is not evidence of any grant by Bubwith to the dean and chapter of the two plots. He died on 17th October 1424, and his will, dated 5th October in that year, referred to 'the chapel which I caused to be made (in the cathedral church) for the chantries of certain chaplains . . . to celebrate divine services for ever there for my soul and the souls of my parents and benefactors . . .'[10] From this it is evident that his chapel was completed before his death, and its services presumably established. The will makes no bequest of the two plots to the dean and chapter, nor does that body appear to have taken any steps to assume ownership of the land. Consequently it remained in the possession of the see. Why did Bubwith not carry out his clear intention, and why was the dean and chapter slow to prompt him to do so ? In the absence of definite evidence it is possible only to hazard a guess. Possibly the dean and chapter had intimated that it did not wish to take possession of the two plots immediately, because either it had no plans for using them forthwith for the benefit of the chantries, or because these seemed sufficiently endowed.

The report of the commissioners in 1543 sets out the endowments of Bubwith's chantries: 'Redy money to be paide by the dean and chapiture as well of the issues frutes and proffectes of the parsonages of Newton and Buckland appropried to the same deane and chapiture, as also of the issues and revenues of the manor of Bickenaller . . .'[11] On 20th March 1427[12] the dean and chapter was empowered to acquire in mortmain the manor of Bicknoller as part satisfaction, to the extent of 10*l*. annually, of the licence granted in 1423 for the acquisition of lands and rents to the yearly value of 40 marks. No licence in mortmain nor grant to the dean and chapter can be traced in respect of the church of Newton (Placey)[13] The chapter may well have judged that these endowments were adequate to secure the annual income of 106*s*. 8*d*. required to pay the stipends of the four chantry priests and to meet such other expenses of the chantries without whatever revenue might accrue from the two plots.

John Stafford followed Bubwith as bishop in 1424, and on his translation to Canterbury in 1443 was succeeded by Thomas Bekynton. Bekynton would naturally have an interest in the two plots, since they had originally been see property, and may have made enquiry about them. He would learn that the land had been designated by Bubwith as a part endowment for his chantries, but that it had never been conveyed to the dean and chapter for this purpose. In order to set matters right, Boleyn and Trevenaunt were nominated as feoffees either by the chapter or by Bekynton, and on 21st September 1451[14] they secured the requisite licence in mortmain to alienate the two plots 'in support of certain charges and works of piety for the safety of the soul of Nicholas (Bubwith) and the souls of his parents and benefactors'.

It now only remained to make good the title of the feoffees, and this Bekynton did on 27th September 1451[15] by making a grant to them of the two plots, in which reference was omitted to the support of works of piety for the benefit of Bubwith's soul. As if to encourage some action, Bekynton empowered the feoffees to enclose the plots and build upon them; further, that part of the land which encroached upon the churchyard was 'by sufficient authority and for good causes appointed for profane uses'. At the request of Boleyn and Trevenaunt this grant was inspected and confirmed at Westminster on 5th December 1451.[16] Soon it began to look as if progress was being made. On 28th August 1452[17], as we have seen, a commission was appointed to enquire whether it would be to the king's prejudice to grant a licence to the feoffees empowering them to convey the two plots to the dean and chapter, and on 21st July 1453[18] licence was issued to them to alienate in mortmain to the dean and chapter these pieces of land pursuant to the licence grant in 1423.

From an indenture dated 23rd June 1459[19] it appears that the feoffees did in fact so convey the land, although there is no record of the grant. The indenture states that the land on the north side of the market place had been 'enclosed with stone walls and built upon with divers costly buildings or messuages erected at no small expense to the bishop'.

A few months before this, on 8th January,[20] Bekynton took a bond of the dean and chapter in a sum of 400*l.*, apparently (though the purpose is not stated) that they would observe all the provisions relating to his chantry. The altar of this chantry, in a chapel erected by Bekynton on the south side of the quire in the cathedral, was dedicated by him on 13th January 1452, when he celebrated the first mass.[21] He must have received very speedy and satisfactory assurance, or have felt that it was unnecessary to exact the bond of 400*l.*, for two days later he cancelled it,[20] on two conditions: firstly, that the dean and chapter fulfil all statutes and ordinances to be made and sealed by him and all charges to be imposed, concerning his chantry; and secondly, that after acquiring an estate by grant or demise of Thomas Boleyn (now left the sole feoffee by the recent death of Trevenaunt) in certain lands and tenements next to the churchyard, newly built and to be built by the bishop, the dean and chapter shall, when required, convey such lands and tenements to him, his heirs or assignees, for ever.

Nothing more is heard of the two plots as an endowment for Bubwith's chantries. In putting in order the business relating to them it seems that Bekynton, inadvertently or by design, had set aside or circumvented Bubwith's intentions. It is generally believed that Bekynton had endowed his chantry with the revenues accruing from the houses in his 'New Works'[22] but there is no extant evidence to support this belief. The houses passed into the possession of the dean and chapter, and were not reclaimed by Bekynton or by his heirs. The rents of the houses, as received, were credited to the common fund; there is nothing to show that initially they were applied for the benefit of the chantry. We do not know when building started on the sites; it probably began after the feoffees had received the grant of 1451 authorising them to enclose and build upon the two plots. In the year of account 1470/1 the communar recorded the receipt of 18*l*. 16*s*. 8*d*. being the total annual income from fifteen new houses built at his own charges by bishop Bekynton.

In his *Itinerary*[23] John Leland describes the buildings erected on the north side of the market place as they appeared in the 16th century: 'There be xii right exceeding fair houses all uniforme of stone high and fair windoid'. Each house had a bay window of three stories with mullioned windows of seven lights each and an embattled parapet.[24] Leland also states that Bekynton was 'mindid yf he had lyvid lengger to have buildid other xii (houses) on the south side of the market stade . . .'

On 7th January 1625 the chapter decreed, among other things, that 'for every house in the New Workes the tenant for the time being or his assigne shal beare a twelve parte of the charge of the greate goutes in the camery and under the cloyster until it come to the first tenement at the east end.'[25] One of Bekynton's great benefactions to the city of Wells was the gift of a supply of water from St Andrew's well.[26] The water ran in lead pipes 12 inches in circumference from a conduit in the grounds of the Palace, near the well, beneath the camery and the cloisters, and beneath the new houses,[27] which were supplied from the pipes,[28] for the cost of maintaining which the tenants were accordingly made responsible.[29]

When Bekynton made his grant to the feoffees in 1451, the churchyard was bounded on the south and west sides by a crenellated stone wall built under licence from king Edward I granted in 1286.[30] Dr R.D. Reid suggests that 'building probably took place simultaneously on both sides of (this) great wall'.[31] He doubts that the buildings on both sides were subsequently joined 'by knocking holes in the wall'. It is evident, however, from leases and plans that each tenement fronted on to the market place, and backed on to the churchyard; we must assume, therefore, that at an early date in the case of each tenement, the buildings in front of and behind the wall were united to create a single house. The proximity of the backs of the houses to the churchyard explains certain special covenants in leases, and regulations made from time to time by the chapter, designed to obviate nuisances and improprieties.

Thus, in 1541[32] a lease was granted on condition that the tenant should not 'make any stable, nor keep any beast, i.e., horse mare, gelding, rother[33] beast, or any unclean beast, nor bring any hay within the precincts of (his) tenement for feeding and nutriment of any such beast, nor make any waste in or upon the said tenement . . .'

In 1680[34] the chapter decreed that 'every person who liveth in any house bordering upon the churchyard and hath a doore opening into it, shall pay or cause to be paid to the dean and chapter or to the master of the fabric . . . two shillings yearly or their doores into the churchyard to be shut up . . .'; later the fee was increased to three shillings. A warning was given in 1725[35] to the occupiers of houses having doors into the great churchyard . . . that if they suffer any coal, ashes, grains or rubbish from their houses to be placed in the . . . churchyard, their doors will be stopped up'. The erection of railings at the rear of the tenements was apparently not disallowed; in March 1726[36] leave was given to tenants and occupants 'having doors into the churchyard and rails opposite their doors . . . to move their rails out to the trees planted and the gravel walk lately made before their doors;' it was stipulated that the rails must be uniform with those erected by Mr Chancellor Pope,[37] and an additional 1s. was required from each house for the ground added by this means to each tenement.[38] In 1799[39] it was again emphasized that rails must be neat, regular, and uniform, and approved by the chapter; and at the same time occupants were forbidden to beat or brush carpets,[40] to dry clothes,[41] to wash barrels, to throw out ashes or other rubbish, or to drive cattle, wheelbarrows, or any other carriages in or through the churchyard. In a lease made in December 1840[42] these conditions were modified: hay, straw, wood, stone, tile and lime might if necessary be brought into the churchyard if required for repairs, and unavoidable rubbish might be removed, but tenants were forbidden to keep poultry or to allow poultry access to the churchyard, or to cause any nuisance or trespass they must keep the courts behind their houses in a decent and neat manner, befitting consecrated ground. Finally a lease granted in 1843[43] prohibited the use of the premises for a hotel, inn, or tavern, and the use of any rooms as a Post Office, Excise office, auctioneer's sale room, or for any trade or business whatsoever.

Every lease of one of the New Works houses made the tenant proportionately responsible for the cost of maintaining the pipes which carried water from St Andrew's well.[44]

In the articles dealing with individiual houses in the New Works,[45] the modern numberings are given; but traditionally the houses were always numbered and specified in leases, from east and west. Thus property no.48 (Article 30; 3, Market Place), was 'the first house from the west end' (of the New Works). In this system of enumeration 'the sixth house from the west' was followed by 'the sixth house from the east', and so on to 'the first house from the east'. The third house from the west is sometimes designated, the tenth from the east.

In the case of houses built on so confined an area as Bekynton's New Works, lack of a garden was a disadvantage not adequately compensated for by encroachment upon the churchyard. This deficiency was supplied by the allotment to each house of one twelfth of an acre of ground situated on the south side of the lane known as Town Hall Buildings. These gardens, designated on Simes's plan of 1735, as 'Garden Works', lay between the lane and the present recreation ground; the premises of Clares Carlton Ltd now stand partly on the site. On some of the gardens, stables coach or gig houses and other buildings were erected by tenants or undertenants; but when a tenant named Traunt(er) built a stable there, he was ordered in October 1684 to take down 'the house which he hath built ... to mak a stable there, and which he doth mak a stable of, contrary to the covenant in his lease, within a month next ensuing, upon the paine of being sued for breach of covenant'[46].

Notes

1. See C1470/1.
2. For these measurements, see Cal. i, p. 435 (R.III, f. 259).

3. See Article 17.
4. Docs. V/7 (1630).
5. *Cal. Pat. Rolls*, 1422–1429, p. 168.
6. Ibid; Cal.i, p. 405.
7. *SRS* 2, p. 160.
8. *Cal. Pat. Rolls*, 1440–1452, p. 580.
9. *Cal. Pat. Rolls*, 1452–1461, p. 112.
10. *Register of Henry Chichele*, ed. E.F. Jacob (Oxford, and Canterbury & York Society, 1937) ii, 298–9. See also J.H. Parker, op. cit., p. 45.
11. *SRS* 2, p. 160.
12. *Cal. Pat. Rolls*, 1422–1429, p. 396.
13. North Newton, in the parish of North Petherton.
14. *Cal. Pat. Rolls*, 1452–1461, p. 112.
15. Cal. i, p. 435 (R.III, f. 259).
16. Ibid.
17. *Cal. Pat. Rolls*, 1452–1461, p. 112; see also, *Cal. Pat. Rolls*, 1446–1452, p. 580.
18. *Cal. Pat. Rolls*, 1422–1429, p. 168.
19. Reg. Bekynton, *SRS* 49, p. 322.
20. Cal. i, pp. 466–467.
21. *SRS* 49, p. 175, no. 630.
22. See A.F. Judd, *The Life of Thomas Bekynton* (Chichester, 1961), p. 159.
23. SNH&A. Soc. XXXIII, p. 72.
24. William Worcestre, *Itineraries*, ed. J.H. Harvey (Oxford Medieval Texts, 1969), 294–5. See also *SRS* 49, p. xxxviii.
25. Cal. ii, p. 383.
26. Cal. ii, p. 433; *SRS* 49, p. 170, no. 598.
27. See R.D. Reid, 'The New Works at Wells' in WNH&A.Soc., *Report*, 1930, pp. 27ff.
28. Cf. Cal. ii, p. 452. Warwick Rodwell, *Wells Cathedral: Excavations & Discoveries*, (Friends of Wells Cathedral), 2nd rev. ed. 1980, 14–16.
29. On 23rd June 1459, Bekynton granted licence to the dean and chapter to make at his expense two 'gutters or subterranean passages and to repair the pipes under the pavement of the market place', *SRS* 49, p. 321, no. 1220.
    At a court baron held on 20th October 1666 tenants were fined 3*d.* each for defaulting in scouring and mending 'the mayne gowte that runes through their howeses (Docs. ADD/4024.
30. Cal. i, p. 532.
31. Op. cit., p. 26.
32. L.1535–1545, f. 6.
33. A rother beast was one of bovine kind.
34. Cal. ii, p. 80.
35. Cal. ii, p. 513.
36. Cal. ii, p. 513, and A.1725–1744, f. 4.
37. See above, Articles 21 and 20.
38. Cf. A.1792–1817, p. 200.
39. Ibid, p. 149.
40. For action in connection with an infringement see M.1860–1872, pp. 77, 80.
41. Cf. L.1790–1807, p. 391 (1st April 1801).
42. R.1, p. 309.

43. R.2, p. 7; cf. ibid, p. 207; See Article 19, p. 60, and Article 25, p. 75.
44. See Cal. ii, p. 383.
45. A provisional list of tenants and/or occupants, with many gaps, is provided by Dr R.D. Reid, op. cit., pp. 33–34.
46. A.1683–1704, f. 42d; Cal. ii, p. 455.

APPENDIX II

'The Cedars'

Early in the 13th Century, on the site in The Liberty which lies between 11, The Liberty and College road, on the eastern part of which now stands the mansion called The Cedars, stood three houses. Midmost of these was a house and croft belonging to Reginald de Waltham, who granted it to Adam Lock, the mason to whose designs the nave, north porch, transepts and quire of the cathedral were probably erected.[1] On Lock's death in 1229 his son Thomas inherited both the house and croft, and half an acre of land near Stoberry.[2] In September 1229, with the concurrence of his mother Agnes and his father's executors, Thomas granted the house and croft, and the half acre of land to Roger de Chuyton, canon and chaplain to bishop Jocelin at annual chief rents of 12d. each to John de Palton (Paulton) and Henry de Waltham.[3] The latter, into whose hands the joint ownership of the property had now passed, may have been a son or other relation of Reginald de Waltham. Not long after this last transaction it appears that Henry de Waltham died, for his widow Katherine made similar grant to Roger de Chuyton of the house and croft and the half acre of land, these properties having fallen to her as her dower.[4] This grant was in the nature of a confirmation of the earlier grant; it had the effect of a quitclaim.

Finally, Chuyton granted the house and the whole curtilage, late of Reginald de Waltham, to St. Andrew and the chancellor of Wells,[5] subject to chief rents of 12d. each to John de Palton and Henry de Waltham, and their heirs, and to other charges for the better observance of his (Roger's) obit. The premises were to be conferred upon the schoolmaster for the time being, on condition that on every school day, before the recess, all the scholars should pray for the souls of Roger, his parents and benefactors.[6]

Against the copy of this grant entered in *Liber Albus I*, two marginal notes have been made. The first, in a later hand, seeks to identify Reginald de Waltham's house and croft: 'Note, that this house is now converted into a college for chantry chaplains (*pro mansis annuellariorum capellanorum*[7])'. The college to which this note refers was the college of St Anne and St Catherine, built to accommodate chantry priests[8] who officiated at altars in the cathedral, and founded in pursuance of the will of bishop Ralph Erghum, who died on 10th April 1400.[9] About 1402 the school was transferred to a house near the Tor gate.[10] These were only temporary quarters, from which the school was again moved in 1410, and it can hardly be doubted that the move away from the Mountroy was necessitated by the plan to build the college there; either Waltham's house was due for demolition in order to clear the site or, as the marginal note suggests, it was intended to incorporate it into the new building.

The second marginal note, in a 16th century hand, purports to correct the first: 'No, but (this house) is within the bounds (*infra septum*) of the house in which chancellor Fitzjames now lives'. The later annotator is right, in that the school was moved from its temporary accommodation near the Tor gate to an outbuilding on the north side of the canonical house to which Fitzjames was later collated;[11] but he seems to have confused the two school houses, or to have been unaware that originally the school house was on the site of the chantry college.

Dr Sellers pictures the new chantry college as 'a large dwelling house in which fourteen, and later eighteen chaplains could each have a chamber (*camera*) of his own. It would also have its parlour, dining hall, and kitchen premises'.[12]

The existence of the college was terminated in 1547 by the Act for the dissolution of the chantries,[13] and, with its endowments (but excluding such sums as had been paid by the dean and chapter towards the stipends of the chantry priests), was purchased on 20th April 1548[14] for 728*l*. 0*s*. 2*d*. by John Ayleworth of Northehawe, Herts., then receiver general for Somerset, and William Lacy 'yoman'.

Twenty years later, on 13th December 1568,[15] Ayleworth sold the property for 45*l*. to John Bridgwater, prebendary successively of Combe XI and Compton Bishop, and canon residentiary.[16] Bridgwater next sold the property for 71*l*. on 7th September 1574[17] to David Jones, on whose death it passed to his son and heir, Anthony Jones. He sold it on 4th June 1581 for 112*l*. to Arthur Colinge, clerk, of Lympsham,[18] from whom it passed to Roger Colinge, who, on 23rd March 1607, granted the entire property for a fine of 80*l*. at a rent of 12*d*. yearly to Humphrey Willis[19] for a term of 200 years. From this lease it appears that the property was '. . . late in the tenure of Elizabeth Stone, widow, William Burge, and William Layard', though the nature of their interest is not clear; they may have been trustees. The lease made to

Willis in 1607 seems to have fallen through, for we next find Roger Colinge selling the premises on 7th October 1609 for 160*l*. to William Evans.[20] Evans was still in possesssion in 1629,[21] and after his death it passed to his widow, Ann Evans. In the summer of 1649 the premises were in the possession of 'Mr Barnefielde', and apparently inhabited by John Prickman.[22] Mrs Evans or her tenants had the house in March 1705,[23] but in August 1722[24] 'the house and garden of the late college called Mountroy college' were in the possession of Anne Evans, spinster, and the premises remained in the hands of this family until the death, early in 1750's, of Mary Evans, spinster.[25]

Soon after, on 13th March 1755, the house was bought by Charles Tudway for 3,314*l*.[26] He immediately began the demolition of the building, with the intention of erecting a house on the site. He first obtained plans from Messrs Foord and Jolly of Bath, but these proved unacceptable, being dismissed as 'absurd'. Mr Tudway then came to an agreement, on 13th December 1758, with Thomas Paty of Bristol for the execution of the work, to be completed by the end of March 1761.[27] The new house was duly finished and on 6th November 1761[28] a settlement was made of the total cost, 4871*l*. 16*s*. 9*d*. It is not clear what Richard Jenkins, one of the residentiaries, meant when, in 1780 he referred to the sale by John Bridgwater of the house 'which Mr Tudway is now rebuilding'.[29] The new house remained in the possession of the Tudway family for almost two centuries. The dean and chapter took a lease of it on 1st October 1926, for the use of the Cathedral School,[30] and finally purchased it for that purpose. The modern name of the mansion derives from the plantation of cedar trees opposite on the south.

Notes

1. J.H. Harvey, *English Cathedrals* (London, rev. ed. 1961), pp. 57, 163.
2. Cf. Cal. i, p. 35, ch. cxi.
3. Cal. i, p. 35, ch. cxi, cf. cix; Cal. i, p. 36, ch. cxii; Ch. 23 (Cal. ii, p. 550; Ch. 30 (Cal. ii, p. 551).
4. Ch. 36 (Cal. ii, p. 553, abbr.).
5. This dignity was held at this time by Richard de Kenilword.
6. Ch.30a; Cal. i, p. 35 (ch. cix); cf. quitclaim by John de Palton, Cal. i.35, ch. cx.
7. Cal. i, p. 35, where the marginal note in question has been incorrectly transcribed, *annuellariorum* appearing as *damicellariorum*.
8. They had previously dwelt in Cristesham's inn in the High street, see above Article 69.
9. See R.V. Sellers, 'The Chantry College in the Mountroy of Wells' in WNH&A. Soc. *Report* 1959–1960, 50–51, pp. 5–17.

10. See above, Article 11.
11. *CHW*, Article 6, p. 64.
12. Op. cit., p. 12.
13. 1 Edward VI, cap. 14.
14. *Cal. Pat. Rolls*, 1547–1548, pp. 407–408, *SRS* 77. p. 14.
15. SRO, DD/TD, box 41/3.
16. Bridgwater was also archdeacon of Rochester, and rector of Lincoln college, Oxford; in 1564 he resigned his preferments and went to Douai. He spent the rest of his life abroad, and wrote several treatises in defence of the Roman Church, see Dict. Nat. Biog.
17. SRO, DD/TD box 41/3; *SRS* 51, p. 111, no. 171.
18. Ibid.
19. Humphrey Willis is commemmorated on a notable brass in St Catherine's chapel in Wells cathedral, see A.J. Jewers, *Wells Cathedral, its Inscriptions and Heraldry* (London, 1892), pp. 72–73.
20. SRO, DD/TD box 41/3.
21. L.1624–1681, p. 76.
22. S1649, p. 4.
23. Cal. ii, p. 485.
24. L.1701–39, p. 230. Cal. ii, p. 507.
25. R. V. Sellers, op. cit., pp. 16–17.
26. SRO, DD/TD box 41/3.
27. Ibid.
28. Ibid.
29. WCL, Richard Jenkins, MS, vol. i, p. 135.
30. A.1924–1954, p. 30.

APPENDIX III

Compton's Burgages

A burgage was a freehold property in a borough, held of the lord for a specified annual rent. Compton's burgages were certain properties in High street, Wells, so called because they were once in the tenure of Walter Compton. The properties were a tenement opposite Jacob's well,[1] and the tenement which became known later as the Catherine Wheel.[2] By his will, Compton devised these burgages to the dean and chapter, a gift which led to an inquisition *ad quod damnum* being taken on 8th February 1368[3] by John de Bekynton, the escheator for Somerset, in order to ascertain whether the king might without prejudice to himself accede to the petition of the dean and chapter to possess the properties donated by Compton. The reason for this inquisition was that the burgages were held by the king as lord in chief; the bishop of Bath and Wells held them of the king by knight service, and Compton held them of the bishop at an annual rent of 3s. 4d. The burgage later known as the Catherine Wheel was charged with 8s. payable annually to the vicars choral for the anniversary of John Hubard,[4] anciently founded in the cathedral; and the burgage opposite Jacob's well with 4s. payable yearly to the vicar of St Cuthbert's church for another anniversary founded in that church. The inquisition found that the king might without harm grant the petition of the dean and chapter, and his letters patent to this effect were issued on 20th February 1368.[5] Compton had failed to secure a licence in mortmain sanctioning his bequest, but his omission was overlooked by the king on payment of 10l. by the dean and chapter,[6] the premises being still in the hands of Compton's executors. The bishop (John Barnet) had already, on 10th January 1367[7] granted to the dean and chapter a faculty to take possession of the burgages, saving to himself and his successors the services and rents due and accustomed. Others had an interest in the burgages. Originally they were in the possession of William de Chelworth, from whom they passed to his son and heir, also William de Chelworth, who granted them for life to Alice, relict of Adam Tettebourne (Tottebourne) called Monyour, at a rent of 1d.

223

annually.[8] William de Chelworth jun. also granted the burgages, with other property, on 3rd September 1361[9] to John de Chidiok, knight, and others, for life. another who acquired an interest in the burgages after the death of Alice Tettebourne was William de Byngham, who granted to Walter Compton on 7th October 1361[10] the rent of 1*d*. which she had paid. There is no record of when or how Compton acquired the burgages, but his title is attested by various quitclaims made to him: by William de Chelworth jun.[17] on 13th October 1361, by William de Byngham on the same day,[12] and by John de Chidiock on 6th December 1361;[13] suggesting that Compton had at the latest taken possession by September 1361. It appears that he died before 15th March 1366, for an indenture of appointment and grant made on that date[14] by the dean and chapter recites the provisions of his will, from which we learn that the burgage later known as the Catherine Wheel was then held by Henry Boudich and his wife Joan for their lives, and that Compton's wife Margery had a portion of the wine cellar.

The later history of the two burgages is dealt with in the articles on the Catherine Wheel,[15] and on the house at Jacob's well.[16].

Notes

1. See Article 49.
2. See Article 52.
3. Cal. i, pp. 368, 372; Ch. 309 (Cal. ii, p. 315).
4. See Article 52.
5. Cal. i, p. 367.
6. *Cal. Pat. Rolls*, 1364–1367, p. 381.
7. Cal. i, p. 368.
8. Ch. 358 (Cal. ii, p. 624).
9. Cf. Cal. i, p. 369.
10. Ch. 358 (Cal. ii, p. 624); Cal. i, p. 371.
11. Cal. i, p. 371.
12. Cal. i, p. 372.
13. Cal. i, p. 369.
14. Cal. i, p. 270.
15. Article 52.
16. Article 49.